Empowerment Through Communication

▼ ▼ ▼ ▼ ▼ ▼ ▼

An Introduction to Oral Communication

Barbara Parisi
Long Island University

Barbara Pasternack
Long Island University

KENDALL/HUNT PUBLISHING COMPANY
4050 Westmark Drive Dubuque, Iowa 52002

Photographs by Rodney K. Hurley

ISBN 0-7872-1295-4

Printed in the United States of America
20 19 18 17 16 15 14 13 12

Dedication

To all our students past, present and future, and our families.
Michael and Jonathan Pasternack
Gloria and William Parisi

Contents

Preface

"Language most shows a man; Speak that I may see thee."

Ben Jonson

We wrote this book expressly to be used in a beginning course in oral communication. It covers a myriad of topics including interpersonal skills and multi-cultural and gender issues. Some of the material presented in the book is a direct out-growth of our participation in the Title III grant at the Brooklyn Campus of Long Island University.

It is our hope that our students will benefit from this book and that it will stimulate an interest in the fascinating world of speech and language.

Acknowledgements

To the following colleagues and friends without whose help this would have been an impossible task:
Jonathan Rosenblum,
(dear Jonathan, typist, spelling checker, editor, friend),
Elliot Seiden, Ann Scarcella, Darlene Kinderman, Dean David Cohen, Rodney Hurley, Bill Walsh, Frank Post, and Devabrata Mondol.

I

The Importance of Oral Communication

- ▼ The Process of Human Communication
- ▼ Society and Communication
- ▼ Understanding Culture in Relation to Communication
- ▼ Speaking Ethically

I

The Importance of Oral Communication

You have probably wondered why "Oral Communication" is a required course. You have enough work to do including getting used to a new environment, friends, and teachers. Also, are you ever really going to get up and give a speech? Isn't it sufficient that you are improving your writing and reading skills?

Think about it carefully. You have four ways of exchanging information: reading, writing, speaking, and listening. Doesn't it therefore stand to reason that speech should be part of your curriculum in college?

Specifically, no matter what you try to do to avoid it, you will be making oral presentations in most, if not all, of your classes. Even if you are not required to give a formal speech, you will have to question and/or be questioned. Think of how helpful it will be if you can learn to: a) listen effectively and b) learn how to formulate intelligent questions.

Additionally, although we live in a multicultural society, our spoken English should be clear enough to be understood by our peers and our teachers. Many students come from homes where their parents or spouses speak little or no English or have inflections and rhythmic patterns that differ greatly from standard American English. This in no way means that an individual's cultural heritage should be given up. It does mean however, that it is important to get as much practice in the organization and delivery of spoken English as possible so that the communication of ideas is effective in any situation.

Lastly, it is important to rid yourself of the fear of public speaking. Studies have shown that people are more afraid to speak in public than to fly in an airplane. Remember President Franklin Delano Roosevelt's famous adage: "We have nothing to fear but fear itself." The more you study about speaking in public and the more practice you get, the easier it becomes and the less inhibited you will feel!

We said earlier that it is important to get as much practice in spoken English as possible without necessarily giving up your cultural heritage. It is equally as important to recognize that our cultural backgrounds play an essential part in the way we communicate to others. In the same way that we expect others to understand us and accept our differences, we should learn to understand the cultural habits and mores of people outside of the United States and of those who have emigrated but still retain their own customs and mannerisms.

Remember that language is a reflection of culture! Therefore, people tend to use variations of dialect that reflect their particular cultural, racial, or ethnic backgrounds. Our language, as well as every other language contains a variety of forms called dialects. American English has approximately seven regional dialects: Southern, Eastern New England, Western Pennsylvania, Appalachian, General American, Middle Atlantic, and New York City. Each dialect features unique sounds, word choices, idioms, and grammatical features.[1]

In addition to differences in spoken language, we must learn to accept differences in other aspects of communication, specifically, touching, eye contact, facial expression, and gesture. For example, in some cultures, it is rude to look directly at someone when addressing them. We tend to expect everyone to smile at us, whether they know us or not; it's the "Have a nice day" syndrome. In some cultures, people do not smile all the time. This does not necessarily mean that they are rude or unfeeling. It is simply the way they have been raised. To really understand why oral communication is a required course, you must analyze the process of human communication in its relationship to society, culture, communication, and the importance of your ethical responsibility while interrelating.

The Process of Human Communication

Communication is the sending and receiving of messages which occur within a situation or an environment and can be interrupted by noise. We are constantly changing and so are the people with whom we communicate. Even our environment is changing and while these changes can go unnoticed by us, they affect us greatly. There is nothing static about communication.

These are the elements of communication: source (sender), receiver, message, channel, feedback, noise, and environment. They are interdependent. A simplified look at the process can be viewed in the following model.

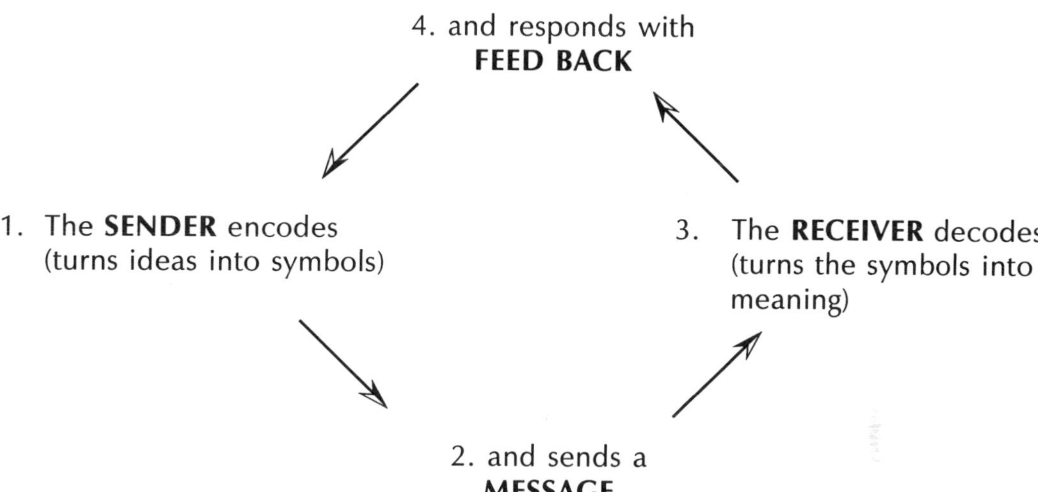

Figure 1. Even though we can talk about the parts of the process individually they are connected with each other.

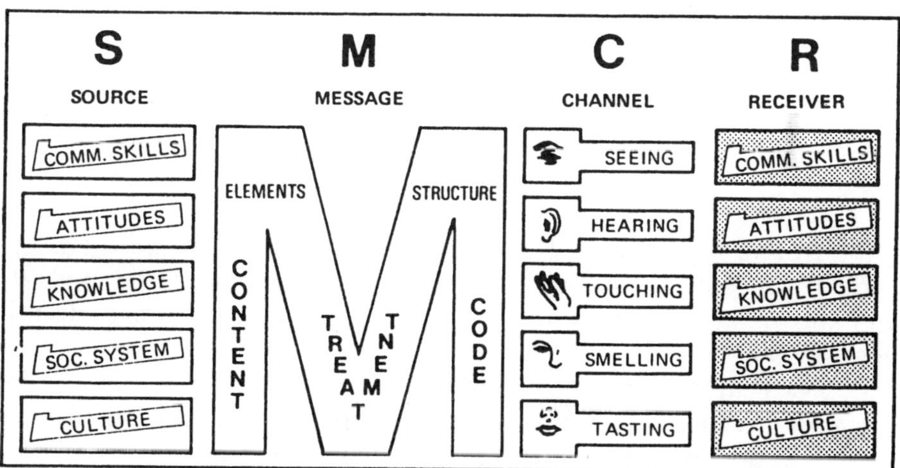

Figure 2. "A Model of the Ingredients in Communication" from *The Process of Communication: an Introduction to Theory and Practice* by David K. Berlo, copyright © 1960 by Holt, Rinehart and Winston, Inc. and renewed 1988 by David K. Berlo, reproduced by permission of the publisher.

To further explain the effects of society on communication we need to look at David Berlo's SMCR Communication Model (see Figure 2). It has four parts which are: the source, message, channel, and receiver. The source, which is the first part of the model, initiates communication by encoding a verbal or nonverbal message.

In Berlo's model the source is composed of five components. The first component in the source category is communication skills — the ability to write, speak, listen, and read are necessary for an effective interchange. Through these skills we can organize ideas, convey these ideas clearly, and use representational body language to support our message.

The source's second component is attitude. Attitude is the approach we use to share our feelings about people or events. We tend to have a better attitude toward sharing feelings through communication with people we trust than with strangers. Our attitudes about things affect what we eventually say.

The third component is knowledge. This refers to what we know about different people, events, objects, or circumstances inherent in a communication situation.

Berlo's fourth component is the social system. Groups that we participate in or roles that we play within those groups help shape our communication.

The fifth and final component of the source is the cultural system. Our communication is affected by values, beliefs, and traditions taught to us by our families and friends.

The second part of Berlo's model is the message which includes all verbal and nonverbal communication we create while encoding. Berlo believes the message is created by the selection and arrangement of the language which shapes the content we eventually receive.

The third part of Berlo's model is the channel which encompasses the use of the five senses — seeing, hearing, smelling, tasting, and touching. These senses aid us in communicating.

The fourth and final part of Berlo's model is the receiver who is responsible for decoding a message. Through the use of our communication skills, our attitudes and knowledge and the effects that our social and cultural system have on us, a message is decoded.

Berlo's SMCR model doesn't include the effect of noise and use of feedback in the communication process. Noise is any kind of interruption in receiving a message. There are two kinds of noise, external which are the physical sounds created from everyday living experiences and internal noises which are the psychological/social sounds we hear inside our own heads. Feedback is the response from the receiver back to the source. By providing feedback, the receiver also functions as a source. The source affected by feedback is a receiver of information. Although Berlo's SMCR Model does leave out two essential elements of noise and feedback in communication, it does provide us a diversified look at the process.

The knowledge of how human beings communicate effectively is probably the most valuable and useful skill we can develop. Through friends, lovers, and our families interpersonal relationships begin, are developed, and sometimes are destroyed. We interact through groups, solving complicated problems, sharing new knowledge, and working out our ideas and experiences. Due to unique interpretation of events a person acts and reacts individually.

Human communication is an ongoing process. Since we are constantly changing, every activity is new and the past can never be repeated. Thus the results of an action can never be negated. The extent of our communication changes as our behavior changes. Remember, communication is dynamic, it can never be erased, and it affects other people.

Communication has two messages. One of the messages is content and is delivered in words. The other tells you how to examine the relationship. Meanings are in people, not in the written word and so, very often, a person hearing someone else's message, will not really understand it's full implication. For example:

> A young man telephones his girlfriend who lives in another city. He is making plans for a rendezvous.
>
> "I have reservations," he says.
>
> She does not respond. There is a long period of silence. He realizes that she thinks he has reservations about coming to see her and tells her that what he means is that he has made train reservations. She breathes a sigh of relief and the plans are made.

Is it no wonder we experience extreme difficulty in communication?

Human communication always takes place within a context. The physical, psychological/social, and temporal dimensions are part of this context. An example of the physical dimension is a tangible environment like your classroom. This environment affects the way you behave. An example of the psychological/social dimension is the games or roles people play, created by norms and mores of our society. Our behavior is determined by these cultural values. Time or the temporal dimension also affects communication. We've always been told that timing in life is everything. Well it's true! Certain sexual innuendos which are considered acceptable today would have at one point in time been considered offensive. For example the Virginia Slims cigarette advertisement which states: "You've come a long way baby!" All three of these dimensions influence each other.

Human communication is the most important part of our daily existence. Most of us do not realize the complexity of the process. We need to develop an understanding of communication so that we can function more effectively in the world.

Society and Communication

The rapid technological advances since the turn of the century created the need to communicate information to different parts of the world in a timely and accurate way. We grew to realize the interdependence between society and communication. In social contexts we create meanings through symbols and objects which members of our group have in common. Certain "in-words" or phrases such as "be cool" and "fresh" are examples. We communicate in a group by valuing the same objects, and by obeying the same norms, mores, and folkways which have our similar values and habits.

Usually we are unaware and unconscious of a group's influence on our behavior. As objects or symbols lose meaning to us we sometimes can see how communication is influenced by society. Through communication we teach, learn, change, and share. It helps us to develop solid relationships which make up the very fabric of society. Through observing society's use of objects or symbols, its social structure, and human interaction, you can see the interdependence between communication and society. By the use of symbols we identify, influence, and communicate our feelings in the social world.

Our social structure creates everyday roles, role expectations, and behavioral consequences. Our major institutions, such as religion, education, politics, family, and business, cause us to take part in a multitude of roles such as family member or group member, student, friend, or employee, each one demanding an understanding of the specific role.

Most of our activities revolve around role playing. Role playing is an extremely important part of life since most of our activities involve the use of roles. We perform these roles according to certain expectations we are conditioned to have. Changes in our roles change our relationships.

Social interaction is understood through the daily roles we play and, by our adjustments, we understand certain patterns which help us to function in society. Social interaction shows the dependency between society and communication. Objects and social structure are products of our communication.

In communication we look for meanings from another person. We might try to predict how a person will respond to certain stimuli. For instance, current gender issues raised between men and women have taught us to look at certain behaviors inherent in the genders and how this affects communication between the sexes. One inherent difference in men and women is asking for directions.

For example:

"A man and a woman were standing beside the information booth at the Washington Folk Life Festival, a sprawling complex of booths and displays. 'You ask,' the man was saying to the woman. 'I don't ask'."The man probably felt that admitting to being unable to find something himself was humiliating, whereas the woman had no problem with "I'm sorry, I don't know."[3] Understanding the gender difference can aid communication.

Social interaction provides the context in which we can communicate but we must understand the social context in which communication occurs. To do this effectively we have to understand how we respond to objects and our social structure. If we study objects, symbols, social structures, and social interaction we understand how to communicate in society.

Understanding Culture in Relation to Communication

In New York City our environment is composed of many different cultures. Education teaches us to appreciate differences and similarities between people, which strengthens intercultural communication by creating valuable conversation. In intercultural communication persons from one culture interact with persons from a different culture. To be able to communicate, these people must study similarities and differences in their values, perceptions, and language.

Effective human communication helps develop a strong sense of self while intercultural communication helps develop a person's cultural sensibilities. When people are content with themselves as individuals they communicate better with people of another culture and they do not create stereotypes. Stereotyping is dangerous in intercultural communication. Remember Archie Bunker!

It's important not to make first judgments based on an initial encounter. Written and spoken language express one's culture in addition to a person's attitudes, beliefs, and values. When people accept a set of cultural values they will usually be more capable of accepting the values of others. Through observing and analyzing cultural values people will realize that differences are not bad. Our perception of things is our reality.

Speaking Ethically

Ethics can be defined as the moral duty and judgment necessary for effective communication. Firstly, we all have a responsibility to communicate ethically with ourselves and others. Although the Bill of Rights guarantees our freedom of speech, "...Congress cannot take away or restrict freedom of speech or freedom of the press. Citizens may protect themselves against damaging insults spoken or written about them by civil lawsuits...."[4] Does that allow us to say what we think even though it may cause harm to others?

Secondly, you must investigate your subject matter fully by distinguishing between facts and opinions. A fact is something that can be proven. For example, it can be proven that the Japanese attacked Pearl Harbor on December 7, 1941, or that Neil Armstrong took a walk on the Moon's surface. However, it cannot as yet be proven that U.F.O.s exist. To investigate a subject fully, you must do library research and consult reliable authorities. You cannot depend upon only one source but must consult a variety of references on your subject. Make sure that you give credit to your sources by using footnotes and a bibliography.

Thirdly, your content should be delivered in an honest manner. This means that outdated information, half truths, lies, and unsupported assumptions must be avoided.

Fourthly, you must respect your audience's intelligence. Your speech should be geared towards the type of group you are addressing. This does not mean that you talk down to or patronize your audience but respect their backgrounds and interests. Always define technical terms and be certain that all your ideas are fully explained.

Be aware that you are always influencing others when you speak to a group. There is power in communication and you must realize that responsibility. Communication between people has consequences. People make right and wrong choices in their lives, and they have a right to these choices. Unethical communication forces individuals to make decisions they might not normally make and to reject choices they might usually make. Ethical communication allows freedom for individuals to use information to make their own choices based on sound mental analysis. It is not easy to determine if individuals can make their own ethical decisions, however; this variable creates the human condition.

▼ ▼ ▼ Chapter I Key Terms

Oral Communication	Verbal Message
Dialects	NonVerbal Message
Human Communication	Physical Dimension
Messages	Psychological/Social Dimension
Environment	Temporal Dimension
Noise	Role Playing
Source	Symbols
Receiver	Stereotypes
Channel	

Feedback
Encode
Decode
Ethics
Facts
Opinion

▼▼▼ Endnotes

1. Doris Balin Bianchi, Wayne Bond, Gerald Kandel, and Ann Seidler. *Easily Understood*, 2nd ed., New Jersey: Avery Publishing Group, Inc., 1983. p. 10.

2. David K. Berlo. *The Process of Communication*. New York: Holt, Rinehart and Winston, 1966. p. 27.

3. Deborah Tannen. *You Just Don't Understand, Women and Men in Conversation*. New York: Ballantine Books, 1990. p. 61.

4. Floyd G. Cullop. *The Constitution of the U.S.* New York: Penguin Books, 1984.

II

Intrapersonal—Interpersonal

- Our Belief System
- The Johari Window
- Self-Concept
- Perception
- Defense Mechanisms
- Conflict and Conflict Management

II

Intrapersonal—Interpersonal

As a college freshman did you ever say: "Can I do college work? Will I be able to make friends? So and so is popular and finds it easy to deal with new situations, why can't I? Do I really belong in college?" These questions illustrate the way in which we communicate with ourselves. *Intrapersonal* is communication with oneself. Before you can effectively communicate with others, you have to understand yourself.

Have you ever wondered why you have difficulty communicating your ideas and beliefs to others? There is a tendency in our modern, technological world to set up barriers to communication, protective devices such as defense mechanisms that never allow us to develop close personal relationships, or to understand ourselves clearly.

Understanding ourselves, really getting to know what makes us behave the way we do, is what is meant by intrapersonal communication. Contrary to popular belief, there is nothing wrong with talking to ourselves. "Who in the world am I? Ah, that's the great puzzle!"[1] By learning to communicate with our innerselves we develop self-awareness. Once we can accomplish this, our *interpersonal* communication skills, how we express our feelings and emotions in relationships with our friends, colleagues, and families can be improved.

Sometimes it is almost frightening to look into ourselves. Consider Lucy's behavior in this "Peanuts" cartoon.

Being able to face pain and disappointment, or the realization that hard work is what we need, helps us to achieve our goals. Consider the student who says: "I'm really dumb. I'll never pass math, why don't I just give up?" Instead of facing the problem by exploring why it may be difficult to ask for help from a fellow student or professor, we sometimes give up. The ability to convey one's problems to someone else is *interpersonal* communication.

This same situation can be applied to an oral communication course. How many times have you heard yourself or others say, "How can I give a speech? I have nothing to say; I can't even think of a topic."

Everyone has something to say, to offer an opinion, to relate an experience or to argue a point. Unless you can examine and understand your innermost feelings, attitudes, values, and beliefs your response will be, "I can't think of a thing to say."

What are your everyday experiences? How did you feel about an item in the news, a person you met, a loved one's troubles? You do not live in a vacuum; you are responsive to everything around you. The idea is to develop the awareness of how your "self" perceives your experiences.

Our Belief System

Interpersonal communication involves the sending and receiving of verbal or nonverbal messages to or from another person or group. Expressing yourself through spoken language is verbal communication. By nonverbal we mean those gestures and personal habits that reveal to others what we feel or think. For instance, the way we walk into a room can indicate whether we are angry or sad.

A straight back or hunched shoulders are indicators of what we want to pass on to others in the room whether we are aware of it or not. Facial expressions reveal information we sometimes don't want others to know. Have you ever experienced trying to hide something from a friend only to have the friend say, "Something is wrong, I can see it on your face."

Verbal communication, of course, is much more evident. However, it is not uncommon for people to engage in "polite conversation" when they cannot relate to an individual or a group because of differences in background and experiences. When individuals have similar experiences, it becomes easier to communicate interpersonally. Additionally, if there is trust in a relationship, communication is more effective.

Our belief system is the way we as individuals perceive what is true to us about our world. Often, even when in great danger, our belief system helps us. Despite the knowledge that capture by the Gestapo was imminent, Anne Frank, in her diary wrote: "I still believe that people are really good at heart. I simply can't build up my hopes on a foundation consisting of confusion, misery, and death...I must uphold my ideals, for perhaps the time will come when I shall be able to carry them out."[2] Contained in our belief system are our attitudes, values, and beliefs.

Belief can be conscious or unconscious statements which we use to communicate our feelings such as true and false statements or good and bad perceptions of situations. For instance: "I'll never learn to drive a car. After all, my brother and father tell me women are terrible drivers. They're probably right. That's why I get so nervous when I'm behind the wheel. Oh, well, there's always public transportation."

An attitude is an organization of our beliefs which allows us to respond in a predisposed way toward a situation or an object. Consider this example: "My mother, father, and sister are all poor in math. It seems to run in the family. I know I'll fail the course. How can I possibly pass when my brother and sister both failed?"

A value is a belief that a certain goal is better than other possible goals. Values influence the way we conduct our lives and behave with people. Some examples of values are: to behave with compassion in situations, to listen and respect others, or to provide security for ourselves and our loved ones.

Belief systems are developed during the course of our lives. Therefore, they are quite complex and usually there is a need to adjust to them as we experience new situations. However, some people are afraid to change and are resistant to examine their belief systems. Examination of our belief systems can allow us to examine ourselves, avoid conflict, and possibly even change our way of feeling. It is true that we communicate more effectively with people whose belief systems are similar to our own. That's why it is important for us to understand how we perceive our world. If we understand our own system we can have an open discussion with people whose belief systems are different from ours. Through the use of the Johari Window our perceptions of ourselves increase, helping us to develop a stronger self-concept.

The Johari Window

The Johari Window was developed by Joe Luft and Harry Ingham to identify a person's areas of self.[3] Using this model, many questions are raised. For example: What do we want others to know about us? How much can a person really tell about us? How much do we know about ourselves?

	Known to self	Unknown to self
Known to others	OPEN	BLIND
Unknown to others	HIDDEN	UNKNOWN

Self-disclosure is the willingness to share information, opinions, and feelings with someone you trust. It involves taking quite a risk. To self-disclose effectively you have to understand yourself. The open box of the model represents the feelings, opinions, and information that we know about ourselves and others know about us. For example: where you went to school; your job; where you live; how many siblings you have.

The blind box of the model represents information about ourselves of which we are unaware but is clearly seen by others. For example: tapping a pen or pencil on a desk; cracking gum; talking with your mouth full.

The hidden box represents the feelings and information that we keep hidden from others and no one else can discover, such as the real reasons for not getting into a university of your choice. By choosing not to tell, you keep it hidden. The closed box represents the information, feelings, and opinions that are completely unknown to us and others. An example of this might be a parent who observes her son playing the piano by ear and the realization by both of them that he has natural talent which should be pursued.

With each separate person we communicate with a different balance of the Johari Window. This understanding will create a strong step toward analyzing your interpersonal relationships.

Self-Concept

Self-concept or self-image is the way you feel about yourself. There are people who have poor self-concepts and those of us who have more positive self-concepts. An example of a negative self-concept can be found in the following little poem:

I Can't Go Back to School

The cat! The Cat!
She ate my hat!
I don't know where my shirt is!
Just look at this sweater!
I wish it looked better!
Just look how thick the dirt is!
How can I dress?
My hair's a mess!
I look just like a fool!
I can't go back to school like this!
I can't go back to school![4]

Some examples of positive self-concepts are: "I want to be an actress. I know I'm up against fierce competition, but I'm talented and if I try my best and work very hard, I'm sure I'll make it!" Or, "I'm studying hard and I know I'll make the Dean's list this semester."

Self-concept begins in childhood and develops throughout adolescence. By the time we are ready to go to college our self-concepts are formed. However, psychologists believe that self-concepts continue to grow and develop through the mid-thirties and forties. Self-concepts are developed through our relationships with others. To improve your relationships with others you need to be open in your communication.

Below is a Positive/Negative Self-Image chart. Ask yourself: What image do I relate to?

A positive self-image	
Capable	I know how to do it, or I can find out.
Intelligent	I'm smart — I can figure it out.
Creative	I do things with a "flair," I'm a good problem solver.
Attractive	I like the way I look — I do things to enhance my appearance.
Self-responsible	I take responsibility for myself and my life. I don't blame others.
Good communicator	I relate well to people, I understand them and they understand me.
Courageous	I'm not afraid to take chances, if they make sense.
Confident	I'll make it!
Assertive	I stand up for my rights and beliefs without hurting anyone else and trampling on their rights.
Happy	I enjoy life.
Purposeful	I know where I'm going. I set goals and expect to reach them.
Loving	I'm warm, caring, sincere, and capable of intimate relationships.
Deserving	I have a right to the best life. I deserve it.
Likable	I like myself and expect others to like me.
Secure	Even when things go wrong I know that ultimately it will all work out right.
Open	I share easily with others. I'm not afraid for others to know me.
Successful	I achieve what I desire.

A positive self-image (continued)

Wealthy (optional)	I expect to make a great deal of money. (Wealthy may or may not be a part of the positive self-image. Some people do not equate money with success or happiness — believe it or not!)

A Negative Self-Image

Incapable	I can't do it. (So I won't try.)
Not intelligent	I'm not smart. (So I won't trouble my brain.)
Noncreative	I do things in a very ordinary way. I have difficulty solving problems.
Unattractive	I don't like the way I look. (There's no sense trying to do much about it.)
Lacking in self-responsibility	It's not my fault, everything went wrong. Let's see who I should blame.
Poor communicator	People don't understand me and I don't understand them. It's their problem.
Fearful	I can't take a chance.
Lacking in confidence	I'm not going to make it. (Why bother to try?)
Nonassertive/ aggressive	No sense standing up for my rights, I'll never get what I need anyhow/I'll trample over anyone to get what I need, otherwise I'll never get it.
Unhappy	I don't enjoy life.
Purposeless	I don't know where I want to go or what I want to do in life.
Unloving	I'm not a "people" person. I'm not affectionate. Real intimacy is not for me.
Undeserving	I haven't got any right to be rich, to be successful, to be happy. I'd feel guilty. I have no right to be richer, healthier, etc., than my father, mother, brother, etc.

A negative self-image (continued)

Unlikable	I don't like myself, so why should anyone else like me?
Insecure	Things always go wrong and I know that it's just another sign that nothing works out for me.
Closed/withdrawn defensive	I don't like to be around people/I don't want people to know the real me. They're out to get me, I better get them first.
Unsuccessful	I never achieve what I desire. (So why bother to try?)
Poor	I will always be!

This chart offers examples of the way we could feel about ourselves which might have been shaped by our background and life experiences. In the past thirty years we have had a resurgence toward examining our cultural backgrounds. Today we are aware of our personal ethnic identities and how they affect communication. This cultural awareness is part of understanding our self-images.

Perception

Very often in life people realize that there's more to a situation than meets the eye. Can we really see everything as clearly as we think we can? Sometimes as we interpret information incorrectly we are told — "Well that's your perception of the situation." Is our perception accurate or not?

Perception is the process by which we can create meanings from our lives. It is developed from a person's educational background, race, sex, environment, and past experiences. Therefore, our perception is selective and influenced by our beliefs, values, and attitudes. Even if our backgrounds are similar, with almost identical abilities, while observing an experience we do not necessarily see and hear the same things. Is the glass half empty or half full? Remember, a person's perception will allow a definition to this answer. Through our five senses taste, sound, sight, touch, and smell we perceive information. However, we do interpret messages through our own set of attitudes, beliefs, and values. We see what we want to see and use the process of selective perception to protect ourselves. These defense mechanisms can cause conflict.

Defense Mechanisms

The roles which we play can create a perception of us by others. The environment, our own personal needs and drives, and other people influence our role-taking behavior. Defense mechanisms confuse people's perception of us and our perceptions of others. They play a great part in our *interpersonal* relationships. The way in which we perceive ourselves influences the way we communicate with others. A more positive self-concept makes it easier to express feelings to someone else. If we are secure in our own belief systems and values, we can more easily relate to others.

How many times have you heard a classmate say "I don't have to go to speech class today. Even though I'm scheduled to give a speech, the professor will never get to me, he's so far behind, there are too many before me."

More than likely, rather than admit to being unprepared, this student *rationalized* by blaming the instructor. This defense mechanism, rationalization, is a technique many of us use to protect ourselves.

Similar to rationalization is *projection*, which is another way to avoid taking responsibility for our own shortcomings. "It wasn't my fault I failed the course, the instructor is a tough grader." Sound familiar? It's often difficult to accept our own failures. By *projecting* on to someone else, we help to maintain our self-esteem.

Another common defense mechanism is displacement. We sometimes use a close friend or a family member as a target to vent our anger or frustration if we cannot confront a person who presents a threat to us. For example, someone you thought was a good friend had betrayed you by repeating something you told them in confidence. You are hurt, but instead of confronting the friend, you scream at your younger sibling for no apparent reason. Wouldn't it be better to confront the person who betrayed your confidence? Even though it may be anxiety provoking, getting feelings out into the open is much better than using an innocent person as a scapegoat.

Regression is returning to a time that may be easier to deal with. It may be an emotional and/or intellectual early stage of development. Someone who finds as an adult that life's problems are overwhelming may resort to infantile behavior such as temper tantrums.

Another common defense mechanism is compensation. If a person feels lacking in a particular behavior or situation, he may compensate by doing something that is more positive. Many people who stutter, for instance, become lawyers, actors, or politicians. This particular defense mechanism can be helpful if not overused.

Denial occurs when a person finds reality too difficult to deal with. Although this is one way in which we can protect ourselves, it can be dangerous if repeated too often. Refusing to visit the doctor when someone is in pain is an example of denial. "There's nothing wrong with me, the doctor will only make me sick."

We tend to *fantasize* when life becomes too stressful. It's a hot day toward the end of the semester. You have final exams coming up and several term papers all due on the same day. It's easier to pretend you're on a beach in the Bahamas sipping Piña Coladas than contending with all the pressures.

These are just a few examples of the more common defense mechanisms. Try to recognize them in your own behavior and remember that they are all quite normal if not used excessively. Once you are able to recognize defensive responses in your behavior towards yourself and others, you will find it much easier to communicate both inter-and intrapersonally.

Conflict and Conflict Management

"When two people's paths cross, there is bound to be a conflict of interest: We can't both stand on the same spot without one of us standing on the other's foot. If no one steps aside, someone will get stepped on. You and I are not the same person, so some of our wants will be different and conflict is inevitable. Because we can't both get our way, we may find ourselves in a power struggle."[5] This example illustrates one kind of conflict.

There are many types of conflict. Whenever we find ourselves unable to decide upon one goal or another or whether or not to enter a new situation we are conflicted—"Should I or shouldn't I?" There is conflict in almost everything we do. We can usually deal with it and it is no longer a problem. However, there are times when it becomes almost impossible to deal with, and we find ourselves in a dilemma that appears unsolvable.

When two people disagree, they often fail to realize that conflict is inevitable in human relationships. Have you ever seen or heard of a relationship in which there is total agreement? Some conflict is healthy. The trick is to recognize that which can be constructive and that which is destructive. Unfortunately, unhealthy or destructive conflict is all too common and can seriously interfere with interpersonal relationships as well as playing havoc with intrapersonal awareness. Frequently, if inner conflicts cannot be resolved, we tend to torment ourselves with self-directed anger and frustration. In the same way, if conflicts with others seem irreconcilable, relationships suffer. It's the approach you take that might make constructive criticism become destructive.

The language you use and the tone of your voice reveal your attitude towards the other person. How many times have you found yourself turning away from an acquaintance because of the way in which he spoke to you? Has a parent ever said to you: "Use a different tone of voice when you speak to me!"?

Learning to listen to the way you sound and monitoring yourself vocally can help your relationships. The idea is to find a way to cooperate with the other person and to recognize that a good, healthy argument often results in creating a closer relationship.

Often, in our closest relationships with family members, we keep our feelings so locked in that eventually we find ourselves raging both inwardly and outwardly. Consider the following example from Vivian Gornick's sensitive and revealing memoir about her relationship with her mother:

> My relationship with my mother is not good, and as our lives accumulate it often seems to worsen. We are locked into a narrow channel of acquaintance, intense and binding. For years at a time there is an exhaustion, a kind of softening, between us. Then the rage comes up again, hot and clear, erotic in its power to compel attention. These days it is bad between us. My mother's way of 'dealing' with the bad times is to accuse me loudly and publicly of the truth. Whenever she sees me she says, "You hate me. I know you hate me." I'll be visiting her and she'll say to anyone who happens to be in the room — a neighbor, a friend, my brother, or one of my nieces — "She hates me. What she has against me I don't know, but she hates me." She is equally capable of stopping a stranger on the street when we're out walking and saying. "This is my daughter. She hates me." Then she'll turn to me and plead, "What did I do to you, you should hate me so?" I never answer. I know she's burning and I'm glad to let her burn. Why not? I'm burning too.[6]

Unfortunately, this conflict was reinforced over a period of many years. The more a painful situation is avoided, the more it is reinforced.

We are often afraid of disclosing our deepest feelings to a close friend or family member. It is important to realize that being self-assertive does not necessarily mean the loss of a relationship.

Let's take a different example. Suppose you are angry and upset because you feel your speech professor is unfair to you. Your grades on speeches are consistently lower than those of your classmates. The professor's critiques seem harsh, and your outlines are bleeding with red marks. You are afraid you may fail the course. You would like nothing better than to tell the professor to "go fly a kite" or worse. Of course, this would get you nowhere and probably alienate the professor. Instead of losing your temper a better alternative would be to find out the professor's office hours and make an appointment to meet privately to discuss your problem. More often than not, this has beneficial results. It all depends upon your attitude and keeping a cool head.

Discussing your problem doesn't always work. Sometimes you have to be assertive, especially when you know you are being treated unfairly. Unfortunately, being overly assertive or aggressive can occasionally result in a loss of friendship, a lowering of a grade, a loss of a promotion, or raise in pay. Be careful not to confuse assertiveness with aggressiveness. Being assertive means the ability to express your views without hurting the other person. Aggressiveness is attempting to get what you want without taking the other person's feelings into consideration. For example, Tanya has been waiting in line for an hour to purchase tickets for a hit show. Liza tries to cut in front of her. Tanya assertively says: "I've been in line for a long time, I guess you're eager to purchase tickets but I was here first!"

An aggressive response would be: "Who do you think you are? You have no right to cut in front of me, I was here first!" You have to sit down and consider how important it is to your personal sense of worth to assert yourself in certain situations. It is up to you as an individual to evaluate the situation and decide whether to approach assertively or not. Approaching a problem head on is not easy and conflicts are not always resolved in the way you would like them to be. But having a positive attitude always helps. Dan Greenburg, in his wonderfully funny and poignant book called *How to Make Yourself Miserable*, lists seventeen basic pessimistic philosophies.[7] Read them carefully.

How many of them have applied to you in trying to resolve conflicts?

1. I can't do it.
2. I never could do anything right.
3. I have the worst luck in the world.
4. I don't have a chance, so why try?
5. I'm all thumbs.
6. I'd only get hurt.
7. It would never work.
8. It's not in the stars.
9. It's never been done before.
10. It's not who you are, it's who you know.
11. It's too late now.
12. It's later than you think.
13. You can't take it with you.
14. What good could come of it?
15. The piper must be paid.
16. The wages of sin is death.
17. The paths of glory lead but to the grave.

Remember that although your personal view of a problem in a relationship is of utmost importance to you, the other person's feelings have to be taken into consideration. Resolving a conflict can never be one-sided. For example: Marie is a college freshman who is living away from home for the first time. She finds that she hates dormitory life and wants to share an apartment off campus with two girls, one of whom is a senior and has experienced being on her own for several years. Marie calls her father and tells him of her plans. He refuses and angrily tells her that she is too young for such a move and he will not pay for an apartment. They quarrel and Marie hangs up the phone in a crying rage. When she thinks it over, she finds she has several alternatives. She tries to problem-solve to resolve her conflict with her father. One, she could try to get a job and pay for the apartment on her own, but this is unrealistic because she could never earn enough at a part time job to pay her share of the rent. Two, she could take a leave of absence, get a full-time position and plan to go back to college when she has saved enough money. Three, she could call her father and ask him to explain why he feels she shouldn't move out of the dorm at this time. Perhaps they could reach some kind of compromise such as having her finish out her freshman year in the dormitory and then allowing her to move out.

It is important for Marie to understand her father's point of view. When she finally decides to call him, he explains that he thinks she is too young and inexperienced to take on the responsibilities of an apartment at present, but that he would consider allowing her to do it in her sophomore or junior year if she could prove to him that she is serious about her studies and mature enough to do both.

Remember, it is much better to approach a conflict by trying to solve the problem than to become hostile and silently build up anxieties that could eventually alienate friends and family members. Healthy *intrapersonal* relationships help to create positive *interpersonal* attitudes. The way we relate to our families and friends reflects the manner in which we relate to ourselves.

▼ ▼ ▼ Chapter II Key Terms

Intrapersonal
Interpersonal
Gestures
Belief System
Self-Disclosure
Self-Concept
Perception
Cultural Awareness
Defense Mechanisims
Conflict
Conflict Management
Assertive
Aggressive

▼ ▼ ▼ Endnotes

1. Evans, Bergan. *Lewis Carroll: Alice's Adventures in Wonderland II. Dictionary of Quotations*. New York: Delacorte Press. 1968. p. 616.

2. Frank, Anne. *Anne Frank, The Diary of a Young Girl*. New York: Doubleday & Co. 1967. p. 237.

3. Reprinted from *Of Human Interaction* by Joseph Luft, by permission of Mayfield Publishing Company (formerly National Press Books), 1969.

4. Hearn, Michael Patrick. *The Place My Words Are Looking For* selected by Paul B. Janeczko. New York: Bradbury Press. 1990. p. 14.

5. Tannen, Deborah. *You Just Don't Understand, Women and Men in Conversation*. New York: Ballantine Books, 1990. p. 149.

6. Gornick, Vivian. *Fierce Attachments*. New York: Simon & Schuster Inc. 1987. p. 6.

7. Greenburg, Dan. *How to Make Yourself Miserable*. New York: Random House. 1966. p. 38.

III

Gender: Nonverbal Communication, Spoken Language, and Listening

- Nonverbal Communication
- Gender-Based Nonverbal Behavior
- Theoretical Concepts of Sex-Role Development
- Spoken Lanugage
- Listening

III

Gender: Nonverbal Communication, Spoken Language, and Listening

There are many ways in which we communicate to others through nonverbal means such as gestures, facial expressions, and body movement. A dancer can communicate a whole story through graceful movements. A painter or sculptor conveys his or her messages through artistic works. A young child can merely point to a refrigerator and a parent understands if the child is hungry or thirsty. The changing nature of our society has resulted in new developments between the nonverbal relationships of men and women. Today we can see gender differences in the nonverbal behaviors of perception, listening, and empathy. Most psychologists believe these differences are biologically rooted, as well as socially, psychologically, and culturally influenced.

Nonverbal Communication

There are a number of nonverbal behavioral codes that men and women use. These are proxemics, kinesics, tactile communication, paralinguistics, and clothing choices. Gender differences are clearly revealed in our nonverbal behavior.

Proxemics is an individual's understanding and use of space. Under the category of proxemics there are two parts: personal space and territoriality. Personal space is the distance a person keeps between himself or herself and other people. We are rarely conscious of our spatial needs but we are very conscious when we feel someone has invaded that space. Studies have shown that women tend to need less personal space than men but tend to react more negatively when their side space has been invaded. Men react more negatively than women in direct face-to-face encounters with people.

There are different rules about personal space which people follow and these rules will vary with cultural differences. In the United States there are accepted informal distance rules that Americans respect which allow people to feel comfortable while communicating. There are four categories: intimate, personal, social, and public distance. Intimate distance, which usually varies from touching to eighteen inches apart, is not usually used by Americans in public. This space is used by family members or loved ones in private settings. Personal distance, which starts at about eighteen inches to four feet, is used by friends who maintain this close distance to show liking. Social distance, usually four to twelve feet, is used in business to create a normal work atmosphere. Four to seven feet shows a closer relationship than seven to twelve feet which is reserved for strangers. Public distance, from twelve feet and beyond, is used by a speaker talking to a large group. Those who understand and respect other people's personal space are usually more effective communicators.

The concept of territoriality explains the need for humans as well as animals to create, develop, and maintain certain spaces as their own. Unlike personal space which is the space that is around us as we move, territoriality is a fixed area. The walled rooms in our houses or our outside fences are examples of territoriality.

Once our personal identities are developed we can control social interaction by creating either barriers or bridges through our daily communication. Certain studies have shown that women are less territorial than men. For example, in their homes men usually have garages, dens, workrooms, and office spaces as well as their own furniture devoted to their needs. Womens' rooms, on the other hand, are generally used by the entire family.

Kinesics refers to a person's body movement, facial expressions, gestures, touching and eye contact. Sometimes our nonverbal body language expresses our emotions more clearly than our verbal language. Nonverbal language can reflect gender differences. For instance, eye contact can be a person's nonverbal way of reaching or rejecting another person. Women usually establish much more eye contact than do men. Facial expressions show the emotional involvement of people in a given situation. Women tend to use more facial expressions than men. For example, they tend to smile more. However, women use less gestures than do men. Touching, an act of affection or aggression, is the access of a person to another person's physical body, and women usually touch more frequently than men.

Paralanguage refers to verbal characteristics people use to communicate their ideas. These characteristics consist of pitch, rate, inflection, volume, quality, pronunciation, and articulation. Paralanguage reveals a great deal of meaning from our written language.

Pitch refers to the high and low tones of our voices. Rate is how quickly or slowly we speak. Gender differences in voices are produced by the different size of our vocal chords in the larynx. We associate men with having lower pitched voice due to longer, thicker vocal chords. Inflection is the pitch change we use to express meaning. Volume is how softly or how loudly we speak. The quality of our voices is revealed through such characteristics as harshness, nasality, stridency, or breathiness. Pronunciation and articulation allow us to say words clearly and crisply.

In addition to our voices and bodies, the clothing we wear reveals a nonverbal message about ourselves. It can show gender, age, role in a group, status, values, or lifestyle possibilities, occupation, nationality, socioeconomic changes, personality, and sexual desires. Our clothing reflects our individuality as well as providing warmth and comfort.

For at least one hundred years books and magazines have been giving us helpful tips on what we should wear to be successful. Even more recently, *Dress for Success* by John T. Molloy has effectively described for us how to select our clothes for corporate life.

Today's different cultural groups wear clothing of national origin creating a sense of ethnic identity. Personal pride is developed by this fashion statement as well as possibly a political statement. From the late 60s to the present, ethnic dress was high fashion. Clothing has always shown the social position of its wearer.

Women's clothing has invariably reflected society's mores. Styles of clothing for women in America were not radically affected until the acceptance of slacks in the late 1960s and early 70s. Although clothes can help convey a person's gender, certain clothes break gender boundaries.

Colors in fashion can be compared to the tone of voice in speaking. Tone of voice conveys a meaning just the way different fabrics, color, and trimming convey different messages. Dress is a nonverbal language and even when we don't want to convey a message we are still saying something to someone. The clothing we choose to wear makes a statement about ourselves.

Gender Based Nonverbal Behavior

Do women gossip more than men? Of course not. Conversations between women and men reveal that neither sex necessarily talks more than the other. A number of the researchers see significance, however, in the studies that show men interrupting, or otherwise dominating, women's speech — traditionally in our society, women have had neither speaking rights nor economic status, and so they have used different linguistic strategies to obtain their goals. However, both sexes can control and change the topic of discussion, interrupt, overlap, and use silence as a means of controlling conversations even though men tend to be dominant in this area. It's important to remember that gender is a biologically based and culturally learned sexual orientation.

The clearest explanation for male/female differences in nonverbal behavior is that we are taught to behave differently through socialization. Women are expected to be more interpersonally sensitive and men are taught to be internal with their emotions. Often enough, men tend to smile less frequently and hardly ever discuss their feelings in public.

Certainly, men and women are biologically different. However, much of our nonverbal behavior is learned through socialization. Therefore, we can analyze and effect change on sex-related issues which affect our nonverbal behavior.

Often verbal and nonverbal language work together to convey a message. Sometimes nonverbal language can work against us. Are there stereotypes of male and female behavior? Are women soft-spoken, insecure, and highly emotional? Are men poor listeners, too aggressive, and dominant? If we believe in gender-based stereotypes we are creating a barrier for change in our communication. It's up to us to stop gender from creating a wall between the sexes.

The media also shapes our perceptions of the roles of men and women. Certain magazines written for different groups of people can stereotype women and men as sexual objects. Magazine print advertisements, popular music, television, cartoons, and comic-strips have created stereotypical roles as well. However, today these stereotypes are changing to depict real people in their evolving roles. Change of this nature is a complex process and to be able to change you must understand how sex-roles are developed.

Theoretical Concepts of Sex-Role Development

There are certain clearly defined masculine and feminine personality traits which society deems as appropriate, thereby creating a person's sexual identity. Sexual stereotyping can lead to sexism which is discrimination against individuals based on gender. There are two major theories which try to explain sex-role development. They are the cognitive-developmental theory and the social-learning theory.

The social-learning theory suggests that boy and girl behaviors are developed using their parents as role models. These behaviors are developed in the preschool period. Girls can imitate their mother's role as homemaker and boys might imitate their fathers' repairing of home or car. If you've ever asked your younger sibling to define these roles they usually are able to do so without difficulty.

Children learn these genderized behaviors through a system of rewards and punishments. Parents are influential in development of sex-role behavior that is later reinforced by outside forces such as teachers and other students.

The cognitive-developmental theory which is based on the work of psychologist Jean Piaget states that the understanding of the concepts of masculine and feminine continue to develop in stages until a child is five or six years old. In this theory, children play an active part in labeling their sexual development, imitate sexual behavior, and acquire information which will improve their communication within their surroundings.

The cognitive-developmental theory proposes that children label themselves as boys or girls and then their values acquire masculine or feminine traits. In the social-learning theory a child imitates and is remembered for appropriate behavior. The chart below explains the theoretical concepts of sex role development.

Comparison of the Three Theoretical Positions of Sex-Role Development

Freudian-Identification	Social Learning	Cognitive-Developmental
Role of Innate Characteristics		
Large role; anatomy is destiny; body structure determines personality	No role	Small role; cognitive maturation; structuring of experience; development of sex identity
Role of Child In Learning Process		
Active	Passive	Active
	Motive	
Internal; reduce fear and anxiety	External; reinforcements Internal; expected reinforcements	Internal; desire for competence
Permanence of Learning		
Very permanent and Irreversible	Permanent only if external reinforcements or self reinforcements maintain behavior; difficulty in changing comes from	Semi-permanent once schemata are stabilized change depends on presentation of discrepant information and on the child's cognitive maturity

Comparison (continued)

	internalized self-reinforcements and conditioned emotional responses	
	Sources of Learning	
Parents or parent surrogates	Parents as well as the larger social system	Parents and the larger social system in interaction with the child's cognitive system
	Age of Learning — Sex Identity	
By 4 or 5	Throughout life, but early years are very important	Throughout life, but 3-20 are most important; years between 6-8 and 16-18 are crucial for change in sterotypic beliefs
	Sequence of Events in Sex-Role Acquisition	
1. Oedipus complex emerges	1. a. Perception of parent as model b. Differential reinforcement for same-sex modeling and for sex-appropriate behaviors and interests	1. a. Sex identity b. Valuing of own-sex models
2. Identification with same-sex parent 3. Sex-role identity	2. Differential modeling and imitation 3. Generalization of behaviors	2. Sex-role identity 3. Modeling of same-sex parent, peers, and other adults
4. Imitation of same-sex parent	4. Sex-role identity	4. Attachment to same-sex parent

[1] Irene H. Frieze, Jacquelynne E. Parsons, Paula B. Johnson, Diane N. Ruble, and Gail L. Zellman. *Women and Sex Roles: A Social Psychological Perspective*. New York: W.W. Norton & Company, Inc., 1978.

Spoken Language

Emerson once said: "Use what language you will, you can never say anything but what you are."

No textbook on communication would be complete without a discussion on language. Our lives are often shaped by the language we use. Everything we do involves either spoken or nonverbal language. Although the terms language and communication are often used interchangeably, they are not the same. We communicate before we learn to use language. An infant communicates its needs to the caretakers by crying. To a stranger, the cries may seem the same, but a mother is usually able to differentiate between a cry that means hunger and a cry that means discomfort or pain. At the earliest stage of development, the infant's cries are merely reflexes, but later they have different meanings.

When a message is transmitted to another, it is communication. Language, however, can be differentiated from communication by the use of symbols to convey ideas. Speech is the way language is expressed through the use of meaningful sounds.

As human beings we have the capacity to learn language. We are not born knowing all the symbols and rules of our native language. We learn them as we mature and are exposed to sounds and grammatical structure.

Speech and language are more specific than communication. "We can think of communication as the process of sharing thoughts, ideas, attitudes, feelings, and desires with others. Communication is the function of both speech and language, but we can and do communicate without using either speech or language."[2]

Language has been defined as a set of symbols that a culture has agreed upon to designate and describe people, objects, actions, concepts and relationships of all kinds. Each language has its own structure and the structures have many functions. There are many ways we use language, depending upon our age, sex, cultural background, socioeconomic status and education.

Language may be abstract or concrete. Abstract refers to words that describe something that is not tangible, that we cannot see or touch, such as love, freedom, or happiness. Concrete language describes things that can be seen and touched: a book, chair, or a table.

Additionally, we might use words that are denotative or connotative — denotative words have the actual dictionary definition and connotative words have implied meanings. For instance the word cat is denotative because it refers to a furry, fourlegged feline. The definition of beauty has many meanings but is usually "in the eye of the beholder," therefore it is connotative. "Language not only reveals a person's identity, who he is, but in some way it makes him the person he is."[3]

People have ways of avoiding language that reveals what they really mean, what is painful to them. They do this through the use of euphemisms. A euphemism is a word substitute for something we find difficult to face. For example, when talking about the death of a loved one, it is easier to say "he passed away" or "she has gone on" than he or she died.

Similarly, we employ terms that are not offensive to women and minorities. An illustration of this would be "native Americans" instead of "Indians," (an incorrect label to begin with) although the preferred term is now "indigenous peoples." Do men and women use language differently in any significant ways? In a recent book by Deborah Tannen, *You Just Don't Understand*, an explanation of sex differences in language is given. "Even if they grow up in the same neighborhood, on the same block, or in the same house, girls and boys grow up in different worlds of words. Others talk to them differently and expect and accept ways of talking from them."[4]

Children learn how to talk and converse from their parents and peers. If their parents have foreign or regional accents, children do not necessarily emulate them. However, they might learn to speak using the pronunciation of the region where they were raised. Anthropologists Daniel Maltz and Ruth Borker have summarized research showing that boys and girls have very different ways of talking to their friends. They often play together but boys and girls spend most of their time playing in same-sex groups. Some of the activities they play at are similar. Their favorite games can be different, and thusly their ways of using language in games are separated.

> Boys tend to play outside, in large groups that are hierarchically structured. Their groups have a leader who tells others what to do and how to do it, and resists doing what other boys propose. It is by giving orders and making them stick that high status is negotiated. Another way boys achieve status is to take center stage by telling stories and jokes, by sidetracking or challenging the stories and jokes of others. Boys' games have winners and losers and elaborate systems of rules that are frequently the subjects of arguments. Finally, boys are frequently heard to boast of their skill and argue about who is best at what.
>
> Girls, on the other hand, play in small groups or pairs; the center of a girl's social life is a best friend. Within the group, intimacy is key: Differentiation is measured by relative closeness. In their most frequent games, such as jump rope and hopscotch, everyone gets a turn. Many of their activities (such as playing house) do not have winners or losers. Though some girls are certainly more skilled than others, girls are expected not to boast about it, or show that they think they are better than the others. Girls don't give orders; they express their preferences as suggestions, and suggestions are likely to be accepted. Whereas boys say,

> 'Gimme that!' and 'Get outta here!' girls say, 'Let's do this,' and 'How about doing that?' Anything else is put down as 'bossy.' They don't grab center stage — they don't want it — so they don't challenge each other directly. And much of the time, they simply sit together and talk. Girls are not accustomed to jockeying for status in an obvious way; they are more concerned that they be liked.[5]

In Robin Lakoff's *Language and Women's Place* three areas of sexual differences in language are depicted. They are lexical traits (word choice), phonological traits and syntactic-pragmatic characteristics.

In terms of word choice, Lakoff believes women use a larger number of words to describe things that they are interested in. For example women use colors such as aquamarine or mauve, while men use primary colors. Also, men tend to have specific vocabularies which interest them in topic areas such as sports. Women can use more vocabulary associated with male language than vice versa. In general, larger vocabularies help people to communicate more effectively.

In terms of phonological traits Lakoff stated that women are more likely to use a statement with a rising inflection creating a question. For example "Did you enjoy the play? Pretty good?" Lakoff believes making this statement into a question weakens the communication.

An example of the use of syntactic-pragmatic characteristics occurs in tag questions used by women, such as the question, "it's really good don't you think?" Women also use hedges in their speech such as "you know" or "well" or "like." Lakoff also states that women do not tell jokes as well as men. Sex differences in language tend to reinforce stereotypes of people and create barriers in communication.[6]

As Deborah Tannen says: "We all want, above all, to be heard — but not merely to be heard. We want to be understood — heard for what we think we are saying, for what we know we meant. With increased understanding of the ways women and men use language should come a decrease in frequency of the complaint 'You just don't understand'."[7] If people listen to each other their communication is more effective.

There is no real evidence to support whether men are better listeners than women. However, cultural and gender differences affect behavior and it's difficult to measure listening performances due to these differences.

Listening

Wilson Mizner said: "A good listener is not only popular everywhere, but after a while he knows something." There could never be a truer statement.

Lisa sits in the front row in her American History class. The instructor is lecturing on the causes of the Civil War. Lisa hears every word he says, but her mind is on the date she has for the following Saturday night. What will she wear? Will he like her and ask her for another date? Should she kiss him good night? Suddenly the instructor is asking her to respond to a question. Lisa is startled, she has no idea what the question is. She heard the words, but did not process them. She wasn't listening!

What we often forget or don't realize is that the terms hearing and listening have different meanings. We hear because our ears receive and convert energy in the form of sound into nerve impulses which travel to the brain. It is the sensory perception of sound. Listening, on the other hand, is a process of interpreting what we hear and evaluating the meaning. How well we hear sounds depends upon the sensitivity of our ears. To listen and really comprehend the content of what we hear takes energy, hard work and motivation.

The importance of listening actively cannot be stressed enough. How can we communicate without listening? A student cannot learn without listening to what the professor is saying. A parent cannot know what a child is feeling without listening to his needs. A worker needs to really listen to directives in order to know exactly what the job entails.

Passive listening doesn't demand the same kind of concentration as active listening. A wife may say to her husband: "You never listen to me." He responds by saying: "I heard every word you said." "Then tell me who is coming to dinner tomorrow night?" "How should I know?" he answers. "You see, I told you you weren't listening!" she replies. He has *heard* his wife but wasn't actively listening.

Listening is most often taken for granted. It's something we think we do all the time, but how often have you forgotten a lecture the moment you stepped out of the classroom? More people than not have poor listening habits, or else set up barriers to the process without realizing why they do it. Some of these barriers include:

- Selective listening — that is choosing what we want to listen to and shutting out the rest of a message or speech. It's similar to "turning off" our ears to television or radio commercials and waiting for the program to resume before we listen again.
- Distracting noise — allowing street noises or loud conversation to interfere with our ability to listen. Some people are able to concentrate on the speaker no matter what distractions occur, others cannot shut out extraneous sounds.
- Sometimes we become too easily distracted by our own thoughts and personal concerns to concentrate on what someone else is saying. Lisa, if you remember, was too involved in thinking about her date and therefore unable to attentively listen to the instructor.
- There is a tendency among many people to pay more attention to the physical attributes of a speaker than listen to what he or she is saying. Placing too much emphasis on whether someone is too fat or too thin, how the person is dressed, etc., can distract us from listening to them.
- Sometimes we tend to formulate a response to what a speaker is saying before we hear the whole message.
- Personal bias can be a barrier to effective listening. If we go to a political debate, for example, the tendency is to listen to the candidate of our choice and not pay much attention to the others. Wouldn't it be better if we paid equal attention to both and therefore be able to determine why our choice is best?

Teachers are usually aware of the student who stares, eyes front, seemingly attentive and listening to the lecture, but like Lisa, when questioned, cannot even remember what the subject of the lecture is. This student has been pretending to listen perhaps because the subject is difficult and therefore seems boring, or because of distractions such as family problems or outside noise.

On the next page are ten keys to follow which will help you become a good listener.

▼ Ten Keys to Effective Listening ▼

	The Bad Listener	The Good Listener
1. Find areas of interest	Tunes out dry subject.	Opportunist asks "What's in it for me?"
2. Judge content, not delivery	Tunes out if delivery is poor.	Judges content, skips over delivery errors.
3. Hold your fire	Tends to enter into argument.	Doesn't judge until comprehension complete.
4. Listen for ideas	Listens for facts.	Listens for central theme.
5. Be flexible	Takes intensive notes using only one system.	Takes fewer notes Uses 4-5 different systems, depending on speakers.
6. Work at listening	Shows no energy output. Attention is faked.	Works hard, exhibits active body state.
7. Resist distractions	Distracted easily.	Fights or avoids distractions, tolerates bad habits, knows how to concentrate.
8. Exercise your mind	Resists difficult expository material; seeks light, recreational material	Uses heavier material as exercise for the mind.
9. Keep your mind open	Reacts to emotional words.	Interprets color words; does not get hung up on them.
10. Capitalize on fact that thought is faster than speech	Tends to daydream with slow speakers.	Challenges, anticipates mentally, summarizes, weighs the evidence, listens between the lines to tone of voice.

Effective listening can be learned. The first step is to evaluate the different types of listening and understand exactly what the purposes are, and secondly to learn what is meant by poor listening habits. Once these two steps are accomplished, there are actual ways to improve listening skills. Remember that listening is an active process, which means that it requires effort on the part of the receiver. When you listen to music or television while working in the kitchen, you are engaged in passive listening. No one is going to quiz you and you don't have to feed back any information. In active listening, however, you are really working and taking the situation seriously.

As students, what you want and need to do is to retain what you have heard. Many instructors base their exams on what you learned from their lectures in addition to what you have read in the textbook. Therefore, it is important that you not only actively listen, but take effective notes. Being a skilled note taker does not mean trying to write down every thing the lecturer says. Many students make the mistake of trying to take massive notes, a task that is virtually impossible, except maybe for a court stenographer.

The best way to take notes is to listen for the main point of a speech or lecture and then use key words when writing them down. Keep your notes as brief and clear as possible and always review them later.

In concluding this chapter, remember that your gender should have nothing to do with your ability to listen. Your desire to be an effective communicator will help you learn this skill. Sex is a biological category and gender is learned behavior, a culture designated to male and female activities. We are always redefining traditionally male and female roles conveyed through the use of spoken and nonverbal language. The changing nature of society has created quite a bit of chaos in the understanding of gender relationships between women and men. Women and men should not communicate differently. As people we need flexibility in our perception and empathic behavior to handle varied communication situations.

▼ ▼ ▼ Chapter III Key Terms

Gender
Listening
Empathy
Proxemics
Kinesics
Tactile Communication
Paralinguistics
Paralanguage
Language
Abstract Language
Concrete Language
Denotative Words
Connotative Words
Euphemisms
Lexical Traits
Phonological Traits

Socialization
Social-Learning Theory
Cognitive-Development Theory
Syntactic-Pragmatic Characteristics
Selective Listening

▼▼▼ Endnotes

1. Irene H. Frieze, Jacquelynne E. Parsons, Paula B. Johnson, Diane N. Ruble, and Gail L. Zellman. *Women and Sex Roles: A Social Psychological Perspective*. New York: W.W. Norton & Company, Inc., 1978.
2. Sharon L. James. *Normal Language Acquisition*. Boston, Ma.: College-Hill Press, 1990. p. 4.
3. John Stewart, ed. *Bridges Not Walls*. Philippines: Addison-Wesley Publishing Co., 1977. p. 63.
4. Deborah Tannen, Ph.d. *You Just Don't Understand*. New York: Ballantine Books, 1990. p. 43.
5. Tannen. pp. 43-44.
6. Robin Lakoff. *Language and Woman's Place*. New York: Harper & Row, 1975.
7. Tannen. *You Just Don't Understand*. p. 48.

IV

Delivery

- ▼ Remember—Nervous Is Normal!
- ▼ Breathing for Speech
- ▼ Accent Reduction
- ▼ The International Phonetic Alphabet and Guides to Foreign Speakers of American English

IV

Delivery

You are sitting in your speech class awaiting your turn to speak. Will I be next? I wish I were a thousand miles from here. Why did I take this class? Even though it is required, I could have put it off until my senior year. Who needs this? I'm never going to be a public speaker.

Call it what you will, stage or speech fright, heightened feeling, or communication apprehension is something everyone experiences when having to deliver an oral presentation. Even actors with years of experience have been known to feel butterflies in the pits of their stomachs while waiting in the wings to go on stage.

Stage fright, or better yet anxiety, has many different physical manifestations. These may take the form of dryness of the mouth, sweating palms, weak knees, swaying bodies, shortness of breath, or aimless pacing back and forth.

So, what can you do to alleviate these fears? Here are several helpful techniques you can use.

First, choose a subject of interest to you of which you have some previous knowledge. Second, be well prepared by practicing from an outline in front of a select audience. Once in front of the classroom choose friendly faces in three parts of the audience. Concentrate on delivering the message and not on what the audience may be thinking. Familiarize yourself with the environment in which you will be speaking. Lastly, learn to realize that you still have plenty of time to work things out with your speech instructor whose opinion you need to help you undertake those first challenges of preparation.

Remember — Nervous Is Normal!

You must learn to trust yourself! With each classroom experience and with the professor becoming less of a stranger and the audience becoming more familiar to you, public speaking will seem less of a threat. Speech is your natural gift, and, as you pay attention to what you look like, you must pay attention to what you sound like and how you convey your message.

Often what is missing is not only the sense of the message, but the color and vitality with which the message must be delivered. Through the use of inflection and intonation spoken language comes alive. Intonation refers to the melody of language and each language has its own intonation pattern. Inflection is the rise and fall of the pitch level within a word or phrase. For example, when the word "no" is uttered with a rising inflection, the meaning can change to "maybe." A downward inflection on the same word means an affirmative "no."

In addition to inflection and intonation, emphasis created by stressing important words helps to convey meaning. Decide which words you want to emphasize and then you will notice that the pitch will be higher, your volume louder, and the duration of the vowel sounds longer.

Other important aspects of delivery are rate (how rapidly or slowly you speak), pausing, and phrasing. Through the use of effective pausing and phrasing, your rate will become appropriate to the message. Variations of pitch, rate, and volume help to create an effective delivery.

If in practice you notice that you are tense, swaying, and moving aimlessly, plant your feet firmly on the floor and relax the upper part of your body. Breathe deeply so you relax and have enough air to support your voice. Your body movement, eye contact with the audience, use of appropriate gestures, and your physical appearance add to the overall success of your presentation.

Breathing for Speech

Breathing deeply is an excellent way to relax and you need to relax to speak well. Also, if you are aware of proper breathing for speech, you will find that your vocal tone is much stronger and your phrasing clearer.

Breath, of course, is life sustaining. We don't think about it much unless we are ill and find breathing difficult. When we breathe quietly, that is, not for speech, the periods of inhalation and exhalation are approximately equal. However, since we speak on exhaled air, the period of exhalation for speech is longer. The breathing we use for speaking is also deeper or certainly should be.

If you can learn diaphragmatic and/or abdominal breathing you will find that you have much greater control over your exhaled air and therefore a stronger vocal quality. There are many exercises for this type of breathing. You have to be careful not to use clavicular breathing, that is raising your shoulders and clavicle (collar bone) while speaking. Try it and you will find that you are breathing in a shallow manner and your voice will sound strained and tense. An exercise you might try is: Breathe deeply from the abdomen. Yawn, stretch your arms, and breathe again. Lie down, knees raised, feet and back on the floor. As you breathe, mark the movement of your abdomen and try to minimize the movement of your chest. Now stand and walk about the room, swinging your arms freely and tasting the air as you breathe it in.

The *yawn* is the ideal breath because it comes from a relaxed body and because it takes in a substantial quantity of air in an unforced manner. Deep body breathing, as deep as possible, gives the voice its fullest support and the body its fullest relaxation. Breathing effectively is important because it helps to create the way you sound.

Here are some sentences you can use to practice your breath control and articulation:

- Greta Garbo gobbled gargonza.
- Six thick thistle sticks.
- He is literally literary.
- Peggy Babcock. Peggy Babcock.
- Tonight is a light night, there's no need to use a night light on a light night like this.
- Should such a shapely sash such shabby stitches show?
- Last year I could not hear with either ear.
- Still the sinking steamer sank.
- Standing on the doorstep welcoming him in.
- Leonard laid a long ladder lengthwise on the lawn.
- He asks that thousands be held to answer with oaths.
- Hundreds wandered up and down the length and breadth of the land for months.
- Three-thousandths of an inch is the width of the line.

- This is the zither he asks for.
- In the production of plosives the breath stream is stopped.
- It is estimated that three-fifths of the earth's surface is covered by the seas.
- A fly and a flea in a flue were imprisoned, so what could they do? Said the fly, "Let us flee!" "Let us fly!" said the flea, so they flew through a flaw in the flue.
- Three months ago the thief was seen in the thick of the thicket.
- She stood at the door of Mrs. Smith's fish-sauce shop welcoming him.
- You're a regular wreck, with a crick in your neck, and no wonder you snore, for your head's on the floor, and you've needles and pins from your soles to your shins, and your flesh is a-creep, for your left leg's asleep, and you've a cramp in your toes, and a fly on your nose, and some fluff in your lung, and a feverish tongue, and a thirst that's intense, and a general sense that you haven't been sleeping in clover.
- The perfectly purple bird unfurled his curled wings and whirled over the world.
- Painted pomp of pleasure's proud parade.
- Three gray geese on the green grass grazing.
- Some folks say I lisp; when I say "soup", "soft soap", or something similar. I perceive it myself.
- Bill had a billboard. Bill also had a board bill. The board bill bored Bill so that Bill sold the billboard to pay his board bill, the board bill no longer bored Bill.
- Amidst the mists and coldest frosts with stoutest wrists and sternest boasts, he thrusts his fists against the posts and still insists he sees the ghosts.
- The weary wanderer wondered wistfully whether winsome Winifred would weep.
- When and where will you go and why?
- The queen was a coquette.

- They know not whence, nor whither, where, nor why.
- Judge not that ye be not judged, for with that judgment ye judge ye shall be judged.
- The clumsy kitchen clock click-clacked.
- Did you enjoy the rich shrimp salad?
- The very merry Mary crossed the ferry in a furry coat.
- A lonely lily lying all alone along a lonely lane.
- Alone, alone, all, all alone.

Accent Reduction

When your grandmother was in school, she may have been required to take a class in diction or elocution as it was then called. Although there have always been variations in spoken American English arising from the diverse populations in our cities, many teachers of speech recognized only one way to speak properly, ignoring cultural differences in dialect. "Dialect is a term used for a variety of a language with features of pronunciation, grammar, or vocabulary that distinguish it from other varieties (dialects) of the same language."[1] Today we recognize differences in dialects and discuss them in speech classes.

By the time you were six or seven years old, your speech pattern was pretty much developed, that is, the manner in which you produce specific speech sounds, your pronunciation, was established. Your speech reflected the way your parents spoke. You probably completed your schooling without paying much attention to the way you speak. Now that you are in college and enrolled in an oral communication course, your instructor mentions Standard American English Speech and its importance in your life.

What is meant by "standard" speech? Although there may be slight variations, standard American speech is that pattern of speaking used and approved by the majority of informed, socially aware individuals in a given geographical area. Obviously, that means that the standard in New York City and its environs is different from the standard in Boston, Los Angeles, or Chicago.

Some authorities recognize what is known as General American Speech or General American Dialect (GAD). For example, Kenneth C. Crannell states: "Although General American Speech is a much debated and, according to some experts, dated term, it has been deliberately chosen to indicate the speech generally used in the Midwest, West, and Northwest. General American contains fewer distinguishing speech characteristics than the speeches of any of the other regions."[2]

Not too long ago, a New York dialect was all too common in the college classroom. Today, in the 90s there has been an influx of new immigrants from various parts of the world phasing out "New Yorkese" as you can read in the *New York Times* article of February 14, 1993 by Deborah Sontag.[3]

Oy Gevalt! New Yawkese An Endangered Dialect?

Deborah Sontag

Tawk to a young New Yawkuh dese days and de foist ting you may notice is dat he aw she don't tawk like dis no maw.

Although New Yorkers' emphatic, finger-in-the-chest style of talking is alive and well, the oi of Toidy-Toid Street, the er of Erster Bar and the dises, dems and doses of legend have gone the way of Automats, Ebbets Field and American-born taxi drivers.

New Yawk Tawk at its purest persists in the city's few white ethnic enclaves, among older New Yorkers, and in movies about the mob and television shows about detectives. But on the playgrounds and in the offices of daily New York life, the pungent dialect that brands New Yorkers in the popular American imagination seems to be fading into history.

Creeping Gumbelism

In fact, just as California claimed the Dodgers, the Giants and the "Tonight" show, it has also grabbed the tongues of many middle-class New Yorkers. Across the country, the regional dialects of many other educated Americans, in this increasingly mobile and television-saturated society, are also becoming muted.

"We all sound like TV announcers," said William Stewart, a sociolinguist who teaches at the CUNY Graduate Center. "West Coast norms have taken over the whole country."

But no city's identity cleaves so closely to its dialect as that of New York. And as the accent fades, the question of what is replacing it—if anything beyond a group of ethnically Balkanized dialects—goes to the heart of New York City's changing persona.

As New York City increasingly becomes a multiracial city, with large numbers of new immigrants from the Caribbean, Latin American and Asia, it is only natural that a language shaped for decades by Irish, Italian and Eastern European settlers should change. The changes are evolving and difficult to define. But an immigrant child looking for linguistic role models at a public school is more likely to meet American-born children speaking variations of black, Puerto Rican English than the New Yawkese of yore, or yaw.

"Certainly, the Yiddishisms that were part of my dialect as a child have disappeared among the Puerto Ricans on the East Harlem block I'm studying," said Ana Celia Zentella, a linguist at Hunter College. "They all say, 'Yo!' and 'What's up?', but they wouldn't know words like shmatte and shiksa and oy gevalt and oy vay."

Christopher Lockner, 26, a counterman at the Pastrami King in Kew Gardens, Queens, prides himself on being a speaker of genuine New Yorkese. "I'll put it to you this way—we are a dying breed," he said, "I got a 7-year-old brothuh who has no accent watsoevuh. The kid's great, there's nothing wrong with him, but it's like he talks more laid-back, like his mouth is easier on the words."

Certainly traces of the dialect spoken by Mr. Lockner can still be found in every neighborhood of the city and among all ethnic and racial groups. In some instances, the purest New Yawk tawk has just moved to the suburbs to Long Island and the Oranges in New Jersey. But linguists say it is unlikely to find a stable home there once a New Yorker becomes upwardly mobile, his accent tends to fade with time, self-consciousness and outside influences.

Some, however, believe that police officers will keep the language alive. They seem to wear the tawk as a badge of identity.

The New York accent, variously called Bowery Dialect, Brooklynese and New Yorkese, has always been a point of both pride and shame. On the one hand, it was considered unrefined, something to be erased through education. On the other, it was gloried in a code that linked New Yorkers in colorful communication that was both common and exclusive.

Barrier to Advancement

But many older New Yorkers, including such expressive types as Henny Youngman and Edward L. Koch, assert that they do not speak the dialect or that it has never existed outside Jimmy Durante movies.

At the Friar's Club in Manhattan recently, Mr. Youngman declared of the New York dialect: "There was never such a thing." (A nearby diner joked, "Take his accent, pohleez!")

And Mr. Koch, noting that his grammar was perfect because he had studied Latin acknowledged only, "My intonation is not Midwest." And he added that the death of strong New York dialect should not be mourned.

"I would not want our kids to go back to dis and dem," he said. "I think it would be hah-rubble. It would cost them many rungs."

In the 1890s, when E.H. Babbit, a linguist, conducted one of the first studies of the English of New York City, nearly everyone transformed the "er" sound to an "oi" sound, as in "Foist" and "Toid" Avenues, said Charles Cairns, a linguistics professor at Queens College.

Foreign Accent to Immigrants

On the elevated tracks at 81st Street in Brooklyn, for example, 81 of 100 train guards passing through the station yelled out, "Eighty-foist!" Mr. Babbitt found. Some linguists believe the Irish immigrants of the 18th and 19th centuries imported the "oi" or "awy" sound, which also transformed liars into lawyers.

Mr. Babbit found, however, that new immigrants were not picking it up. "Outsiders, unless they come to New York very young, rarely adopt it; but the genuine born-and-bred New Yorker rarely escapes it," he wrote.

A century later, when Martin Gross, the principal of Public School 14 in Corona, Queens, recently told his class of fourth graders about his friend who has "poiple coitains" on the window in his living room, the students dissolved into giggles.

"There's Americans all over the place and they don't talk funny like that!" said Nabeel Tahir, who like almost everyone else in his class is from an immigrant family.

In the traditional New York City dialect that Nabeel and his classmates do not speak, "t's" are swallowed in words like bottle and made sibilant in words like time. Singer rhymes with finger. Words like nude drop any hint of a y before the u. Them turns to dem, and thing to ting. Bad, bag, cab, and cash take a low, long front vowel. And, among the most persistent traits, coffee is cawfee, regular or light.

A Matter of Class

Most typically, the classic New Yorker drops "r's" after vowels where they should be pronounced, as in flowuh powhu, and adds them when they do not exist as in idea(r) and Cuber (home of Fidel).

William Labov, a linguist who published a definitive description of New York dialect in 1964, researched the use of "r" in a study at Saks, Macys and S. Klein. Employees at each store were asked where a department like women's shoes could be found in order to elicit the answer, "fourth floor."

At Saks, the ritziest of the stores, employees were most likely to pronounce the r; at Klein's, the bargain basement, they were most likely to drop it.

Linguists generally agree that local dialects are most likely to develop and persist in working-class and poorer communities whose residents do not have much contact with other ways of speaking.

A Subway Ride to Eloquence

"When you're looking at someone's verbal repertoire, you have to look at the social networks they're in," Professor Zentella said. "If young people from East Harlem go downtown to offices with a lot of different kinds of people, that changes not only their language but their hair styles and the way they dress."

Watching television, going away to college and moving in this increasingly mobile society all chip away at the regional accents of many Americans. Judy Schwarz, a 45-year-old teacher who grew up in Flatbush, said she "tawked the tawk" until she left the state to go to college.

"It was like someone took a vacuum cleaner to all the really noticeable parts of my accent," Mrs. Schwarz said recently, on a visit to her old neighborhood from her new home in Philadelphia. "When I would go home for vacations, they told me I was starting to sound like I was British."

The evolution and devolution of dialects is a complicated linguistic matter. Miriam R. Eisenstein, a sociolinguist at New York University, said that salient features of a dialect often begin to disappear when speakers become conscious of them—particularly if the features are caricatured or stigmatized.

"When Archie Bunker went on the air saying 'terlet' for toilet, its use in New York began to decline," Ms. Eisenstein said. "Likewise, when comedians began mockingly saying muddah and faddah, people developed the attitude that dropping the r was a definite sign of lack of mental development."

Often people who consider themselves upwardly mobile try to erase features of dialect brought to their attention, just as immigrants or children of immigrants often strive to erase the traces of their native tongue.

"Sometime, I intentionally try to lose the accent totally, to assimilate," said Nilsa Buon, a Puerto Rican woman who grew up in East Harlam. "Sometime, I'm like, what the heck, it's too much of an effort."

As close to a million new immigrants settled in the city during the last decade, the English of New York City was pushed and pulled in new and often subtle directions. "When you have lots of people coming in from different language backgrounds, what they're bringing is going to influence what emerges as the lingua franca," said Clifford Hill, a linguist at Columbia University.

And it is still unclear whether a new, citywide dialect will emerge—or whether new New Yorkers, particularly young ones, will gravitate toward the sounds and rhythms of the black English and Spanish-influenced English of school playgrounds or toward the more homogenized accents of television newscasters.

Do you find that your accent gets in your way when trying to communicate with a friend or when interviewing for a job or when speaking in front of a class? Read the article called "When an Accent Becomes an Issue" by Raymond Hernandez of *The New York Times* of March 2, 1993.[4]

▼ Immigrants Turn to Speech Classes to Reduce Sting of Bias ▼

Raymond Hernandez

When Carmen Friedman, an immigrant from Colombia, began dating the man who would become her husband, she felt embarrassed because she mispronounced his first name, Joseph, as "Yoseph."

When she started a job as a substitute teacher a year ago, she dreaded going to work, becoming nauseated at the thought of having to speak in front of a new class.

Finally, when she realized that her accent had not diminished, even after nearly five years in the United States, she became so unnerved by the idea of not fitting in that she paid for lessons to eliminate her accent.

"I don't want my accent to hurt my self-esteem anymore," said Mrs. Friedman, who is 31 years old and lives in Queens. "I know I can get my point across in English, but I don't want to feel uncomfortable every time I say something."

Still an Impediment

As the ethnic composition of New York City and the nation changes under a growing tide of immigration, accents are still an impediment, even a stigma, for millions of people in school, at work and in social settings.

Aside from the differences of comprehension that thick accents may create, immigrants say that their experiences often reflect an underlying bias against them. But they feel their choice is between speech lessons or exclusion.

Saying they face ridicule, condescension or hostility, many immigrants go to great lengths to reduce their accents and speak like natives, often seeking speech therapists and tutors for help.

And in a few isolated cases, people who have felt discriminated against because of their accents have turned to the courts, making formal complaints like those filed for years by victims of racial and ethnic discrimination.

"People still think that there is no problem with being intolerant over the way other people speak," said Charles Cairns, a professor of linguistics at Queens College and the City University of New York Graduate Center. "They feel that it's acceptable to criticize or discriminate against people with nonstandard ways of speaking English."

Turning to Speech Lessons

Even though experts say such sentiments amount to bias, immigrants have turned to speech lessons offered by tutors, private companies and colleges. Although it is difficult to determine how many people have taken such courses, experts say they are becoming increasingly popular among immigrants.

Pace University, for instance, offers about four voice and diction courses each semester that include lessons on accent reduction, up from about two classes five years ago. At New York Speech Improvement Services in Manhattan, more than half of the 200 clients that come weekly are immigrants.

At the same time, many immigrants who are fluent in English are debating whether they need such courses at all and whether by taking them they are surrendering their cultural identity.

"Sometimes native Americans act like they have never heard a person with an accent," said Galo Conde, a New York City public-school teacher who arrived from Colombia 20 years ago and who says he has often been snubbed by others, including his students, because of his accent. "But I think when you have an accent it gives you a certain originality, something that is singular, something that is yours."

Divisions Aren't New

The divisions and debate over accents and dialects have long been a part of American culture, from condescension toward a Southern drawl or Brooklynese to the question of whether black English is a legitimate dialect to the more recent issue of whether Caribbean schoolchildren in New York City who speak dialectal English should be entitled to lessons in English as a second language.

"Speech has always been a popular indicator of education and intelligence," said Sam Chwat, a speech therapist and director of New York Speech Improvement Services who counts among his accomplishments teaching Robert De Niro to shed his New York accent for his role in "Cape Fear." "To me, it is cosmetic. It has nothing to do with your logic, fund of information or ability to problem-solve."

Yet remarks, gibes and ridicule about accents arouse anger, insecurity and shame among their targets, leaving many immigrants feeling cheated of the chance to assimilate.

Making Accent an Issue

One such person, a Dominican woman from Queens, enrolled reluctantly in accent-elimination classes last month after the corporation she worked for made an issue of her accent in her last two job reviews.

The woman, a 48-year-old senior accountant who spoke on the condition of anonymity because she feared losing her job, learned English within a few years of arriving in the United States in 1967 and later earned a master's degree in business at St. John's University.

But in otherwise positive job reviews recently, she said, her managers complained that they often could not understand her because of her thick accent. She found the criticism absurd, particularly since no one had previously raised the issue during her more than 20 years of employment there, but she went to a speech-evaluation clinic nonetheless.

"They said there was no problem understanding me," she said of the people at the clinic.

Now she is suspicious and angry, wondering if the criticism was concocted to keep her from being promoted, as she hopes to be. "I think this whole thing has been fabricated to keep me from advancing within the company," she said. With much bitterness, the woman said she chose to conform rather than complain.

"It's been a very sad experience for me," she added.

Attitudes Reflect Biases

Experts who study the interaction between social behavior and language say that attitudes toward accents often reflect other biases. Many people, for instance, view a French accent as romantic while they dismiss as incomprehensible the accents of immigrants from Asian or Latin American countries.

"Our linguistic perceptions fall along class and racial lines in the country," said Randolph Wills, managing attorney for New York City's Human Rights Commission, which in the last year investigated three cases in which people said they were denied jobs because of their accents. One company settled with a complainant and the other cases are pending.

The bias arises daily in many ways and places, in a report last February, the United States Commission on Civil Rights identified discrimination against Asian-Americans in the workplace, citing, among other things, discrimination against those with accents, in Westfield, Mass., hundreds signed a petition last summer to bar teachers with accents from teaching young children.

A Federal Lawsuit

Last year, the Federal Equal Employment Opportunity Commission filed its first lawsuit on the issue, accusing a California company of discrimination after it dismissed an employee who was a native of India because the company felt his accent was not good for its image. Officials and experts predict that similar cases will arise as more immigrants arrive.

"The issue seems to have come of age," said Raj K. Gupta, executive assistant to the agency's commissioner, referring to a flurry of letters and telephone calls from people who, after having learned about the first lawsuit, described similar cases of bias to the agency.

Many more immigrants, however, live silently amid what they describe as hostility toward them because of the way they speak.

Ten years ago, when Mari Santana was studying broadcasting at Montclair, N.J., a professor urged her to change her major suggesting that her accent would be a liability, she said, "'It's still not too late for you to change your major'." she recalled him telling her each time she entered his class, "'You'll never get a job'."

A Course She Didn't Need

Demoralized, Ms. Santana, a native of the Dominican Republic, enrolled in a speech course, but the instructor felt she did not need the lessons and asked her to leave to make room for someone who did.

Ms. Santana, whose accent is slight, felt desperate. "It became an obsession for me to graduate and move on," she said. In 1983, Ms. Santana finished college and has since worked as a reporter in both English and Spanish-language television.

She is now an anchorwoman for the evening news at a local Spanish-language station, Channel 47, and acknowledges that during her career, she has met a few people who are put off by the way she speaks English. She has come to see character, however, even charm, in her accent. "I have to be me," she said, although she adds that she is taking diction courses to broader her job prospects.

Some linguists question the value of accent-reduction instruction, arguing that accents should not be treated as impairments, particularly when they do not hurt communication. Some even say the lessons prey on fears, while those who teach the courses maintain that they help bolster self-confidence.

"I question the need for an accent-correction course when the person can already be understood," said Angela Parrino, an assistant professor of applied linguistics at Hunter College who teaches an accent reduction class at Queens College.

No Promises

The other morning, on the first day of her new class, Ms. Parrino made no promises to her students about what they would sound like when the course ended in May. Instead, she stressed the importance of speaking clearly and carefully, while pointing out the among native Americans there is a diversity of speech patterns and dialects.

One student in the class, John Castillo, a 22-year-old from Colombia, feels that the course is critical to his future. "To tell you the truth," he said during a break, "this class is my last hope. If it doesn't work out, I'm going back to my country."

The problem, he said, is that he feels his accent sets him apart from others, even though he has lived in this country for nine years. He graduated from Newtown High School in Queens and is now a junior at Queens College.

"I was practically raised in this country," he said, speaking in a soft, lilting accent. "But I have this accent. Does that mean I'm not an American? I don't know."

The speech pattern you have been using all of your life may differ from the concept of General American Speech. It might be influenced by your African-American, Asian-American, Latino, Russian, or Creole background. If you are reluctant to give up your speech pattern for fear of losing touch with your culture, you don't have to! What we suggest is that you realize that a clear speech pattern is an important tool not only in the college classroom but also in the outside world.

Remember, your speech pattern, or accent, is only faulty if it interferes with what you are trying to say. If your listeners are more aware of how you are saying something than they are of what you are saying, then you might want to correct your accent.

If Eliza Doolittle, the *My Fair Lady* of *Pygmalion*, could change her Cockney accent, you certainly can learn to change those few customary diction characteristics that interfere with the clarity and meaning of what you are saying.

If you decide you want to improve your speech, don't be afraid to ask your instructor for help. Your speech class is the best place to correct any diction problem. Don't wait until you are in an interview situation where you are in competition with others and subject to evaluation by the interviewer.

The best way to check your pronunciation is by using the phonetic alphabet to find the desired manner and place of speech sounds. The words you speak are made up of individual phonemes (sounds) which should be articulated clearly. Unfortunately, English spelling has little to do with the way words are pronounced. Phonetics helps you to break down a word into its distinctive sounds and gives you a visual clue in recognizing how a word should be pronounced. There are several phonetic dictionaries in your library, or if these are unavailable, you can check the diacritical pronunciation key in any good standard dictionary. Also, listen carefully to your instructor and to those speakers who are considered to be experts.

Earlier in our discussion, we mentioned Standard American Speech and dialects. Dialects are fairly consistent variations from Standard American English and are associated with particular groups of people who live in the same area. If you listen carefully to African-American dialect, for example, you will find that it is not totally different from so-called Standard American Speech. The problem is, when is a dialect appropriate? This has to be your decision based on what you learn from your own experiences and from your speech class. Learn to listen to yourself in order to become aware of how you sound to yourself and to others.

The International Phonetic Alphabet and Guides to Foreign Speakers of American English

The International Phonetic Alphabet has been in existence since 1888, and its core is the Roman Alphabet, our basic symbol system. Since it was designed by a group of European scholars, many of the symbols which had to be added to the Roman Alphabet system may look strange to you. We operate for spelling purposes with the twenty six letters of the Roman Alphabet, but we actually produce more than forty sounds in spoken English. This has been an unending problem not only for those whose native tongue is English, but a problem of great complexity for those who learn our language after they have learned their own. Our spelling patterns in English are highly unphonetic; that is, they do not look like what they sound like. A very simple example is "school" which in phonetic transcription looks like (skul), and therefore looks more like what it sounds like.

When you turn to the dictionary to determine the preferred pronunciation of a word you will see different symbols used originally by Websters known as the diacritical marking system. We believe the phonetic system is more precise, more highly individualized with one sound per symbol and one symbol per sound. Phonetics is not a language; it is only a system of symbols representing sounds.

On the following pages is the sound system of American English (IPA) to be used by you.

SOUND SYSTEM OF AMERICAN ENGLISH

Consonant Sounds

IPA Symbols	Examples					Dictionary Symbol
Plosives						
/p/	pay	cup	supper	stopped		p
/b/	buy	rub	rubber	robbed		b
/t/	take	hit	letter	missed		t
/d/	dime	hide	ladder	wanted		d
/k/	keep	take	banker	ache		k
/g/	go	egg	again			g
Fricatives						
/s/	sit	bus	past	cats		s
/z/	zero	does	easy	dogs		z
/ʃ/	she	cash	issue	ocean	motion	sh
/ʒ/		beige	leisure			zh
/f/	fish	rough	laughing	physics		f
/v/	very	have	ever			v
/θ/	think	earth	nothing			th
/ð/	these	breathe	brother			th
/h/	house		ahead	who		h
Affricates						
/tʃ/	church	each	capture	cello		ch
/ʤ/	jump	judge	danger	page	giant	j
Nasals						
/m/	me	come	summer			m
/n/	no	run	money	hand	know	n
/ŋ/		sing	singing			ŋ
Lateral and Glides						
/l/	like	pool	allow	glass		l
/w/	we		award	quart		w
/hw/	when		nowhere	what		hw
/r/	rain		sorry	grow		r
/j/	you		onion	music	million	y

Vowel Sounds

IPA Symbols	Examples					Dictionary Symbol
Front						
/i/	eat	meet	ski	believe		ē
/ɪ/	it	city	different			i
/e/, /er/#	ate	obey	rain	pay		ā
/ɛ/	red	ready	sweater	guest	egg	ĕ
/æ/	at	sad	hand	salmon		ă
Back						
/u/	too	sue	chew	fruit	rude	o͞o ü
/ʊ/	wood	would	push	crook		o͝o u̇
/o/, /oʊ/#	go	hello	stone	widow		ō
/ɔ/	all	jaw	taught	boss	thought	ô ŏ
/a/	arm	calm	stop	clock	father	ä o
Central						
/ʌ/*	under	cut	sun	son	flood	u ŭ
/ə/**	among	banana	above	Russia		ə
/ɜˆ/*	murder	bird	world	search	purpose	ər ûr
/ɚ/**	father	actor	scholar			ər
Diphthong						
/eɪ/	late	raid	rain	strange		ā
/aɪ/	time	cry	lie	why	sigh	ī
/ɔɪ/	boy	oil	noise			oi
/aʊ/***	now	house	doubt	power		ou au
/ɪɚ/##	peer	sheer	beer			ê
/ɛɚ/##	pear	share	bear			â
/ɔɚ/##	pour	shore	bore			
/ʊɚ/##	poor	sure	boor			

* Stressed syllables
** The 'schwa' is used in unstressed syllables.
*** /aʊ/ is also acceptable
\# The diphthongs [eɪ]and [oʊ] are variations of the /e/ and /o/ phonemes. For practical teaching purposes, the /eɪ/ and /oʊ/ are indicated phenomically to signal differences in meaning in General American Dialect.
\#\# In certain regions such as New York City, New England, and in the South, where /r/ is omitted, the variants [ɪə, ɛə, ɔə, ʊə] are often heard. For practical teaching purposes, the variants listed in the chart are indicated phonemically to signal difference in meaning in General American Dialect. Phonemic representations are usually /ɪr, ɛr, ɔr, ʊr/.

5 Joyce Buck and Irene Alterbaum. *Listen Speak: Pathways to Better Speech,* 2nd edition. Dubuque, Iowa: Kendall Hunt Publishers, 1991. pp. 10-11.

The following charts are for those students for whom English is a second language. The problems that arise in spoken American English for many non-native speakers are commonly known as sound substitutions and distortions, and in some cases additions of sounds where they do not necessarily belong.

Keep in mind that not all nonnative speakers have the same difficulties. Check the charts below and become aware of those sounds with which you have problems.

If you come from a Spanish-speaking country, you should be aware of the following:

Sound Substitution	Sample Word	Phonetic Transcription
d for ð (voiced th)	this	dɪs/ðɪs
t for θ (unvoiced th)	think	tiŋk/θɪŋk
b for v	very	berɪ/verɪ
s for z	zoo	su/zu
ng for n	been	bɪŋ/bɪn
ʤ for j	you	ʤu/ju
tʃ for ʃ	shoe	tʃu/ʃu
ʃ for tʃ	cheap	ʃip/tʃip
i for ɪ	if	if/ɪf
ɪ for i	beet	bɪt/bit

Note: Spanish-speaking individuals may add a sound such as a vowel to a word in which it does not belong, such as ɛ in ɛscrit. Trilled "r" sounds are also common. In English we do not trill the r.

If you are French speaking, be aware of the following:

Sound Substitution	Sample Word	Phonetic Transcription
ɪ for i	beet	bɪt/bit
i for ɪ	slip	slip/slɪp
ɛ for æ	man*	mɛn/mæn
ʃ for tʃ	choose	ʃuz/tʃuz
ʒ for ʤ	jam	ʒæm/ʤæm
z for ð	that	zæt/ðæt
s for θ	thin	sɪn/θɪn
_for h (this sound is omitted)	hat	æt/hæt

*This vowel sound is nasalized and often the final consonant (in this case "n") is omitted.
**The word is "street." There should be no vowel preceding it.

Note: In French the "r" sound as in "red" is trilled, that is, made in the back of the throat or using the tongue tip. In English the "r" is made by pulling the tongue back to the center of the palate.

If you come from an Asian country such as China, be aware of the following:

Sound Substitution	Sample Word	Phonetic Transcription
i for ɪ	fit	fit/fɪt
r for l	blue	bru/blu
l for r	brake	blek/brek
ts for tʃ	chew	tsu/tʃu
d for ð	this	dɪs/ðis
z for ð	this	zis/ðis
s for z	is	ɪs/ɪz

Note: For Korean students the sound of [ɝ] as in world is difficult to pronounce.
Sometimes final consonants such as s, t or d are omitted and may also be omitted in the middle of words.

If your native language is Russian, be careful of the following:

Sound Substitution	Sample Word	Phonetic Transcription
ɪ for i	deep	dɪp/dip
i for ɪ	dip	dip/dɪp
a for ʌ	but	bat/bʌt
ɔ for o	boat	bɔt/bot
v for w	work	vɝk/wɝk
w for v	visit	wɪzɪt/vɪzɪt
f for v	alive	əlaɪf/əlaɪv
z or d for	that	zœt/ðœt dœt/ðœt
s or t for	throw	sro/θro tro/θro

Note: A [g] is often added to [ng] in the middle and end of words such as "ringing" or "singing." Sometimes the sound of [g] is substituted for an [h].

Following are some word lists for practice:

Voiced th [ð]
the
their
this
that
those
these
mother
father
brother
bathe

[r]
run
race
right
raw
rub
reason
rule
rock
brown
ring
wrong

[ʃ]
shoe
shine
shake
ship
shell
shop
shin
cash
mash
lash

[s]
sue
some
same
sorry
sin
soap
basket
fuss
mass
sauce

Unvoiced th [θ]
thin
throw
think
thimble
thumb
Thursday
bathtub
birthday
arithmetic
bath

[l]
look
lace
light
law
left
lion
library
lonely
blue
yellow
long

[tʃ]
chew
China
choke
chip
cherry
chop
chin
catch
match
latch

[z]
zoo
zone
zebra
exist (has the z sound)
zinc
busy (has the z sound)
easy (has the z sound)
buzz
Thursday (has the z sound)
breeze

[dʒ]
jam
jello
jet
joke
jewel
jump
just
joy
budget
danger

[w]
went
west
wine
wail
wet
wane
wary
wow
worse
wise

[i]
beat
deed
feet
heat
heel
meet
neat
seat
peal
seal

[o]
oak
oat
old
coat
hole
open
row
bow
slow

[j]
yam
yellow
yet
yoke
yule
yawn
your
year
amuse
senior

[v]
vent
vest
vine
vale
vet
vain
vary
vow
verse
vise

[ɪ]
bit
did
fit
hit
hill
mitt
knit
sit
pill
sill

[ɔ]
ball
bought
bald
caught
hall
off
raw
bore
slaw

[ʌ]
up
under
come
club
double
mother
ugly
oven
young
study
touch
public

[h]
hot
habit
heart
hope
hand
he
hole
happen
behind
how
ahead
hello

A good delivery depends on your ability to use your nervous energy to your own advantage. Use your breath to relax as well as support your speech sounds. By using all of the techniques discussed in this section you will feel secure and confident to speak in public.

▼ ▼ ▼ Chapter IV Key Terms

Inflection	Inhalation
Intonation	Exhalation
Emphasis	Diaphragmatic Breathing
Pitch	Abdominal Breathing
Volume	Clavicular Breathing
Rate	Dialect
Duration	Pronounciation
Pausing	Phoneme
Phrasing	Diacritical Marking System
Articulation	International Phonetic Alphabet (IPA)

▼ ▼ ▼ Endnotes

1. Jon Eisenson. *Voice and Diction,* 5th edition. New York: MacMillan, 1985. p. 45.
2. Kenneth C. Crannell. *Voice and Articulation,* 2nd edition. California: Wadsworth, 1991. p. 346.
3. Sontag, Deborah. "Oy Gevalt! New Yawkese An Endangered Dialect?", *The New York Times*. 14 February 1990. p. 1.
4. Hernandez, Raymond. "When an Accent Becomes an Issue," *The New York Times*. 2 March 1993. sec. B, p. 1.
5. Joyce Buck and Irene Alterbaum. *Listen Speak: Pathways to Better Speech,* 2nd edition. Dubuque, Iowa: Kendall Hunt Publishers, 1991. pp. 10-11.

V

Creating Effective Presentations

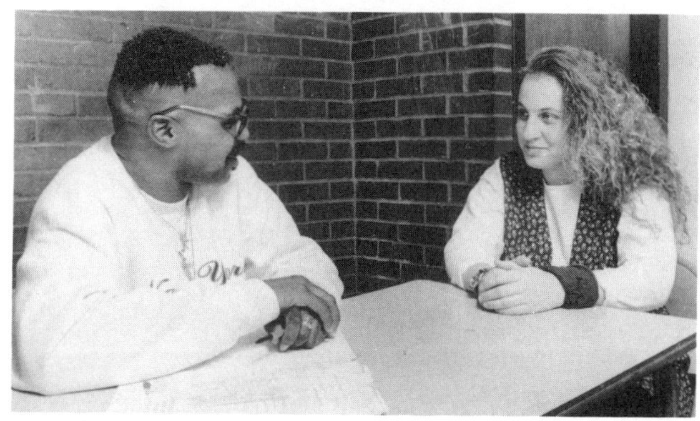

- The Treasured Library: Gathering Materials
- The Library
- The Media
- The Interview
- Your Personal Experiences
- Note Taking
- Outlining: Introduction, Body, Conclusion
- Styles of Presentation
- Patterns of Organization
- Supporting Your Speech
- Bibliography
- Visual Aids

▼▼▼▼▼▼▼▼▼▼▼▼▼▼▼▼▼▼▼▼ V

Creating Effective Presentations

The Treasured Library: Gathering Materials

The first question students usually ask when the instructor assigns a speech is "what shall I talk about?" The second question is always "where will I find information?" What you will talk about depends upon the assignment and purpose of your speech. Once you have decided upon a topic and know the specific purpose, either to inform or to persuade, your next step is to locate appropriate information to support your main idea.

The Library

Your best source of information for any topic is your library card catalog (or library computer). In the card catalog you will find books listed alphabetically by author, subject, and title. If you have no specific books in mind, look for the subject word in the card catalog. Sometimes there will be a card entry with the notation to "See" or "See also" other subject headings. Most of the books you will need can be taken home, but there are many books on reserve and you may use them in the reading room of the library. If you are not familiar with how to use the card catalog, ask your librarians. They are trained to help you. Don't be afraid to ask!

In addition to the card catalog, you have a wide variety of periodicals and reference books to choose from. Virtually every profession is represented in journals and abstracts, from arts and sciences to business administration. If you want to consult one of these journals or abstracts, there are periodical indexes which may be found in a special section of your library. Almost all scholarly journals and some popular periodicals have their own annual indexes. There are also reference books which are on open shelves in all libraries. Although they may not be taken home, they are easy to use and should be consulted when preparing a speech. These include encyclopedias which can give you a broad overview and always include a bibliography of additional suggested readings.

The Media

The media is another way of gathering information. Radio and television broadcasts can be very informative, especially those dealing with current political and social issues. Sometimes, for a small fee, you can send to the station for a transcript of an entire interview or panel discussion.

Newspapers and magazines are also useful in gathering information for your speech. They are especially helpful in finding appropriate quotations and anecdotes.

The Interview

A fascinating and rewarding way to gather information is by interviewing a person who is an expert on a particular topic. As students in a University, you have experts in almost every area available to you. Most professors are willing to answer questions if you make an appointment to see them during their office hours. There are also people in your community who are available and who will be able to help you. For example, your congressman can answer questions on current political issues; your local precinct police captain can answer questions on crime in the community or the high school principal in your area is a good source of information concerning educational policies in the schools. Your parents and friends, as well, have varied backgrounds and interests and may often provide information you won't find in books.

If you ask questions fairly, with an open, pleasant manner, most people are willing to help!

Your Personal Experiences

Never underestimate your own personal experiences and interests. You make your speech unique! Take a few minutes to sit down and search through those little compartments of your mind that store experiences and knowledge. Although your awareness of a subject may not be considered "factual" material, it can supply important and interesting details to support your main idea. After all, it is *your* point of view that makes a speech original.

Note Taking

Once you have gathered all your materials together, it is important that you keep track of all the information. The best way to do this is to take careful notes. Separate index cards or sheets of paper make your note taking easier. Direct quotes must be taken down word for word, but other information can be put in your own words. Always include your sources in your notes, so that you know where each idea came from and can always document your information if questioned.

It is important to start gathering your materials as soon as possible. As soon as you know your topic and have a specific date for your speech, start planning your research.

Outlining: Introduction, Body, Conclusion

As your first speech assignment you have been asked to present something about your life to your fellow classmates. What do you do first? Of course the instructor says you can choose your own way to present this information. What does this mean to you? You are probably thinking to yourself, how do I do this? And by now anxiety is controlling your feelings. But, relax — you can really do this if you follow a few major concepts.

You must create a specific purpose and central idea (basic thesis statements) to express the main ideas you will be presenting. Develop main points and subpoints which support the specific purpose and the central idea. Analyze, evaluate, and choose an appropriate pattern of arrangement, such as chronological, topical, or spatial, problem-solution or cause-effect which will show the relationship and create organization between the main points. A well-structured speech is created by using three parts — the Introduction, the Body, and the Conclusion.

It has been proven by successful people that they can do more activities in one day than other people because they can organize their time more effectively. A person who speaks for a long time does not necessarily say as much as a person who has learned to state things clearly in a properly organized way.

Good organization is important for three reasons: First, it lets you say exactly what you need to within a given time. Second, it helps the audience to follow your logic more effectively and remember what you've said. And third, it helps you to cover what you've planned to say.

An outline is the most efficient way of presenting your material. Once you can outline well you will find it easier to talk to your audience in an extemporaneous manner.

Through years of coaching students on speech outlining techniques we've noticed that many students feel compelled to write out their entire speech word for word and then create an outline from this text. Our recommendation is that you write only an outline of phrases and words, however, whatever method works best for you is the one you should use.

The Introduction to a speech is probably the hardest and most important part to create and develop. Your Introduction should be designed to let the audience know your topic and establish the topic's importance to them. Also, your Introduction should capture and establish a rapport with your audience.

How do you create a good Introduction? Through the use of a five-step plan: 1) attention-getter (A/G), 2) specific purpose (S/P), 3) central idea (C/I), 4) value statement (V/S), and 5) transition (T), you can provide the audience the essential ingredients needed to follow your particular speech topic.

An attention-getter is used to stimulate the audience's senses and thus engage them to your topic. For example you could use a question, quote, dramatic story, poem or song lyric, or a statistic. These techniques could startle, create curiosity, establish credibility, and motivate your audience to listen on.

The second step of the Introduction should be your specific purpose. As quoted from Stephen Lucas' *The Art of Public Speaking*, a specific purpose "should focus on one aspect of a topic. You should be able to state your specific purpose in a single infinitive phrase (to inform my audience about...; to persuade my audience to...) that indicates *precisely* what you hope to accomplish with your speech."[1]

Your specific purpose and your central idea should not be in the form of a question. They should be declarative statements. A central idea is exactly what your speech will be about. Lucas states a central idea is "a concise statement of what you *expect to say*. Sometimes it is called the thesis statement....that refines and sharpens the specific purpose statement."[2]

A value statement creates relevance and motivates the audience to listen to your speech. Your transition is a statement which connects your Introduction to your Body. Here is an example of an effective Introduction:

A/G Sing — "Oh what a beautiful morning." How many of you recognize this melody?

S/P Well, today I'd like to inform you about the major musical comedy successes of collaborators Richard Rodgers and Oscar Hammerstein III.

C/I *Oklahoma, Carousel, South Pacific, The King and I, Flower Drum Song*, and *The Sound of Music* are some of their most renowned productions due to their strong themes, plot lines, musical scores, and well-developed characterizations.

V/S If you have never seen these productions before you may develop a love of this genre from my speech.

Transition Let's start with *Oklahoma*.

The body of your speech should consist of main points which come directly from your specific purpose and central idea and these main points are broken down into subpoints which further support and develop your ideas.

Your Conclusion is more likely to be remembered than what you have said in the Body of your speech. So, you need to clearly restate your specific purpose and central idea and use some sort of effective closing statement. Remember: Never introduce new and unanswerable ideas in your conclusion.

We would like to leave you with a simple way to remember speech format:

Introduction: Tell them what you're going to tell them.

Body: Tell them.

Conclusion: Tell them what you told them.

Remember, an outline is a way of thinking on paper to see if you have things in the proper order and to make certain you've included all elements. A prepared speech should evolve from research to a rough outline to a second outline (and a third, fourth, if necessary) to a final outline. The movement from rough outline to final outline is dictated by changes you will want to make in the order of the speech or the concentration of the information.

Standard outline sequence:

I.				(Main point)
	A.			(Subpoint)
	B.			(Subpoint)
		1.		(Sub-subpoint)
		2.		(Sub-subpoint)
			a.	(Sub-sub-subpoint)
			b.	(Sub-sub-subpoint)
			(1)	(Sub-sub-sub-subpoint)
			(2)	(Sub-sub-sub-subpoint)
II.				
				etc.

There is no need to label points as Subpoint, etc., because the numbering/letter system makes it clear.

It is best to use phrases rather than full sentences in an outline because you are concerned only with the skeleton of the speech. The text of the speech are the words *you* speak.

There is logic to an outline. For example, if there is a I level, there is also a II level; if an A, then a B; if a 1, then a 2. The principle here is: If there are not at least two subdivisions of a concept, then there cannot be any subdivision at all. Furthermore, an outline lets you determine the relative importance of a point. You know that a I level is of equal importance with a II level, and A is equal to a B. This helps the audience focus on the relative value of points within a speech.

Styles of Presentation

There are four different styles of presentation of a speech:

1. Reading from a manuscript
2. Memorization
3. Speaking impromptu
4. Speaking extemporaneously

Speaking from a manuscript is a style used by professional speakers who need to deliver long and complicated messages accurately. It is a difficult style to master since you have to make every word sound as if it is coming from you naturally. It is used primarily by politicians and prominent public speakers so that they do not misstate even a single word.

When trying to commit a speech to memory, it is easy to lose your train of thought. You might also try to memorize a particular vocal pitch or quality thus creating an unnatural delivery.

An impromptu speech is one delivered without any previous preparation. It is primarily used when a person is asked to say a few words at a social function.

An extemporaneous speech differs from impromptu. It contains a well-developed outline which allows you to speak naturally to your audience without losing your train of thought.

Patterns of Organization

There are five basic patterns of organization used by speech writers. They are topical, chronological, spatial, problem-solution, and causal or cause-effect. The topical pattern is the most commonly used arrangement of organizations and consists of breaking the speech up into its component parts creating subtopics.

Topic — Preparation for the Graduate Record Examination

Review of:

1. English Grammar
2. Reading Comprehension
3. Analogies
4. Logic
5. Mathematics

The chronological pattern is used to show time order as in a series of events or explaining a process.

Topic — Being a College Freshman

1. Application to college
2. Interview and Placement Tests
3. Acceptance and Freshman Orientation
4. Adjustment to first year

The spatial pattern is used to present physical areas following a certain direction. This pattern could explain something from top to bottom, right to left, or North to South. For example: Manifest Destiny in the United States.

Topical, chronological, and spatial patterns are used most often in informative speeches.

The problem-solution pattern is used in a persuasive speech. You present the problems to your audience and show a viable solution for these problems.

Topic — Fast Food

Problem: High Sodium and Fat content; can cause health problems if eaten in excess; does not provide balanced diet. Solution: Eat in moderation.

The causal pattern shows cause-effect relationship. You present the cause and show its effect or vice versa.

Topic — Effects of Cigarette Smoke

1. Lung cancer
2. Heart disease
3. Dangers of secondhand smoke

From your specific purpose and central idea, main points need to be developed. Write these main points in your outline first as complete sentences or phrases. When you are more comfortable with your material, then turn them into shorter phrases or words. Main points will be supported by sub-points. The pattern you choose for the organization of your speech should depend on the effect and purpose you are trying to create. Therefore, consider the patterns of arrangement to help you organize your speech in a logical fashion. The following is an outline revision sheet to help you structure your outline:

▾ Outline Revision Sheet ▾

Outline Format

- Correct your outline format
- Complete sentences, phrases, and words

Audience Analysis and Adaptation

- Be sensitive to audience demographics such as age, sex, educational background, racial and ethnic background, religion, and economic and social status
- The subject matter should be interesting to your audience
- Knowledge level of your audience

Specific Purpose

- You need a specific purpose
- The specific purpose needs to be precise
- The specific purpose should not be too broad
- The specific purpose should be appropriate for your audience

Central Idea

- You need a central idea
- The central idea must be clear
- The central idea should not be too broad

Introduction

- Add attention-getting material
- Attention-getting material must grab the listener's attention and interest
- Remember to include your value statement

Transition Between Introduction and Body

- Add a transition
- Your transition needs to be effective

Body

- The body of the speech must show a pattern of organization
- You should not make too many main points
- Your main points must be clear
- Your main points must support the central idea
- Provide strong support for all of your points
- Use visual aids

Transitions Between Main Points

- Add transitions between main points
- Transitions need to be effective

Transitions Between Body and Conclusion

- Add a transition
- Transition needs to be effective

Conclusion

- Add a conclusion
- Remember to have a closing statement
- Restate your specific purpose and central idea
- Do not put any new ideas in your conclusion

Bibliography

- Needs bibliography
- Bibliographical entries must be written correctly

Visual Aids

- List the visual aids needed for your performance

Supporting Your Speech

Okay, you've researched, organized, and outlined your speech. You have gathered all the necessary materials and now you're ready to put it together and practice it. Your next and probably most important task is to determine how you are going to get your message across to your audience. You want your audience not only to listen to you, but to remember what you say.

There are certain rhetorical devices you can use to give your speech life and make it interesting. These devices are similar to those used in the advertisements you see and hear everyday. For example, if a famous person endorses a product, consumers tend to associate that product with that person. This particular technique is called a testimonial. Speakers can use this device as well. An authority figure's quotation can be useful in backing up a statement you make, and the audience might accept your ideas more readily.

Several "figures of speech" that you may recognize from your English classes can be used to make your public address more effective. For instance, comparisons such as metaphors and similes make language much more interesting than merely making simple statements. A simile is a figure of speech expressing comparison or similarity by using terms such as like or as. It is more explicit than a metaphor which only implies a comparison. The poet Wallace Stevens in his lovely poem: "The House Was Quiet and the World Was Calm" used similes effectively such as "the summer night is like a perfection of thought...."[3] The Reverend Martin Luther King Jr. used similes and metaphors to enhance his memorable "I Have a Dream" speech. "...We will not be satisfied until justice rolls down like waters, and righteousness like a mighty stream"[4] is a simile. "Now is the time to rise from the dark and desolate valley of segregation to the sunlit path of racial injustice,"[5] is a metaphor. We must be careful, however, not to use cliches such as, "poor as a church mouse," "big as a house," or "pretty as a picture." Giving human qualities to inanimate objects or ideas is called personification, which can be effective if original and not overused.

Illustration creates a word picture giving a more realistic meaning to your speech and holding the attention of your audience. Everyone likes a story and it is easier to remember the main point of a speech when you have a strong illustration to support it. An excerpt from Jesse Jackson's speech to the Democratic National Convention on July 20, 1988 is an example of a vivid illustration: "America's not a blanket woven from one thread, one color, one cloth. When I was a child growing up in Greenville, South Carolina, and grandmother could not afford a blanket, she didn't complain and we did not freeze. Instead, she took pieces of old cloth — patches, wool, silk, gaberdine, crockersack on the patches — barely good enough to wipe off your shoes with. But they didn't stay that way very long. With sturdy hands and a strong cord, she sewed them together into a quilt, a thing of beauty and power and culture."[6]

If you want your audience to sympathize with a person who is homeless, merely telling them that a young woman is hungry and begging on the street may not impress them. However, if you compare the meals that await your audience in their comfortable homes with the shelter and meager meal the young woman is expecting, the audience will have something to relate to. Similar to comparison is contrast. Charles Dickens used the device of contrast at the beginning of *A Tale of Two Cities* when he wrote, "It was the best of times, it was the worst of times...."[7]

Repetition can be an effective device if when it is used your vocal tone changes so that the phrase doesn't sound static. Martin Luther King Jr. used this device effectively when he repeated the phrase "I have a dream" throughout his memorable civil rights speech.

Two other devices, which are excellent ways of getting your ideas across to an audience, are rhetorical questions and statistics. These are also effective means of introducing or concluding a speech.

A rhetorical question is one which doesn't require a reply because either the answer is obvious such as "Do you know what today is?" or one which gets people to start thinking along particular lines such as "Do you want to die in a war thousands of miles away from home?"

Statistics are helpful if they are not just listed but used to intrigue your listeners. If you say in an antismoking speech "Do you know that approximately 50,000 deaths a year are caused by smoking cigarettes?" your audience will sit up and listen. Of course you have to support your statistics with additional evidence.

Another way to make your presentation more effective is through the use of visual aids. They supply interest, variety, and clarity. There are many kinds of visual aids including charts, maps, photographs, and models.

Bibliography

Remember all speeches need a bibliography. Frank Post of Long Island University explains clearly how to put together a annotated: "The New Annotated Bibliography is a reference tool that you will prepare for your informative and persuasive speeches, as well as for your dramatic reading. Use at least three reference sources in each of your bibliographies. The bibliography should be delivered in the format of the Modern Language Association (MLA). Begin with listing your sources, followed by a brief statement. The statement should not just summarize the article. Your bibliographic statement should critically examine and connect the article to your topic. Following, in proper MLA format, are sample bibliographic entries for a videotape, a book, and a magazine article. You should duplicate the punctuation, underlining, capitalization, i.e, the style, that is demonstrated below. If you do not know how to cite a specific source, refer to the *MLA Handbook for Writers of Research Papers*. This reference guide is available in most bookstores and libraries. It is highly recommended that you purchase a copy as you will use it throughout your college and professional career.

(1/2" from top) Your Name

(now 1" margins all around)

(Center Title)

(Topic)

Annotated Bibliography

(two spaces down and therefore double-spaced, indent 5 spaces after first line)

Kiss of the Spiderwoman. Dir. Hector Babenco. With William Hurt and Raul Julia. Warner Brothers, 1985. Begin your citation directly after the period following the year or page number. You should really think about how you will apply your videotape and readings to your speech. Consider these entries as notes to yourself. (Video tape sample)

Puig, Manuel. *Kiss of the Spiderwoman*. New York: Vantage Books, 1990. Notice the periods, spacing, colons. Be sure to type your annotated bibliography. (Novel sample)

Smith, Marilyn. "Manuel Puig's Novels." *Time*. 30 Feb. 1988: 133-36. The numbers here indicate pages. Abbreviate the month. Each entry should be about 5 lines. Have fun! Good Luck! (Magazine sample)

Visual Aids

As the term itself implies, a visual aid is the use of an object, picture, map, etc., to help clarify and enhance your speech. Visual aids can be wonderful devices if not over-used, if they relate to your topic and are large enough for your audience to see. As with anything else, there is an art to using a visual aid. You have to make sure that you don't rely on it too much or you will take away precious time from your actual speech. Visual aids are especially useful in a demonstration speech or when explaining something technical or for reinforcement of an idea you want your audience to remember.

We live in a highly visual society. Years ago, before the advent of television, people listened to the radio. They had to use their imaginations to visualize characters in a play, actions, clothing, etc. Now, of course, television is the major medium of entertainment and news for many people. Unfortunately we no longer have to use our imaginations, it's all done for us on the screen. Audiences expect visualization. Think back to your favorite teacher in high school or your most effective professor in college. More than likely they used the chalk board when explaining an important point, or hung maps in front of the room or perhaps brought in an historical item to share with the class. We know a wonderful history professor whose favorite topic is the Civil War. When teaching it to the class, he brings in hats from the Union army and the Confederacy and an authentic firearm (unloaded of course) which he takes apart to show his students how it was used, thereby also explaining the horrors of war.

Remember your early elementary school experiences? Show and Tell was a favorite assignment. Well, now that you're in a college speech class, you have a chance to re-create your Show and Tell presentation, only in a mature, carefully prepared manner.

Here are several kinds of visual aids you can use depending upon the topic of your speech. Objects or models (reproductions of the actual object): for example, if you are giving a speech on how to use a Poloroid camera, the camera itself would certainly be a plus. You can even take a picture of your audience. Or if you are talking about the complexity of the human ear, a model of the ear with detachable parts would make your presentation clear and concrete.

Reproductions: these include pictures, plans, slides, photographs, film strips, video tapes, drawings, etc. The kind of reproduction you use, its size and shape depends upon the size of your audience and the room in which you are speaking.

Let's say you plan to speak on the plight of the homeless in New York City. Pictures of homeless men and women or even a video tape if you can find one would bring your message across with strength, and the audience would tend to keep these pictures in their minds.

Graphs, diagrams, and charts: A graph indicating the decline of the dollar in the past two decades would give clarity to a speech on this topic. Of course the graph would have to be large enough and simple enough for everyone to see and understand.

Here are some points to keep in mind when using visual aids:

1. If you use the chalk board make sure your back is not to the audience. There is a tendency to face the board when writing on it.

2. Choose visual aids that are large enough to be seen by everyone in the audience. Holding a small photograph is almost like using no visual aids at all.
3. Practice using your visual aids. Make certain you are comfortable with them so that your presentation runs smoothly.
4. Remember to keep talking and maintain your eye contact. We have observed students who forget to speak while demonstrating how to do something, thereby losing the attention of the audience. Also, long pauses while demonstrating a process can put your audience to sleep.
5. Try to set up your visual aids before you begin your speech. If this is not possible take up as little time as you can and don't allow your visual aids to become a distraction.
6. Try to avoid passing around leaflets or pictures especially during your speech. If you have handouts, it's best to distribute them before you start or after you have completed your speech.

Visual aids can be helpful and add color and vitality to your speech if they are carefully prepared and used skillfully. To give an effective presentation you must first research your topic, then author your speech in the style of presentation required, making sure that your body has a clear pattern of organization. Remember to support your speech with rhetorical devices and consider using visual aids to make your speech clearer to your audience.

▾ ▾ ▾ Chapter V Key Terms

Outlining
Introduction
Body
Conclusion
Specific Purpose
Central Idea
Main Points
Subpoints
Patterns of Organization
Chronological
Topical
Spatial
Problem-Solution
Cause-Effect (Causal)
Extemporaneous
Rapport
Value Statement
Transition
Manuscript
Memorization
Impromptu
Testimonial
Simile
Metaphor
Illustration
Comparison/Contrast
Repetition
Statistics
Visual Aids

▼ ▼ ▼ Endnotes

1. Stephen Lucas. *The Art of Public Speaking*. New York: Random House, 1983. p. 49.

2. Lucas. p. 55.

3. Hayden Carruth, Ed. *The Voice That Is Great within Us: American Poetry of the Twentieth Century*. New York: Bantam Books, 1970. p. 40.

4. Lucas. p. 373.

5. Lucas. p. 397.

6. Diane Ravitch, Ed. *The American Reader*. New York: Harper Collins Publisher, 1990. p. 368

7. Charles Dickens. *A Tale of Two Cities*. New York: Tom Doherty Associates, 1989. p. 3.

VI

Oral Presentations

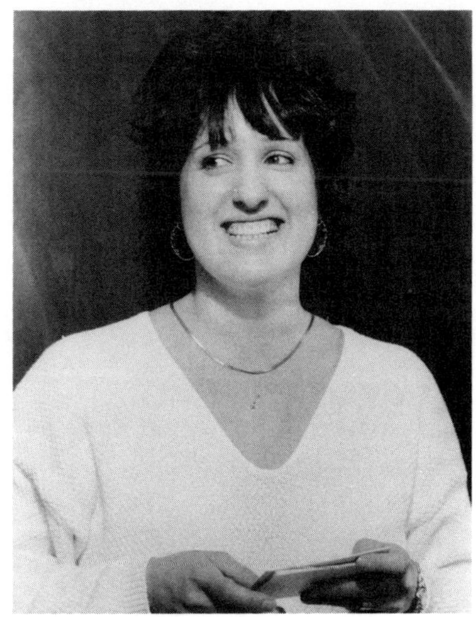

- Oral Interpretation
- Analyzing Your Selection
- Oral Interpretation Analysis Sheet
- Differences Between Oral Interpretation and Acting
- Rehearsing Oral Interpretation for Presentation
- Oral Interpretation Scoring
- The Rehearsal Process
- The Performance
- Selections

VI

Oral Presentations

There are many types of oral presentations. In the next four chapters, you will learn about oral interpretation — the art of reading aloud, group discussion, and informative and persuasive speeches. Once these types are explained and you have had the opportunity to prepare your class projects, you may then decide which you like the best.

Oral Interpretation

How many times have you found yourself falling asleep in a classroom and you hadn't felt tired when you came in the door? There are certain kinds of voices that just put us to sleep. Usually these voices are expressionless, therefore we cannot really solicit meaning from them.

As a student in a speech class, you have probably never thought about the power of your voice to express your feelings. But without this ability you will find yourself powerless in an overwhelming situation. Stop — think about it — how effectively do you use your voice and when might you use your voice more effectively? If you don't really know the answers to these questions, think back to when you were a child.

As a child, it was always a lot of fun to have one of your parents read to you. Dramatized renditions of *The Cat in the Hat*, *Charlotte's Web*, *Grimm's Fairy Tales*, or the Disney classics gave these books life. It is a great art to read aloud effectively. The ability to hear the sounds of descriptive words, can add greatly to the impact of a story. To recreate the author's meaning of a work gives pleasure to the reader as well as the audience.

Oral interpretation is the art of communicating the author's meaning of a literary work to an audience. The speaker is the interpreter whose job it is to emotionally, intellectually, and artistically communicate a message through the use of a trained voice and body.

The purpose of studying the technique of oral interpretation is to increase your ability to communicate clearly the emotional content of a message, an important skill no matter what career you ultimately choose.

Analyzing Your Selection

To analyze how to begin to interpret a literary work, you must first discover the author's meaning and then present it clearly to your audience. To find the author's meaning, ask the question: what did the author feel and think? By using the journalistic questions, who, what, when, where, why, and how, you will be able to understand fully the meaning of the material.

In your selection, there may be characters whose motivations need to be examined and understood. Sometimes a literary piece does not tell a story or give us a picture of a person but creates a mood revealing particular images or feelings. Through the use of picturesque language the mood of a work is depicted. The meaning of the piece can also be created through the use of sounds. Words like beep, bang, and boom — onomatopoeia — can create special moods.

Here is a series of questions which can help you to discover the author's meaning:

1. Who is speaking and who is listening?
2. Who are the characters?
3. Where do they live?
4. Where does the action take place?
5. What is happening to the characters?
6. What specific feelings do they arouse in you?
7. What is the mood of your piece?
8. What is the theme, plot, and climax of your work?
9. What in your background gives you an appreciation of this selection?

Hopefully this analysis sheet will help you understand your selection:

▾ Oral Interpretation Analysis Sheet ▾

The name of the selection ______________________________

The author of the selection ______________________________

Who is the speaker in the selection? ______________________________

Who is the listener in the selection? ______________________________

Where does the action take place? ______________________________

When does the action take place? ______________________________

Give a plot description ______________________________

____

____

____

What lines contain the climax? ______________________________

____

____

____

What lines reveal the mood of this selection? ______________________________

____

____

____

What is the theme of this selection? ______________________________

____

____

____

How does this selection relate to your life? ______________________________

____

____

____

Differences between Oral Interpretation and Acting

It is important to understand the differences between oral interpretation and acting. Although the oral interpreter reads a manuscript to reveal the *internal* life of a character, he does not physically recreate the *external* life of a character. An interpreter uses only voice and possibly a few gestures to suggest the characterization. Also the interpreter in many cases uses the manuscript as part of the performance as opposed to the actor who memorizes the entire text.

Both the interpreter and the actor must feel the emotions in the chosen selection. They must both study the characters and come to understand the characters' motivation as well as their language, speech rhythms, and choice of words which reflect their personalities and emotional states.

Rehearsing Oral Interpretation for Presentation

In the first rehearsal the performer must maintain eye contact directly with the audience, which is called an open focus. A closed focus may be developed when the performer's eye contact is above the heads of the audience. The performer's eye position during a performance differentiates one character from another.

By the second rehearsal students must feel comfortable with the text of their selections. Choices of selections for interpretation should not contain any technical jargon, difficult words, obscenities, or embarrassing scenes or ideas, or any materials that may inhibit their classmates. Time constraints and audience analysis should be discussed when preparing for the final presentation.

In rehearsal, the five vocal variables of pitch, emphasis, volume, tempo, and pausing should be considered and used. The craft of scoring should be learned. This refers to marking the selection with various symbols that act as visual cues to direct changes in the vocal variables. Scoring, which can also aid in eye contact and phrasing, is generated by the student's interpretation of the author's meaning of the selection.

Oral Interpretation Scoring

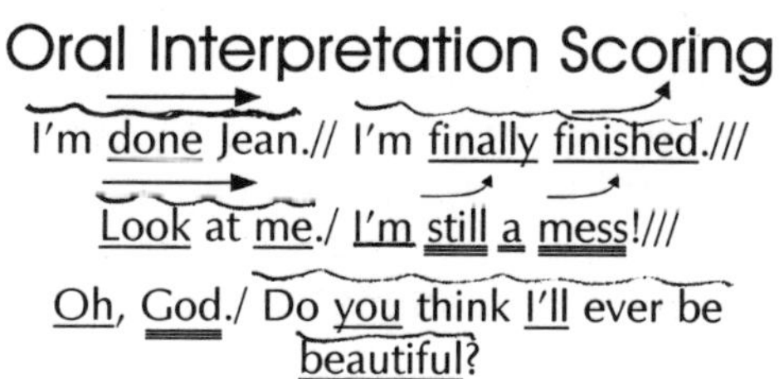

PITCH *an arrow*: indicates whether to raise pitch, lower pitch, or maintain the same pitch.

EMPHASIS *an underscore*: indicates the degree of word stress; the more stress, the more underscores.

VOLUME *from musical notation*: a < with the point facing left = increased volume; a > facing the right = decreased volume.

TEMPO *a wavy line*: the more undulations, the faster the rate.

PAUSE *a slashed line*: the more slashed lines, the longer the pause.

In rehearsal three, students can record their selections on audio tape and critique the recording.

Throughout rehearsals four, five, and six, students can continue to rehearse their selections as well as work on physical and vocal warm-up exercises. Finally, each student should rehearse in the room where the selection will be presented, practicing their physical positioning for the actual performance.

The hardest decision for a student is to determine what genre — prose, poetry, or drama — can be selected for an oral interpretation assignment. Each genre poses a different set of problems for the interpreter. Once a selection is chosen rehearsals can begin.

Before presenting your oral interpretation project you need to write an introduction to help the audience understand your selection. Included in this introduction should be: 1) the name of your selection, 2) the author, 3) background information which will help the audience to follow your piece, 4) how your piece relates to life today, and 5) the mood setting.

The Rehearsal Process

Rehearse aloud your introduction and selection. Stand straight and give your introduction in a conversational style by talking directly to the would-be audience. Hold your script in one hand, with the other lightly placed on the open book. This hand is then free for gesturing. Rehearse frequently. Pause and then begin to read your selection. You should become so familiar with the selection that you can lift your eyes from the page and establish eye contact with the audience. Hold your manuscript high enough for easy reading without having to bob your head up and down as you look from audience to book. Put yourself into what you are reading. Be alert and animated and let this interest show in your face, voice, and body.

The Performance

At the start of your performance, establish eye contact with the audience, and then give your introduction. Communicate the attitude that you are prepared and interested in what you are going to read.

After your introduction, pause, and then read your selection as you rehearsed it. Pronounce the words clearly and read slowly enough to be understood. Many beginning students have the tendency to rush through their selections. When you are through, try your best to maintain the mood you have created. Don't destroy it by abrupt movements or by running back to your seat. Remember, while you are in front of your audience, you are performing!

The following is an evaluation sheet showing the general criteria for grading in oral interpretation.

Oral Interpretation Grading Sheet

Selection

1. Appropriate for reader and audience ______

Introduction

2. Conversational delivery ______
3. Appropriate information ______

Content

4. Author's meaning communicated ______
5. Author's feeling communicated ______
6. Climax communicated ______

Voice

7. Appropriate expression ______
8. Adequate volume ______
9. Appropriate rate ______
10. Clear articulation ______
11. Correct pronunciation ______

Body

12. Expressive face ______
13. Responsive body ______
14. Adequate eye contact ______
15. Unobtrusive handling of script ______

Additional comments:

Here is a variety of possible prose, poetry, or dramatic monologues which can be used for the oral interpretation project.

Poetry

Song of the Open Road
Walt Whitman

1

Afoot and light-hearted I take to the open road,
Healthy, free, the world before me,
The long brown path before me leading wherever I choose.

Henceforth I ask not good-fortune, I myself am good-fortune,
Henceforth I whimper no more, postpone no more, need nothing,
Done with indoor complaints, libraries, querulous criticisms,
Strong and content I travel the open road.

The earth, that is sufficient,
I do not want the constellations any nearer,
I know they are very well where they are,
I know they suffice for those who belong to them.

(Still here I carry my old delicious burdens,
I carry them, men and women, I carry them with me wherever I go,
I swear it is impossible for me to get rid of them,
I am fill'd with them, and I will fill them in return.)

5

From this hour I ordain myself loos'd of limits and imaginary lines,
Going where I list, my own master total and absolute,
Listening to others, considering well what they say,
Pausing, searching, receiving, contemplating,

Gently, but with undeniable will, divesting myself of the holds that
would hold me.
I inhale great draughts of space,
The east and the west are mine, and the north and the south are mine,
I am larger, better than I thought,
I did not know I held so much goodness.

All seems beautiful to me,
I can repeat over to men and women, You have done such good to me
I would do the same to you,
I will recruit for myself and you as I go,
I will scatter myself among men and women as I go,
I will toss a new gladness and roughness among them,
Whoever denies me it shall not trouble me,
Whoever accepts me he or she shall be blessed and shall bless me.

9

Allons! whoever you are come travel with me!
Travelling with me you find what never tires.
The earth never tires,
The earth is rude, silent, incomprehensible at first, Nature is rude
and incomprehensible at first,
Be not discouraged, keep on, there are divine things well envelop'd.
I swear to you there are divine things more beautiful than words
can tell.

15

Allons! the road is before us!
It is safe—I have tried it—my own feet have tried it well—be not
detain'd!
Let the paper remain on the desk unwritten, and the book on the shelf
unopen'd!
Let the tools remain in the workshop! let the money remain unearn'd!
Let the school stand! mind not the cry of the teacher!

Let the preacher preach in his pulpit! let the lawyer plead in the court,
    and the judge expound the law.
Camerado, I give you my hand!
I give you my love more precious than money,
I give you myself before preaching or law;
Will you give me yourself? will you come travel with me?
Shall we stick by each other as long as we live?

Dream Deferred
Langston Hughes

What happens to a dream deferred?

Does it dry up
like a raisin in the sun?
Or fester like a sore—
And then run?
Does it stink like rotten meat?
Or crust and sugar over—
like a syrupy sweet?

Maybe it just sags
like a heavy load.

Or does it explode?

▼ ▼ ▼ ▼ ▼

Living in Sin
Adrienne Rich

She had thought the studio would keep itself;
no dust upon the furniture of love.
Half heresy, to wish the taps less vocal,
the panes relieved of grime. A plate of pears,

a piano with a Persian shawl, a cat
stalking the picturesque amusing mouse
had risen at his urging.
Not that at five each separate stair would writhe
under the milkman's tramp; that morning light
so coldly would delineate the scraps
of last night's cheese and three sepulchral bottles;
that on the kitchen shelf among the saucers
a pair of beetle-eyes would fix her own—
envoy from some village in the moldings...
Meanwhile, he, with a yawn,
sounded a dozen notes upon the keyboard,
declared it out of tune, shrugged at the mirror,
rubbed at his beard, went out for cigarettes;
while she, jeered by the minor demons,
pulled back the sheets and made the bed and found
a towel to dust the table-top,
and let the coffee-pot boil over on the stove.
By evening she was back in love again,
thought not so wholly but throughout the night
she woke sometimes to feel the daylight coming
like a relentless milkman up the stairs.

The Road Not Taken

Robert Frost

Two roads diverged in a yellow wood,
And sorry I could not travel both
And be one traveler, long I stood
And looked down one as far as I could
To where it bent in the undergrowth;

Then took the other, as just as fair,
And having perhaps the better claim,
Because it was grassy and wanted wear;
Though as for that passing there
Had worn them really about the same,

And both that morning equally lay
In leaves no step had trodden black.
Oh, I kept the first for another day!
Yet knowing how way leads on to way,
I doubted if I should ever come back.

I shall be telling this with a sign
Somewhere ages and ages hence:
Two roads diverged in a wood, and I —
I took the one less traveled by,
And that has made all the difference.

Acquainted with the Night
Robert Frost

I have been one acquainted with the night.
I have walked out in rain—and back in rain.
I have outwalked the furthest city light.

I have looked down the saddest city lane.
I have passed by the watchman on his beat
And dropped my eyes, unwilling to explain.

I have stood still and stopped the sound of feet
When far away an interrupted cry
Came over houses from another street,

But not to call me back or say good-by;
And further still at an unearthly height
One luminary clock against the sky

Proclaimed the time was neither wrong nor right.
I have been one acquainted with the night.

▼ ▼ ▼ ▼ ▼

Mending Wall

Robert Frost

Something there is that doesn't love a wall,
That sends the frozen-ground-swell under it
And spills the upper boulders in the sun,
And makes gaps even two can pass abreast.
The work of hunters is another thing;
I have come after them and made repair
Where they have left not one stone on a stone,
But they would have the rabbit out of hiding,
To please the yelping dogs. The gaps I mean,
No one has seen them made or heard them made,
But at spring mending-time we find them there.
I let my neighbor know beyond the hill;
And on a day we meet to walk the line
And set the wall between us once again.
We keep the wall between us as we go.
To each the boulders that have fallen to each.
And some are loaves and some so nearly balls
We have to use a spell to make them balance:
"Stay where you are until our backs are turned!"
We wear our fingers rough with handling them.
Oh, just another kind of outdoor game,
One on a side. It comes to little more:
There where it is we do not need the wall:
He is all pine and I am apple orchard.
My apple trees will never get across
And eat the cones under his pines, I tell him.
He only says, "Good fences make good neighbors."
Spring is the mischief in me, and I wonder
If I could put a notion in his head:
"*Why* do they make good neighbors? Isn't it
Where there are cows? But here there are no cows.
Before I built a wall I'd ask to know
What I was walling in or walling out,
And to whom I was like to give offense.

Something there is that doesn't love a wall,
That wants it down." I could say "Elves" to him,
But it's not elves exactly, and I'd rather
He said it for himself. I see him there,
Bringing a stone grasped firmly by the top
In each hand, like an old-stone savage armed.
He moves in darkness as it seems to me,
Not of woods only and the shade of trees.
He will not go behind his father's saying,
And he likes having thought of it so well
He says again, "Good fences make good neighbors."

The Unknown Citizen

(to JS/07/M378)
This Marble Monument Is Erected by the State

W.H. Auden

He was found by the Bureau of Statistics to be
One against whom there was no official complaint,
And all the reports on his conduct agree
That, in the modern sense of an old-fashioned word, he was a saint,
For in everything he did he served the Greater Community.
Except for the War till the day he retired
He worked in a factory and never got fired,
But satisfied his employers, Fudge Motors Inc.
Yet he wasn't a scab or odd in his views,
For his Union reports that he paid his dues,
(Our report on his Union shows it was sound)
And our Social Psychology workers found
That he was popular with his mates and liked a drink.
The Press are convinced that he bought a paper every day
And that his reactions to advertisements were normal in every way.

Policies taken out in his name prove that he was fully insured,
And his Health-card shows he was once in hospital but left it cured.
Both Producers Research and High-Grade Living declare
He was fully sensible to the advantages of the Installment Plan
And had everything necessary to the Modern Man,
A phonograph, a radio, a car and a frigidaire.
Our researchers into Public Opinion are content
That he held the proper opinions for the time of year;
When there was peace, he was for peace; when there was war, he went.
He was married and added five children to our population,
Which our Eugenist says was the right number for a parent of his generation,
And our teachers report that he never interfered with their education.
Was he free? Was he happy? The questions is absurd:
Had anything been wrong, we should certainly have heard.

Richard Cory

Edwin Arlington Robinson

Whenever Richard Cory went down town,
We people on the pavement looked at him:
He was a gentleman from sole to crown,
Clean favored, and imperially slim.

And he was always quietly arrayed,
And he was always human when he talked;
But still he fluttered pulses when he said,
"Good-morning," and he glittered when he walked.

And he was rich—yes, richer than a king—
And admirably schooled in every grace:
In fine, we thought that he was everything
To make us wish that we were in his place.

So on we worked, and waited for the light,
And went without the meat, and cursed the bread;

And Richard Cory, one calm summer night,
Went home and put a bullet through his head.

From *THE CHILDREN OF THE NIGHT* by Edwin Arlington Robinson (New York: Charles Scribner's Sons, © 1987).

The Walrus and the Carpenter
Lewis Carroll

The sun was shining on the sea,
   Shining with all his might:
He did his very best to make
   The billows smooth and bright—
And this was odd, because it was
   The middle of the night.

The moon was shining sulkily,
   Because she thought the sun
Had got no business to be there
   After the day was done—
"It's very rude of him," she said,
   "To come and spoil the fun!"

The sea was wet as wet could be.
   The sands were dry as dry.
You could not see a cloud, because
   No cloud was in the sky:
No birds were flying overhead—
   There were no birds to fly.

The Walrus and the Carpenter
   Were walking close at hand:
They wept like anything to see
   Such quantities of sand:
"If this were only cleared away,"
   They said, "it *would* be grand!"

"If seven maids with seven mops
 Swept it for half a year,
Do you suppose," the Walrus said,
 "That they could get it clear?"
"I doubt it," said the Carpenter,
 And shed a bitter tear.

"O Oysters, come and walk with us!"
 The Walrus did beseech.
"A pleasant walk, a pleasant talk,
 Along the briny beach:
We cannot do with more than four,
 To give a hand to each."

The eldest Oyster looked at him,
 But never a word he said:
The eldest Oyster winked his eye
 And shook his heavy head—
Meaning to say he did not choose
 To leave the oyster-bed.

But four young Oysters hurried up,
 All eager for the treat:
Their coats were brushed, their faces washed,
 Their shoes were clean and neat—
And this was odd, because, you know,
 They hadn't any feet.

Four other Oysters followed them,
 And yet another four;
And thick and fast they came at last,
 And more, and more, and more—
All hopping through the frothy waves,
 And scrambling to the shore.

The Walrus and the Carpenter
 Walked on a mile or so,
And then they rested on a rock
 Conveniently low:
And all the little Oysters stood
 And waited in a row.

"The time has come," the Walrus said,
"To talk of many things:
Of shoes—and ships—and sealing-wax—
Of cabbages—and kings—
And why the sea is boiling hot—
and whether pigs have wings."

"But wait a bit," the Oysters cried,
"Before we have our chat;
For some of us are out of breath,
And all of us are fat!"
"No hurry!" said the Carpenter.
They thanked him much for that.

"A loaf of bread," the Walrus said,
"Is what we chiefly need:
Pepper and vinegar besides
Are very good indeed—
Now, if you're ready, Oysters dear,
We can begin to feed."

"But not on us!" the Oysters cried,
Turning a little blue.
"After such kindness, that would be
A dismal thing to do!"
"The night is fine," the Walrus said.
"Do you admire the view?

"It was so kind of you to come!
And you are very nice!"
The Carpenter said nothing but
"Cut us another slice:
I wish you were not quite so deaf—
I've had to ask you twice!"

"It seems a shame," the Walrus said,
"To play them such a trick,
After we've brought them out so far,
And made them trot so quick!"
The Carpenter said nothing but
"The butter's spread too thick!"

"I weep for you," the Walrus said:
"I deeply sympathize."
With sobs and tears he sorted out
Those of the largest size,
Holding his pocket-handkerchief
Before his streaming eyes.

"O Oysters," said the Carpenter,
"You've had a pleasant run!
Shall we be trotting home again?"
But answer came there none—
And this was scarcely odd, because
They'd eaten every one.

Jabberwocky
Lewis Carroll

'Twas brillig, and the slithy toves
Did gyre and gimble in the wabe:
All mimsy were the borogoves,
And the mome raths outgrabe.
"Beware the Jabberwock, my son!
The jaws that bite, the claws that catch!
Beware the Jubjub bird, and shun
The frumious Bandersnatch!"

He took his vorpal sword in hand;
Long time the manxome foe he sought—
So rested he by the Tumtum tree,
And stood awhile in thought.

And, as in uffish thought he stood,
The Jabberwock, with eyes of flame,
Came whiffling through the tulgey wood,
And burbled as it came!

One, two! One, two! And through and through
The vorpal blade went snicker-snack!
He left it dead, and with its head
He went galumphing back.

"And hast though slain the Jabberwock?
Come to my arms, my beamish boy!
O frabjous day! Callooh, Callay!"
He chortled in his joy.

'Twas brillig, and the slithy toves
Did gyre and gimble in the wabe:
All mimsy were the borogoves,
And the mome raths outgrabe.

Goblin Market

Christina Rossetti

She cried, "Laura," up the garden,
"Did you miss me?
Come and kiss me.
Never mind my bruises,
Hug me, kiss me, suck my juices
Squeezed from goblin fruits for you,
Goblin pulp and goblin dew.
Eat me, drink me, love me;
Laura, make much of me;
For your sake I have braved the glen
And had to do with goblin merchant men."
Laura started from her chair,
Flung her arms up in the air,
Clutched her hair:
"Lizzie, Lizzie, have you tasted
For my sake the fruit forbidden?
Must your light like mine be hidden,
Your young life like mine be wasted,
Undone in mine undoing,
And ruined in my ruin,

Thirsty, cankered, goblin-ridden?"—
She clung about her sister,
Kissed and kissed and kissed her:
Tears once again
Refreshed her shrunken eyes,
Dropping like rain
After long sultry drouth;
Shaking with anguish fear, and pain,
She kissed and kissed her with a hungry mouth.
   Her lips began to scorch,
That juice was wormwood to her tongue,
She loathes the feast:
Writhing as one possessed she leaped and sung,
Rent all her robe, and wrung
Her hands in lamentable haste,
And beat her breast.
Her locks streamed like the torch
Borne by a racer at full speed,
Or like the mane of horses in their flight,
Or like an eagle when she stems the light
Straight toward the sun,
Or like a caged thing freed,
Or like a flying hag when armies run.
   Swift fire spread through her veins, knocked at her heart,
Met the fire smouldering there
And overbore its lesser flame;
She gorged on bitterness without a name:
Ah! fool, to choose such part
Of soul-consuming care!
Sense failed in the mortal strife:
Like the watch-tower of a town
Which an earthquake shatters down,
Like a lightning-stricken mast,
Like a wind-uprooted tree
Spun about,
Like a foam-topped waterspout
Cast down headlong in the sea,
She fell at last:
Pleasure past and anguish past.

▼ ▼ ▼ ▼ ▼

The Raven
▼ *Edgar Allan Poe* ▼

Once upon a midnight dreary, while I pondered weak and weary,
Over many a quaint and curious volume of forgotten lore,
While I nodded, nearly napping, suddenly there came a tapping,
As of some one gently rapping, rapping at my chamber door.
"'Tis some visitor," I muttered, "tapping at my chamber door—
Only this and nothing more."

Ah, distinctly I remember it was in the bleak December,
And each separate dying ember wrought its ghost upon the floor.
Eagerly I wished the morrow;—vainly I had sought to borrow
From my books surcease of sorrow—sorrow for the lost Lenore—
For the rare and radiant maiden whom the angels name Lenore—
Nameless here for evermore.

And the silken sad uncertain rustling of each purple curtain
Thrilled me—filled me with fantastic terrors never felt before;
So that now, to still the beating of my heart, I stood repeating,
"'Tis some visitor entreating entrance at my chamber door—
Some later visitor entreating entrance at my chamber door;—
This it is and nothing more."

Presently my soul grew stronger; hesitating then no longer,
"Sir," said I, "or Madam, truly your forgiveness I implore;
But the fact is I was napping, and so gently you came rapping,
And so faintly you came tapping, tapping at my chamber door,
That I scarce was sure I heard you"—here I opened wide the door;—
Darkness there, and nothing more.

Deep into that darkness peering, long I stood there wondering, fearing,
Doubting, dreaming dreams no mortals every dared to dream before;
But the silence was unbroken, and the stillness gave no token,
And the only word there spoken was the whispered word, "Lenore!"
This I whispered, and an echo murmured back the word, "Lenore!"—
Merely this and nothing more.

Back into the chamber turning, all my soul within me burning,
Soon again I heard a tapping somewhat louder than before.
"Surely," said I, "surely that is something at my window lattice;
Let me see, then, what thereat is, and this mystery explore—
Let my heart be still a moment and this mystery explore;—
'Tis the wind and nothing more."

Open here I flung the shutter, when, with many a flirt and flutter,
In there stepped a stately raven of the saintly days of yore;
Not the least obeisance made he; not a minute stopped or stayed he;
But, with mien of lord or lady, perched above my chamber door—
Perched upon a bust of Pallas just above my chamber door—
Perched, and sat, and nothing more.

Then this ebony bird beguiling my sad fancy into smiling,
By the grave and stern decorum of the countenance it wore,
"Though thy crest be shorn and shaven, thou," I said, "art sure no craven,
Ghastly grim and ancient raven wandering from the Nightly shore—
Tell me what thy lordly name is on the Night's Plutonian shore!"
Quoth the raven, "Nevermore."

Much I marvelled this ungainly fowl to hear discourse so plainly,
Though its answer little meaning—little relevancy bore;
For we cannot help agreeing that no living human being
Ever yet was blessed with seeing bird above his chamber door—
Bird or beast upon the sculptured bust above his chamber door,
With such name as "Nevermore."

But the raven, sitting lonely on the placid bust, spoke only
That one word, as if his soul in that one word did he outpour.
Nothing farther then he uttered—not a feather then he fluttered—
Till I scarcely more than muttered, "Other friends have flown before—
On the morrow *he* will leave me as my hopes have flown before."
Then the bird said, "Nevermore."

Startled at the stillness broken by reply so aptly spoken,
"Doubtless," said I, "what it utters is its only stock and store,
Caught from some unhappy master whom unmerciful Disaster

Followed fast and followed faster till his songs one burden bore—
Till the dirges of his Hope that melancholy burden bore
Of 'Never—nevermore.'"

But the raven still beguiling all my sad soul into smiling,
Straight I wheeled a cushioned seat in front of bird and bust and door;
There, upon the velvet sinking, I betook myself to linking
Fancy unto fancy, thinking what this ominous bird of yore—
What this grim, ungainly, ghastly, gaunt, and ominous bird of yore
Meant in croaking "Nevermore."

This I sat engaged in guessing, but no syllable expressing
To the fowl whose fiery eyes now burned into my bosom's core;
This and more I sat divining, with my head at ease reclining
On the cushion's velvet lining that the lamplight gloated o'er,
But whose velvet violet lining with the lamplight gloating o'er,
She shall press, ah, nevermore!

Then, methought, the air grew denser, perfumed from an unseen censer
Swung by angels whose faint foot-falls tinkled on the tufted floor.
"Wretch," I cried, "thy God hath lent thee—by these angels he hath sent
Respite—respite and nepenthe from thy memories of Lenore!
Quaff, oh quaff this kind nepenthe and forget this lost Lenore!"
Quoth the raven, "Nevermore."

"Prophet!" said I, "thing of evil!— prophet still, if bird or devil!—
Whether Tempter sent, or whether tempest tossed thee here ashore,
Desolate, yet all undaunted, on this desert land enchanted—
On this home by Horror haunted,—tell me truly, I implore—
Is there—*is* there balm in Gilead?—tell me—tell me, I implore!"
Quoth the raven, "Nevermore."

"Prophet!" said I, "thing of evil!—prophet still, if bird or devil!
By that heaven that bends above us—by that God we both adore—
Tell this soul with sorrow laden if, within the distant Aidenn,
It shall clasp a sainted maiden whom the angels name Lenore—
Clasp a rare and radiant maiden whom the angels name Lenore."
Quoth the raven, "Nevermore."

"Be that word our sign of parting, bird or fiend!" I shrieked, upstarting—
"Get thee back into the tempest and the Night's Plutonian shore!
Leave no black plume as a token of that lie thy soul hath spoken!
Leave my loneliness unbroken!— quit the bust above my door!
Take thy beak from out my heart, and take thy form from off my door!"
Quoth the raven, "Nevermore."

And the raven, never flitting, still is sitting, *still* is sitting
On the pallid bust of Pallas just above my chamber door;
And his eyes have all the seeming of a demon's that is dreaming,
And the lamp-light o'er him streaming throws his shadow on the floor;
And my soul from out that shadow that lies floating on the floor
Shall be lifted—nevermore!

Ulysses

Alfred, Lord Tennyson

It little profits that an idle king,
By this still hearth, among these barren crags,
Matched with an aged wife, I mete and dole
Unequal laws unto a savage race,
That hoard, and sleep, and feed, and know not me.
I cannot rest from travel; I will drink
Life to the lees. All times I have enjoyed
Greatly, have suffered greatly, both with those
That loved me, and alone; on shore, and when
Through scudding drifts the rainy Hyades
Vext the dim sea. I am become a name;
For always roaming with a hungry heart
Much have I seen and known,—cities of men,
And manners, climates, councils, governments,
Myself not least, but honored of them all;
And drunk delight of battle with my peers,
Far on the ringing plains of windy Troy.
I am a part of all that I have met;
Yet all experience is an arch wherethrough
Gleams that untraveled world, whose margin fades

For ever and and for ever when I move.
How dull it is to pause, to make an end,
To rust unburnished, not to shine in use!
As though to breathe were life! Life piled on life
Were all too little, and of one to me
Little remains; but every hour is saved
From that eternal silence, something more,
A bringer of new things; and vile it were
For some three suns to store and hoard myself,
And this grey spirit yearning in desire
To follow knowledge like a sinking star,
Beyond the utmost bound of human thought.

This is my son, mine own Telemachus,
To whom I leave the scepter and the isle—
Well-loved of me, discerning to fulfil
This labor, by slow prudence to make mild
A rugged people, and through soft degrees
Subdue them to the useful and the good.
Most blameless is he, centered in the sphere
Of common duties, decent not to fail
In offices of tenderness, and pay
Meet adoration to my household gods,
When I am gone. He works his work, I mine.

There lies the port; the vessel puffs her sail;
There gloom the dark, broad seas. My mariners,
Souls that have toiled, and wrought, and thought with me—
That ever with a frolic welcome took
The thunder and the sunshine, and opposed
Free hearts, free foreheads—you and I are old;
Old age hath yet his honor and his toil.
Death closes all; but something ere the end,
Some work of noble note, may yet be done,
Not unbecoming men that strove with Gods.
The lights begin to twinkle from the rocks;
The long day wanes; the slow moon climbs; the deep
Moans round with many voices. Come, my friends,
'Tis not too late to seek a newer world.
Push off, and sitting well in order smite

The sounding furrows; for my purpose holds
To sail beyond the sunset, and the baths
Of all the western stars, until I die.
It may be that the gulfs will wash us down;
It may be we shall touch the Happy Isles,
And see the great Achilles, whom we knew.
Though much is taken, much abides; and though
We are not now that strength which in old days
Moved earth and heaven, that which we are, we are:
One equal temper of heroic hearts,
Made weak by time and fate, but strong in will
To strive, to seek, to find, and not to yield.

To His Coy Mistress
Andrew Marvel

Had we but world enough, and time,
This coyness, lady, were no crime.
We would sit down, and think which way
To walk, and pass our long love's day.
Thou by the Indian Ganges' side
Shouldst rubies find; I by the tide
Of Humber would complain. I would
Love you ten years before the Flood,
And you should, if you please, refuse
Till the conversion of the Jews.
My vegetable love should grow
Vaster than empires, and more slow;
An hundred years should go to praise
Thine eyes, and on thy forehead gaze;
Two hundred to adore each breast,
But thirty thousand to the rest;
An age at least to every part,
And the last age should show your heart.
For, lady, you deserve this state,
Nor would I love at lower rate.
But at my back I always hear
Time's winged chariot hurrying near;

And yonder all before us lie
Deserts of vast eternity.
Thy beauty shall no more be found,
Nor, in thy marble vault, shall sound
My echoing song; then worms shall try
That long-preserved virginity,
And your quaint honor turn to dust,
And into ashes all my lust:
The grave's a fine and private place,
But none, I think, do there embrace.
Now therefore, while the youthful hue
Sits on thy skin like morning dew,
And while thy willing soul transpires
At every pore with instant fires,
Now let us sport us while we may,
And now, like amorous birds of prey,
Rather at once our time devour
Than languish in his slow-chapped power.
Let us roll all our strength and all
Our sweetness up into one ball,
And tear our pleasures with rough strife
Thorough the iron gates of life.
Thus, though we cannot make our sun
Stand still, yet we will make him run.

Dover Beach

Matthew Arnold

The sea is calm to-night
The tide is full, the moon lies fair
Upon the straits;—on the French coast the light
Gleams and is gone; the cliffs of England stand,
Glimmering and vast, out in the tranquil bay.
Come to the window, sweet is the night-air!
Only, from the long line of spray
Where the sea meets the moon-blanch'd land,
Listen! you hear the grating roar
Of pebbles which the waves draw back, and fling,

At their return, up the high strand,
Begin, and cease, and then again begin,
With tremulous cadence slow, and bring
The eternal note of sadness in.
Sophocles long ago
Heard it on the Ægean, and it brought
Into his mind the turbid ebb and flow
Of human misery; we
Find also in the sound a thought,
Hearing it by this distant northern sea.

The Sea of Faith
Was once, too, at the full, and round earth's shore
Lay like the folds of a bright girdle furl'd.
But now I only hear
Its melancholy, long, withdrawing roar,
Retreating, to the breath
Of the night-wind, down the vast edges drear
And naked shingles of the world.

Ah, love, let us be true
To one another! for the world, which seems
To lie before us like a land of dreams,
So various, so beautiful, so new,
Hath really neither joy, nor love, nor light,
Nor certitude, nor peace, nor help for pain;
And we are here as on a darkling plain
Swept with confused alarms of struggle and flight,
Where ignorant armies clash by night.

Sonnets

William Shakespeare

Shall I compare thee to a summer's day?
Thou art more lovely and more temperate.
Rough winds do shake the darling buds of May,
And summer's lease hath all too short a date.
Sometime too hot the eye of heaven shines,

And often is his gold complexion dimmed;
And every fair from fair sometimes declines,
By chance, or nature's changing course, untrimmed:
But thy eternal summer shall not fade
Nor lose possession of that fair thou ow'st,
Nor shall Death brag thou wand'rest in his shade
When in eternal lines to time thou grow'st.
So long as men can breathe or eyes can see,
So long lives this, and this gives life to thee.

My mistress'eyes are nothing like the sun
William Shakespeare

My mistress' eyes are nothing like the sun;
Coral is far more red than her lips' red;
If snow be white, why then her breasts are dun;
If hairs be wires, black wires grow on her head.
I have seen roses damasked red and white,
But no such roses see I in her cheeks;
And in some perfumes is there more delight
Than in the breath that from my mistress reeks.
I love to hear her speak, yet well I know
That music hath a far more pleasing sound;
I grant I never saw a goddess go:
My mistress, when she walks, treads on the ground
And yet, by heaven, I think my love as rare
As any she, belied with false compare.

Death, Be Not Proud
John Donne

Death, be not proud, though some have called thee
Mighty and dreadful, for thou art not so;
For those whom thou think'st thou dost overthrow
Die not, poor death, nor yet canst thou kill me.
From rest and sleep, which but thy pictures be,

Much pleasure—then, from thee much more must flow;
And soonest our best men with thee do go,
Rest of their bones and soul's delivery.
Thou art slave to fate, chance, kings, and desperate men,
And dost with poison, war, and sickness dwell;
And poppy or charms can make us sleep as well,
And better than thy stroke. Why swell'st thou then?
One short sleep passed, we wake eternally,
And death shall be no more; death, thou shalt die.

The World Is Too Much with Us

William Wordsworth

The world is too much with us; late and soon,
Getting and spending, we lay waste our powers;
Little we see in Nature that is ours;
We have given our hearts away, a sordid boon!
The sea that bares her bosom to the moon;
The winds that will be howling at all hours,
And are up-gathered now like sleeping flowers;
For this, for everything, we are out of tune;
It moves us not.—Great God! I'd rather be
A Pagan suckled in a creed outworn;
So might I, standing on this pleasant lea,
Have glimpses that would make me less forlorn;
Have sight of Proteus rising from the sea;
Or hear old Triton blow his wreathed horn.

Drama

A Raisin in the Sun
Lorraine Hansberry

Walter *(Violently flinging the coat after her) (The door slams behind her)*

Mama *(Still quietly)* Walter, what is the matter with you?

Walter Matter with me? Ain't nothing the matter with me!

Mama Yes there is. Something eating you up like a crazy man. Something more than me not giving you this money. The past few years I been watching it happen to you. You get all nervous acting and kind of wild in the eyes—*(WALTER jumps up impatiently at her words)* I said sit there now, I'm talking to you!

Walter Mama—I don't need no nagging at me today.

Mama Seem like you getting to a place where you always tied up in some kind of knot about something. But if anybody ask you 'bout it you just yell at 'em and bust out the house and go out and drink somewheres. Walter Lee, people can't live with that. Ruth's a good, patient girl in her way—but you getting to be too much. Boy, don't make the mistake of driving that girl away from you.

Walter Why—what she do for me?

Mama She loves you.

Walter Mama—I'm going out. I want to go off somewhere and be by myself for a while.

Mama I'm sorry 'bout your liquor store, son. It just wasn't the thing for us to do. That's what I want to tell you about—

Walter I got to go out, Mama—
(He rises)

Mama It's dangerous, son.

Walter What's dangerous?

Mama When a man goes outside his home to look for peace.

Walter *(Beseechingly)* Then why can't there never be no peace in this house then?

Mama You done found it in some other house?

Walter No—there ain't no woman! Why do women always think there's a woman somewhere when a man gets restless. *(Picks up the* *check)* Do you know what this money means to me? Do you know what this money can do for us? *(Puts it back)* Mama—Mama—I want so many things . . .

Mama Yes, son—

Walter I want so many things that they are driving me kind of crazy . . . Mama—look at me.

Mama I'm looking at you. You a good-looking boy. You got a job, a nice wife, a fine boy and —

Walter A job. *(Looks at her)* Mama, a job? I open and close car doors all day long. I drive a man around in his limousine and I say, "Yes, sir; no, sir; very good, sir; shall I take the Drive, sir?" Mama, that ain't no kind of job . . . that ain't nothing at all. *(Very quietly)* Mama, I don't know if I can make you understand.

Mama Understand what, baby?

Walter *(Quietly)* Sometimes it's like I can see the future stretched out in front of me—just plain as day. The future, Mama. Hanging over there at the edge of my days. Just waiting for me—a big, looming blank space—full of nothing. Just waiting for me. But it don't have to be *(Pause. Kneeling beside her chair)* Mama—sometimes when I'm downtown and I pass them cool, quiet-looking restaurants where them white boys are sitting back and talking 'bout things . . . sitting there turning deals worth millions of dollars . . . sometimes I see guys don't look much older than me—

Mama Son—how come you talk so much 'bout money?

Walter *(With immense passion)* Because it is life, Mama!

Mama *(Quietly)* Oh—*(Very quietly)* So now it's life. Money is life. Once upon a time freedom used to be life—now it's money. I guess the world really do change . . .

Walter No—it was always money, Mama. We just didn't know about it.

Mama No . . . something has changed. *(She looks at him)* You something new, boy. In my time we was worried about not being lynched and getting to the North if we could and how to stay alive and still have a pinch of dignity too . . . Now here come you and Beneatha—talking 'bout things we ain't never even thought about hardly, me and your daddy. You ain't satisfied or proud of nothing we done. I mean that you had a home; that we kept you out of trouble til you was grown; that you don't have to ride to work on the back of nobody's streetcar— You my children—but how different we done become.

Walter *(A long beat. He pats her head and gets up)* You just don't understand, Mama, you just don't understand.

Mama Son—do you know your wife is expecting another baby? (Walter *stands, stunned, and absorbs what his mother has said*) That's what she wanted to talk to you about. (WALTER *sinks down into a chair*) This ain't for me to be telling—but you ought to know. *(She waits)* I think Ruth is thinking 'bout getting rid of that child.

Walter *(Slowly understanding)*—No—no—Ruth wouldn't do that.

Mama When the world gets ugly enough—a woman will do anything for her family. The part that's already living.

Walter You don't know Ruth, Mama, if you think she would do that.

(RUTH *opens the bedroom door and stands there a little limp.)*

Ruth *(Beaten)* Yes I would too, Walter. *(Pause)* I gave her a five-dollar down payment.

(There is total silence as the man stares at his wife and the mother stares at her son)

Mama *(Presently)* Well—*(Tightly)* Well—son, I'm waiting to hear you say something . . . *(She waits)* I'm waiting to hear how you be your father's son. Be the man he was . . . *(Pause. the silence shouts)* Your wife say she going to destroy your child. And I'm waiting to hear you talk like him and say we a people who give children life, not who destroys them— *(She rises)* I'm waiting to see you stand up and look like your daddy and say we done give up one baby to poverty and that we ain't going to give up nary another one . . . I'm waiting.

Walter Ruth—*(He can say nothing)*

Mama If you a son of mine, tell her! (Walter *picks up his keys and his coat and walks out. She continues, bitterly)* You . . . you are a disgrace to your father's memory. Somebody get me my hat!

Curtain

SCENE THREE

Time: Saturday, moving day, one week later.

Before the curtain rises, RUTH's voice, a strident, dramatic church alto, cuts through the silence.

It is, in the darkness, a triumphant surge, a penetrating statement of expectation: "Oh Lord, I don't feel no ways tired! Children, oh, glory, hallelujah!"

As the curtain rises we see that RUTH is alone in the living room, finishing up the family's packing. It is moving day. She is nailing crates and tying cartons. Beneatha enters, carrying a guitar case, and watches her exuberant sister-in-law.

Ruth Hey!

Beneatha *(Putting away the case)* Hi.

Ruth *(Pointing at a package)* Honey—look in that package there and see what I found on sale this morning at the South Center. *(RUTH gets up and moves to the package and draws out some curtains)* Lookahere—hand-turned hems!

Beneatha How do you know the window size out there?

Ruth *(Who hadn't thought of that)* Oh—Well, they bound to fit something in the whole house. Anyhow, they was too good a bargain to pass up. *(RUTH slaps her head, suddenly remembering something)* Oh, Bennie—I meant to put a special note on that carton over there. That's your mama's good china and she wants 'em to be very careful with it.

Beneatha I'll do it

(BENEATHA *finds a piece of paper and starts to draw large letters on it)*

Ruth You know what I'm going to do soon as I get in that new house?

Beneatha What?

Ruth Honey—I'm going to run me a tub of water up to here . . . *(With her fingers practically up to her nostrils)* And I'm going to get in it—and I am going to sit . . . and sit . . . and sit in that hot water and the first person who knocks to tell *me* to hurry up and come out—

Beneatha Gets shot at sunrise.

Ruth *(Laughing happily)* You said it sister! *(Noticing how large BENEATHA is absent-mindedly making the note)* Honey, they aint' going to read that from no airplane.

Beneatha *(Laughing herself)* I guess I always think things have more emphasis if they are big somehow.

Ruth *(Looking up at her and smiling)* You and your brother seem to have that as a philosophy of life. Lord, that man—done changed so 'round here. You know—you know what we did last night? Me and Walter Lee?

Beneatha What?

Ruth *(Smiling to herself)* We went to the movies. *(Looking at BENEATHA to see if she understands)* We went to the movies.

You know the last time me and Walter went to the movies together?

Beneatha No.

Ruth Me neither. That's how long it been. (*Smiling again*) But we went last night. The picture wasn't much good, but that didn't seem to matter. We went—and we held hands.

Beneatha Oh, Lord!

Ruth We held hands—and you know what?

Beneatha What?

Ruth When we come out of the show it was late and dark and all the stores and things was closed up . . . and it was kind of chilly and there wasn't many people on the streets . . . and we was still holding hands, me and Walter.

Beneatha You're killing me.

(WALTER enters with a large package. His happiness is deep in him; he cannot keep still with his new-found exuberance. He is singing and wiggling and snapping his fingers. He puts his package in a corner and puts a phonograph record, which he has brought in with him, on the record player. As the music, soulful and sensuous, comes up he dances over to RUTH and tries to get her to dance with him. She gives in at last to his raunchiness and in a fit of giggling allows herself to be drawn into his mood. They dip and she melts into his arms in a classic, body-melding "slow drag")

Beneatha *(Regarding them a long time as they dance, then drawing in her breath for a deeply exaggerated comment which she does not particularly mean)* Talk about—olddddddddddddd fashionedddddddddddddd—Negroes!

Walter *(Stopping momentarily)* What kind of Negroes? *(He says this in fun. He is not angry with her today, nor with anyone. He starts to dance with his wife again)*

Beneatha Old-fashioned.

Walter *(As he dances with RUTH)* You know, when these New Negroes have their convention—*(Pointing at his sister)*—that is going to be the chairman of the Committee on Unending Agitation. *(He goes on dancing, then stops)* Race, race, race! . . . Girl, I do believe you are the first person in the history of the entire human race to successfully brainwash yourself. (*BENEATHA breaks up and he goes on dancing. He stops again, enjoying his tease)* Damn, even the N double A C P takes a holiday sometimes!

(BENEATHA and RUTH laugh. He dances with RUTH *some more and starts to laugh and stops and pantomimes someone over an operating table)* I can just see that chick someday looking down at some poor cat on an operating table and before she starts to slice him, she says . . . *(Pulling his sleeves back maliciously)* "By the way, what are your views on civil rights down there? . . .." *(He laughs at her again and starts to dance happily. The bell sounds)*

Beneatha Sticks and stones may break my bones but . . . words will never hurt me!

(BENEATHA goes to the door and opens it as WALTER and RUTH go on with the clowning. BENEATHA is somewhat surprised to see a quiet-looking middle-aged white man in a business suit holding his hat and a briefcase in his hand and consulting a small piece of paper)

Open Admissions

Shirley Lauro

The Characters

Professor Alice Miller — Professor of Speech Communications. Started out to be a Shakespearean scholar. Has been teaching Speech at a city college in New York for 12 years. She is overloaded with work and exhausted. Late thirties. Wears skirt, blouse, sweater, coat, gloves. Carries briefcase.

Calvin Jefferson — 18, a Freshman in Open Admissions Program at the College. Black, powerfully built, handsome, big. At first glance a streetperson, but belied by his intensity. Wears jacket, jeans, cap, sneakers. Has been at the College 3 months, hoping it will work out.

The Place

A cubicle Speech Office at a city college in New York.

The Time

The Present. Late fall. 6 o'clock in the evening.

The play begins at a very high level of tension and intensity and builds from there. The level of intensity is set by CALVIN who enters the play with a desperate urgency, as though he had arrived at the Emergency Room of a Hospital, needing immediate help for a serious problem. He also enters in a state of rage and frustration but is containing these feelings at first. The high level of tension is set by both ALICE and CALVIN and occurs from the moment CALVIN enters. ALICE wants to leave. She does not want the scene to take place. The audience's experience from the start should be as if they had suddenly turned in on the critical round of a boxing match.

CALVIN's speech is "Street Speech" jargon. Run-on sentences and misspellings in the text are for the purpose of helping the actor with the pronunciations and rhythms of the language.

The Speech office of Professor Alice Miller in a city college in New York. A small cubicle with partitions going 3/4 of the way up. Windowless, airless, with a cold antiseptic quality and a strong sense of impersonalness and transience. The cubicle has the contradictory feelings of claustrophobia and alienation at the same time. It is a space used by many teachers during every day of the week.

On the glass-windowed door it says:

SPEECH COMMUNICATIONS DEPT.
Prof. Alice Miller, B.A., M.A., Ph.D.

There are other names beneath that.

In the cubicle there is a desk with nothing on it except a phone, a chair with a raincoat on it, a swivel chair and a portable black board on which has been tacked a diagram of the "Speech Mechanism." Room is bare except for these things.

At Rise: Cubicle is in darkness. Muted light filters through glass window on door from hallway. Eerie feeling. A shadow appears outside door. Someone enters, snapping on light.

It is Alice. She carries a loose stack of essays, a book sack loaded with books and a guide book, one Shakespeare book, two speech books, and a portable cassette recorder. She closes the door, crosses to the desk, puts the keys in her purse, puts purse and booksack down and dials "O."

Alice Outside please. (*Waits for this, then dials a number.*) Debbie? Mommy, honey . . . . A "93"? Terrific! Listen, I just got through. I had to keep the class late to finish . . . So, I can't stop home for dinner. I'm going right to the meeting . . . no, I'll be safe . . . don't worry. But you go put the double lock on, ok? And eat the cold meatloaf. (*She puts essays in book sack.*) See you later. Love you too. (*She kisses the receiver.*) Bye.
(She hangs up, puts on coat, picks up purse and book sack, crosses to door and snaps off light. Then opens door to go. Calvin looms in doorway.)

Alice OOHH! You scared me!

Calvin Yes ma'am, I can see I scared you okay. I'm sorry.

Alice Calvin Washington? 10:30 section?

Calvin Calvin Jefferson, 9:30 section.

Alice Oh, right. Of course. Well, I was just leaving. Something you wanted?

Calvin Yes, Professor Miller. I came to talk to you about my grades. My grade on that Shakespeare project especially.

Alice Oh. Yes. Well. What did you get, Calvin? A "B" wasn't it? Something like that?

Calvin Umhumm. Thass right. Somethin like that...

Alice Yes. Well, look, I don't have office hours today at all. It's very dark already. I just stopped to make a call. But if you'd like to make an appointment for a conference, I'm not booked yet next month. Up 'till then, I'm just jammed.

Calvin Thass two weeks! I need to talk to you right now!

Alice Well what exactly is it about? I mean the grade is self-explanatory—"Good"—"B" work. And I gave you criticism in class the day of the project, didn't I? So what's the problem?

Calvin I wanna sit down and talk about *why* I got that grade! And all my grades in point of fact.

Alice But I don't have office hours today. It's very late and I have another commitment. Maybe tomorrow—(*She tries to leave.*)

Calvin (*voice rising*) I have to talk to you *now*!

Alice Look, tomorrow there's a Faculty Meeting. I can meet you here afterwards . . . around 12:30. Providing Professor Roth's not scheduled to use the desk.

Calvin I got a job tomorrow! Can't you talk to me right now?

Alice But what's it about? I don't see the emergen—

Calvin *(voice rising loudly)* I jiss tole you what it's about! My project and my grades is what it's about!

Alice *(glancing down the hall, not wanting a commotion overheard)* All right! Just stop shouting out here, will you? *(She snaps on light and crosses to desk.)* Come on in. I'll give you a few minutes now.

(He comes in.)

Alice *(She puts purse and book sack down and sits at desk.)* Okay. Now then. What?

Calvin *(Closes door and crosses UC. Silent for a moment, looking at her. Then:)* How come all I ever git from you is "B"?

Alice *(stunned)* What?

Calvin This is the third project I did for you. An all I ever git is "B."

Alice Are you joking? This is what you wanted to talk about? "B" is an excellent grade!

Calvin No it's not? "A" is "excellent." "B" is "good."

Alice You don't think you deserved an "A" on those projects, do you?

Calvin No. But I got to know how to improve myself somehow, so maybe sometime I can try for a "A." I wouldn't even mind on one of those projects if I got a "C." Thass average—if you know what I mean? Or a "D." But all I ever git from you is "B." It don't matter what I do in that Speech Communications Class, seems like. I come in the beginnin a it three months ago? On the Open Admissions? Shoot, I didn't know which end was up. I stood up there and give this speech you assigned on "My Hobby." You remember that?

Alice *(Reads note on desk.)* About basketball?

Calvin Huh-uh. That was Franklin Perkins give that speech. Sits in the back row?

Alice *(Tosses note in wastebasket.)* Oh. Yes. Right. Franklin.

Calvin Umhmm. I give some dumb speech about "The Hobby a Makin Wooden Trays."

Alice Oh, yes. Right. I remember that.

Calvin Except I didn't have no hobby making wooden trays, man. I made one in high school one time, thass all.

Alice *(Leafs through pages of speech books.)* Oh, well, that didn't matter. It was the speech that counted.

Calvin Umhmm? Well, that was the sorriest speech anybody ever heard in their lives! I was scared to death and couldn't put one word in front a the other any way I tried. Supposed to be 5 minutes. Lasted 2! And you give me a "B"!

Alice *(Rises, crosses to DR table and puts speech books down.)* Well, it was your first time up in class, and you showed a lot of enthusiasm and effort. I remember that speech.

Calvin Everybody's firss time up in class, aint' it?

Alice Yes. Of course.

Calvin *(Cross DR to Alice.)* That girl sits nex to me, that Judy Horowitz—firss time she was up in class too. She give that speech about "How to Play the Guitar?" And man, she brought in charts and taught us to read chords and played a piece herself an had memorized the whole speech by heart. An you give her a "B."

Alice *(Crosses to desk, picks up book sack and puts it on desk.)* Well, Judy's organization on her outline was a little shaky as I recall.

Calvin *(Crosses end of desk.)* I didn't even turn no outline in.

Alice *(Picks up purse and puts it on desk)* You didn't

Calvin *(Leans in.)* Huh-uh. Didn't you notice?

Alice Of course! It's—just—well, it's been sometime—*(She quickly takes the grade book from the book sack and looks up his name.)* Let me see, oh, yes. Right. Here, I see. You didn't hand it in...

Calvin Thass right, I didn'.

Alice You better do that before the end of the term.

Calvin I can't. Because I don't know which way to do no outline!

Alice *(Looks up name in grade book and marks it with red pencil.)* Oh. Well . . . that's all right. Don't worry about it okay? *(She puts grade book away.)* Just work on improving yourself in other ways.

Calvin What other ways? Only thing you ever say about anything I ever done in there is how I got to get rid of my "Substandard Urban Speech!"

Alice *(Picks up 2 files from desk and crosses to UCR file cabinet.)* Well, yes, you do! You see, that's your real problem, Calvin! "Substandard Speech." It undercuts your "Positive Comminicator's Image!" Remember how I gave a lecture about that? About how all of you here have Substandard Urban Speech because this is a Sub—an Urban College. *(She puts on gloves.)* Remember? But that's perfectly okay! It's okay! Just like I used to have Substandard Midwestern Speech when I was a student. Remember my explaining about that? How I used to say "crik" for "creek," and "kin" for "can" and "tin" for "ten?" *(She crosses in back of desk and chuckles at herself.)* Oh, and my breathiness! *(She picks up purse.)* That was just my biggest problem of all: Breathiness. I just worked myself to death up at Northwestern U. getting it right straight out of my speech. Now, that's what you have to do too, Calvin. *(She picks up book sack and keys.)* Nothing to be ashamed of—but get it right straight out! *(She is ready to leave. She pats Calvin on the shoulder and crosses UC.)*

Calvin *(Pause. Looks at her.)* Thass how come I keep on gettin "B?"

Alice "That's."

Calvin *(Steps in to Alice.)* Huh?

Alice "That's" Not "Thass." Can't you hear the difference? "That's" one of the words in the Substandard Black Urban Pattern. No final "T's." Undermining your Positive Image . . . labeling you. It's "Street Speech." Harlemese. Don't you remember? I called everyone's attention to your particular syndrome in class the minute you started talking?

(He looks at her, not speaking.)

Alice It's "last," not "lass;" "first," not "firss." That's your friend, that good old "Final T!" Hear it when I talk?

Calvin Sometimes. When you say it, hittin it like that!

Alice Well, you should be going over the exercises on it in the speech book all the time, and recording yourself on your tape recorder. *(She pats book sack.)*

Calvin I don't got no tape recorder.

Alice Well, borrow one! *(She turns away)*

Calvin *(Crosses in back of Alice to her right.)* On that Shakespeare scene I jiss did? Thass why I got a "B"? Because of the "Final T's?"

Alice *(Backs DS a step)* Well, you haven't improved your syndrome, have you?

Calvin How come you keep on answerin me by axin me somethin else?

Alice And that's the other one.

Calvin What "other one"?

Alice Other most prevalent deviation. You said: "ax-ing" me somethin else.

Calvin Thass right. How come you keep axin me somethin else?

Alice "Asking me," Calvin, "asking me!"

Calvin I jiss did!

Alice No, no. Look. That's classic Substandard Black! Text book case. *(She puts purse and book sack down and crosses to diagram on blackboard.)* See, the jaw and teeth are in two different positions for the two sounds, and they make two completely different words! *(She writes "ass-king," and "ax-ing" on the blackboard, pronouncing them in an exaggerated way for him to see.)* "ass-king" and "ax-ing." I am "ass-king" you the question. But, the woodcutter is "ax-ing" down the tree. Can't you hear the difference? *(She picks up his speech book from desk.)* Here. *(Calvin follows her to desk.)*

Alice Go over to page 105. It's called a "Sharp S" problem with a medial position "sk" substitution. See? "skin, screw, scream"—those are "sk" sounds in the Primary Position. "Asking, risking, frisking,—that's medial position. And "flask, task, mask"—that's final position. Now you should be working on those, Calvin. Reading those exercises over and over again. I mean the way you did the Othello scene was just ludicrous: "Good gentlemen, I ax thee-" *(She crosses to the board and points to "ax-ing". She chuckles.)* That meant Othello was chopping the gentlemen down!

Calvin How come I had to do the Othello scene anyhow? Didn git any choice. An Franklin Perkins an Sam Brown an Lester Washington they had to too.

Alice What do you mean?

Calvin An Claudette Jackson an Doreen Simpson an Melba Jones got themselves assigned to Cleopatra on the Nile?

Alice Everyone was assigned!

Calvin Uh-huh. But everybody else had a choice, you know what I mean? That Judy Horowitz, she said you told her she could pick outa five, six different characters. And that boy did his yesterday? That Nick Rizoli? Did the Gravedigger? He said he got three, four to choose off of too.

Alice *(Cross to Calvin)* Well some of the students were "right" for several characters. And you know, Calvin, how we talked in class about Stanislavsky and the importance of "identifying" and "feeling" the part?

Calvin Well how Doreen Simpson "identify" herself some Queen sittin on a barge? How I supposed to "identify" some Othello? I don't!

Alice *(Crosses to blackboard, picks up fallen chalk.)* Oh, Calvin, don't be silly.

Calvin *(Crosses center.)* Well, I don'! I'm not no kind of jealous husband. I haven' got no wife. I don' even got no girlfriend, hardly! And thass what it's all about ain't it? So what's it I'm supposed to "identify" with anyhow?

Alice *(Turns to Calvin)* Oh, Calvin, what are you arguing about? You did a good job?

Calvin "B" job, right?

Alice Yes.

Calvin *(Crosses to Alice)* Well, what's that "B" standin for? Cause I'll tell you somethin you wanna know the truth: I stood up there didn' hardly know the sense a anythin I read, couldn't hardly even read it at all. Only you didn't notice. Wasn't even listenin, sittin there back a the room jiss thumbin through your book.

(Alice crosses to desk.)

Calvin So you know what I done? Skip one whole paragraph, tess you out—you jiss kep thumbin through your book! An then you give me a "B"! *(He has followed Alice to desk.)*

Alice *(Puts papers in box and throws out old coffee cup.)* Well that just shows how well you did the part!

Calvin You wanna give me somethin I could "identify" with, how come you ain' let me do that other dude in the play . . .

Alice Iago?

Calvin Yeah. What is it they calls him? Othello's . . .

Alice Subordinate.

Calvin Go right along there with my speech syndrome, wouldn' it now? See, Iago has to work for the Man. I identifies with him! He gits jealous man. Know what I mean? Or that Gravedigger? Shovelin dirt for his day's work! How come you wouldn't let me do him? Thass the question I wanna ax you!

Alice *(Turns to Calvin.)* "Ask me, " Calvin, "Ask me!"

Calvin *(Steps SR.)* "Ax you?" Okay, man. *(Turns to Alice.)* Miss Shakespeare, Speech Communications 1! *(Crosses UR of Alice.)* Know what I'll "ax" you right here in this room, this day, at this here day right now? I'll "ax" you how come I have been in this here college 3 months on this here Open Admissions and I don't know nothin more than when I came in here? You know what I mean? This supposed to be some big break for me. This here is where all them smart Jewish boys has gone from the Bronx Science and went an become some Big Time Doctors at Bellvue.

An some Big Time Judges in the Family Court an like that there. And now it's supposed to be my turn.

(Alice looks away and Calvin crosses R of Alice)

Calvin You know what I mean? *(He crosses UR.)* An my sister Jonelle took me out of foster care where I been in 6 homes and 5 schools to give me my chance. *(He crosses DR.)* Livin with her an she workin 3 shifts in some "Ladies Restroom" give me my opportunity. An she say she gonna buss her ass git me this education I don't end up on the streets! *(Crosses on a diagonal to Alice.)* Cause I have got brains!

(Alice sits in student chair. Calvin crosses in back, to her left)

Calvin You understand what I am Communicatin to you? My high school has tole me I got brains an can make somethin outta my life if I gits me the chance! And now this here's supposed to be my chance! High school says you folks gonna bring me up to date on my education and git me even. Only nothin is happenin to me in my head except I am getting more and more confused about what I knows and what I don't know! *(He sits in swivel chair.)* So what I wanna "ax" you is: How come you don't sit down with me and teach me which way to git my ideas down instead of givin me a "B."

(Alice rises and crosses UR.)

Calvin I don't even turn no outline in? Jiss give me a "B." *(He rises and crosses R of Alice.)* An Lester a "B"! an Melba a "B"! an Sam a "B"! What's that "B" standin for anyhow? Cause it surely ain't standin for no piece of work!

Alice Calvin don't blame me!

(Calvin crosses DR.)

Alice I'm trying! God knows I'm trying! The times are rough for everyone. I'm a Shakespearean scholar, and they have me teaching beginning Speech. I was supposed to have 12 graduate students a class, 9 classes a week, and they give me 35 Freshmen a class, 20 classes a week. I hear 157 speeches a week! You know what that's like? And I go home late on the subway scared to death! In Graduate School they told me I'd have a first rate career. Then I started here and they said: "Hang on! Things will improve!" But they only got worse . . . and worse! Now I've been here for 12 years and I haven't written one word in my field! I haven't read 5 research books! I'm exhausted . . . and

I'm finished! We all have to bend. I'm just hanging on now . . . supporting my little girl . . . earning a living . . . and that's all . . . *(She crosses to desk.)*

Calvin *(Faces Alice.)* What I'm supposed to do, feel sorry for you? Least you can earn a livin! Clean office, private phone, name on the door with all them B.A.'s, M.A.'s, Ph.D.'s.

Alice You can have those too. *(She crosses DR to Calvin.)* Look, last year we got 10 black students into Ivy League Graduate Programs. And they were no better than you. They were just perceived *(Points to blackboard.)* as better. Now that's the whole key for you . . . to be perceived as better! So you can get good recommendations and do well on interviews. You're good looking and ambitious and you have a fine native intelligence. You can make it, Calvin. All we have to do is work on improving your Positive Communicator's Image . . . by getting rid of that Street Speech. Don't you see?

Calvin See what? What you axin me to see?

Alice "Asking" me to see, Calvin, "Asking" me to see!

Calvin *(Starts out of control at this, enraged, crosses US and bangs on file cabinet.)* Ooooeee! Ooooeee! You wanna see? You wanna see? Oooooeee!

Alice Calvin stop it! STOP IT!

Calvin "Calvin stop it"? "Stop it"? *(Picks up school books from desk.)* There any black professors here?

Alice *(Crosses UR.)* No! They got cut . . . the budget's low . . . they go. . :

Calvin *(interrupting)* Cut? They got CUT? *(Crosses to Alice and backs her to the DS edge of desk.)* Gonna cut you, lady! Gonna cut you, throw you out the f_______ [expletive] throw the f_____ [expletive] books out the f______ [expletive] window, burn it all mother f_____ [expletive] down. F______ [expletive] DOWN!!!

Alice Calvin! Stop it! STOP IT! YOU HEAR ME?

Calvin *(Turns away, center stage.)* I CAN'T!! *YOU* HEAR *ME*? I CAN'T! *YOU* HEAR *ME*? I CAN'T! YOU GOTTA GIVE ME MY EDUCATION! GOTTA TEACH ME! GIVE ME SOMETHING NOW! GIVE ME NOW! NOW! NOW! NOW! NOW! NOW!

(Calvin tears up text book. He starts to pick up torn pages and drops them. He bursts into a wailing, bellowing cry in his anguish and despair, doubled over in pain and grief. It is a while before his sobs subside. Finally, Alice speaks.)

Alice Calvin . . . from the bottom of my heart . . . I want to help you . . .

Calvin *(barely able to speak)* By changin my words? Thass nothin . . . nothin! I got to know them big ideas . . . and which way to git em down . . .

Alice But how can I teach you that? You can't write a paragraph, Calvin . . . or a sentence . . . you can't spell past 4th grade . . . the essay you wrote show that . . .

Calvin *(rises)* What essay?

Alice *(Crosses to UL files, gets essay and hands it to Calvin.)* The autobiographical one . . . you did it the first day . . .

Calvin You said that was for your reference . . . didn't count . . .

Alice Here . . .

Calvin *(Opens it up. Stunned.)* "F"? Why didn't you tell me I failed?

Alice *(Crosses to desk, puts essay down.)* For what?

Calvin *(Still stunned.)* So you could teach me how to write.

Alice *(Crosses DL.)* In 16 weeks?

Calvin *(Still can't believe this.)* You my teacher!

Alice That would take years! And speech is my job. You need a tutor.

Calvin I'm your job. They outa tutors!

Alice *(Turns to him.)* I can't do it, Calvin. And that's the real truth. I'm one person, in one job. And I can't. Do you understand? And even if I could, it wouldn't matter. All that matters is the budget . . . and the curriculum . . . and the grades . . . and how you look . . . and how you talk!

Calvin *(Pause. Absorbing this.)* Then I'm finished, man.

(There is a long pause. Finally:)

Alice *(Gets essay from desk, refiles it and returns to desk.)* No, you're not. If you'll bend and take what I can give you, things will work out for you . . . Trust me . . . Let me help you Calvin . . . Please . . . I can teach you speech . . .

Calvin *(Crosses to US file cabinet. Long pause)* Okay . . . all right, man . . . *(Crosses to student chair and sits.)*

Alice *(Crosses to desk, takes off rain coat and sits in swivel chair.)* Now, then, we'll go through the exercise once then you do it at home . . . please, repeat after me, slowly . . . "asking" . . . "asking" . . . "asking" . . .

Calvin *(long pause)* Ax-ing . . .

Alice Ass-king

Calvin *(During the following, he now turns from Alice, faces, front, and gazes out beyond the audience; on his fourth word, lights begin to fade to black:)*)Ax-ing . . . Aks-ing . . . ass-king . . . asking . . . asking . . . asking . . .

Blackout

End of Play

A Doll's House
Henrik Ibsen

Act III

The same room. The table which was formally by the sofa has been moved into the centre of the room; the chairs surround it as before. The door to the hall stands open. Dance music can be heard from the floor above. Mrs. Linde is seated at the table, absent-mindedly glancing through a book. She is trying to read, but seems unable to keep her mind on it. More than once she turns and listens anxiously towards the front door.

Mrs. Linde (*looks at her watch*) Not here yet. There's not much time left. Please God he hasn't—! *(Listens again.)* Ah, here he is. (*Goes out into the hall and cautiously opens the front door. Footsteps can be heard softly ascending the stairs. She whispers.*) Come in. There's no one here.

Krogstad (*in the doorway*) I found a note from you at my lodgings. What does this mean?

Mrs. Linde I must speak with you.

Krogstad Oh? And must our conversation take place in this house?

Mrs. Linde We couldn't meet at my place; my room has no separate entrance. Come in. We're quite alone. The maids' asleep, and the Helmers are at the dance upstairs.

Krogstad *(Comes into the room)* Well, well! So the Helmers are dancing this evening? Are they indeed?

Mrs. Linde Yes, why not?

Krogstad	True enough. Why not?
Mrs. Linde	Well, Krogstad. You and I must have a talk together.
Krogstad	Have we two anything further to discuss?
Mrs. Linde	We have a great deal to discuss
Krogstad	I wasn't aware of it.
Mrs. Linde	That's because you've never really understood me.
Krogstad	Was there anything to understand? It's the old story, isn't it—a woman chucking a man because something better turns up?
Mrs. Linde	Do you really think I'm so utterly heartless? You think it was easy for me to give you up?
Krogstad	Wasn't it?
Mrs. Linde	Oh, Nils, did you really believe that?
Krogstad	Then why did you write to me the way you did?
Mrs. Linde	I had to. Since I had to break with you, I though it my duty to destroy all the feelings you had for me.
Krogstad	*(clenches his fists)* So that was it. And you did this for money!
Mrs. Linde	You mustn't forget I had a helpless mother to take care of, and two little brothers. We couldn't wait for you, Nils. It would have been so long before you'd had enough to support us.
Krogstad	Maybe. But you had no right to cast me off for someone else.
Mrs. Linde	Perhaps not. I've often asked myself that.
Krogstad	*(more quietly)* When I lost you, it was just as though all solid ground had been swept from under my feet. Look at me. Now I am a shipwrecked man, clinging to a spar.
Mrs. Linde	Help may be near at hand.
Krogstad	It was near. But then you came, and stood between it and me.
Mrs. Linde	I didn't know, Nils. No one told me till today that this job I'd found was yours.
Krogstad	I believe you, since you say so. But now you know, won't you give it up?
Mrs. Linde	No—because it wouldn't help you even if I did.
Krogstad	Wouldn't it? I'd do it all the same.
Mrs. Linde	I've learned to look at things practically. Life and poverty have taught me that.
Krogstad	And life has taught me to distrust fine words.
Mrs. Linde	Then it's taught you a useful lesson. But surely you still believe in actions?
Krogstad	What do you mean?
Mrs. Linde	You said you were like a shipwrecked man clinging to a spar.

Krogstad I have good reason to say it.

Mrs. Linde I'm in the same position as you. No one to care about, no one to care for.

Krogstad You made your own choice.

Mrs. Linde I had no choice—then.

Krogstad Well?

Mrs. Linde Nils, suppose we two shipwrecked souls could join hands?

Krogstad What are you saying?

Mrs. Linde Castaways have a better chance of survival together than on their own.

Krogstad Christine!

Mrs. Linde Why do you suppose I came to this town!

Krogstad You mean—you came because of me?

Mrs. Linde I must work if I'm to find life worth living. I've always worked, for as long as I can remember; it's been the greatest joy of my life—my only joy. But now I'm alone in the world, and I feel so dreadfully lost and empty. There's no joy in working just for oneself. Oh, Nils, give me something—someone—to work for.

Krogstad I don't believe all that. You're just being hysterical and romantic. You want to find an excuse for self-sacrifice.

Mrs. Linde Have you ever known me to be hysterical?

Krogstad You mean you really—? Is it possible? Tell me—you know all about my past?

Mrs. Linde Yes.

Krogstad And you know what people think of me here?

Mrs. Linde You said just now that with me you might have become a different person.

Krogstad I know I could have.

Mrs. Linde Couldn't it still happen?

Krogstad Christine—do you really mean this? Yes—you do—I see it in your face. Have you really the courage—?

Mrs. Linde I need someone to be a mother to; and your children need a mother. And you and I need each other. I believe in you, Nils. I am afraid of nothing—with you.

Krogstad *(clasps her hands)* Thank you, Christine—thank you! Now I shall make the world believe in me as you do! Oh—but I'd forgotten—

Mrs. Linde *(listens)* Ssh! The tarantella! Go quickly, go!

Krogstad Why? What is it?

Mrs. Linde You hear that dance? As soon as it's finished, they'll be coming down.

Krogstad All right, I'll go. It's no good, Christine. I'd forgotten—you don't know what I've just done to the Helmers.

Mrs. Linde Yes, Nils. I know.

Krogstad And yet you'd still have the courage to—?

Mrs. Linde I know what despair can drive a man like you to.

Krogstad Oh, if only I could undo this!

Mrs. Linde You can. Your letter is still lying in the box.

Krogstad Are you sure?

Mrs. Linde Quite sure. But—

Krogstad *(looks searchingly at her)* Is that why you're doing this? You want to save your friend at any price? Tell me the truth. Is that the reason?

Mrs. Linde Nils, a woman who has sold herself once for the sake of others doesn't make the same mistake again.

Krogstad I shall demand my letter back.

Mrs. Linde No, no.

Krogstad Of course I shall. I shall stay here till Helmer comes down. I'll tell him he must give me back my letter—I'll say it was only to do with my dismissal, and that I don't want him to read it—

Mrs. Linde No, Nils, you mustn't ask for that letter back.

Krogstad But—tell me—wasn't that the real reason you asked me to come here?

Mrs. Linde Yes—at first, when I was frightened. But a day has passed since then, and in that time I've seen incredible things happen in this house. Helmer must know the truth. This unhappy secret of Nora's must be revealed. They must come to a full understanding; there must be an end of all these shiftings and evasions.

Krogstad Very well. If you're prepared to risk it. But one thing I can do—and at once—

Mrs. Linde *(listens)* Hurry! Go, go! The dance is over. We aren't safe here another moment.

Krogstad I'll wait for you downstairs.

Mrs. Linde Yes, do. You can see me home.

Krogstad I've never been so happy in my life before!

He goes out through the front door. The door leading from the room into the hall remains open

Mrs. Linde *(tidies the room a little and gets her hat and coat)* What a change! Oh, what a change! Someone to work for—to live for!

A home to bring joy into! I won't let this chance of happiness slip through my fingers. Oh, why don't they come? *(Listens.)* Ah, here they are. I must get my coat on.

She takes her hat and coat. Helmer's and Nora's voices become audible outside. A key is turned in the lock and Helmer leads Nora almost forcibly into the hall. She is dressed in an Italian costume with a large black shawl. He is in evening dress, with a black cloak.

Nora *(still in the doorway, resisting him)* No, no, no—not in here! I want to go back upstairs. I don't want to leave so early.

Helmer But my dearest Nora—

Nora Oh, please, Torvald, please! Just another hour!

Helmer Not another minute, Nora, my sweet. You know what we agreed. Come along, now. Into the drawing-room. You'll catch cold if you stay out here.

He leads her, despite her efforts to resist him, gently into the room.

Mrs. Linde Good evening.

Nora Christine!

Helmer Oh, hullo, Mrs. Linde. You still here?

Mrs. Linde Please forgive me. I did so want to see Nora in her costume.

Nora Have you been sitting here waiting for me?

Mrs. Linde Yes. I got here too late, I'm afraid. You'd already gone up. And I felt I really couldn't go back home without seeing you.

Helmer *(takes off Nora's shawl)* Well, take a good look at her. She's worth looking at, don't you think? Isn't she beautiful, Mrs. Linde?

Mrs. Linde Oh, yes, indeed—

Helmer Isn't she unbelievably beautiful? Everyone at the party said so. But dreadfully stubborn she is, bless her pretty little heart. What's to be done about that? Would you believe it, I practically had to use force to get her away!

Nora Oh, Torvald, you're going to regret not letting me stay—just half an hour longer.

Helmer Hear that, Mrs. Linde? She dances her tarantella—makes a roaring success—and very well deserved—though possibly a trifle too realistic—more so than was aesthetically necessary, strictly speaking. But never mind that. Main thing is—she had a success—roaring success. Was I going to let her stay on after that and spoil the impression? No, thank you. I took my beautiful little Capri signorina—my capricious little Capricienne, what?—under my arm—a swift round of the ballroom, a curtsey to the company, and, as they say in novels, the beautiful apparition disappeared! An exit should always be dramatic, Mrs. Linde. But unfortunately that's just what I can't get Nora to realize. I say, it's hot in here. *(Throws his cloak on a chair and opens the door to his study.)* What's this? It's dark in here. Ah, yes, of course—excuse me. *(Goes in and lights a couple of candles.)*

Nora *(whispers swiftly, breathlessly)* Well?

Mrs. Linde *(quietly)* I've spoken to him.

Nora Yes?

Mrs. Linde Nora—you must tell your husband everything.

Nora *(dully)* I knew it.

Mrs. Linde You've nothing to fear from Krogstad. But you must tell him.

Nora I shan't tell him anything.

Mrs. Linde Then the letter will.

Nora Thank you, Christine. Now I know what I must do. Ssh!

Helmer *(returns)* Well, Mrs. Linde, finished admiring her?

Mrs. Linde Yes. Now I must say good night.

Helmer Oh, already? Does this knitting belong to you?

Mrs. Linde *(takes it)* Thank you, yes. I nearly forgot it.

Helmer You knit, then?

Mrs. Linde Why, yes?

Helmer Know what? You ought to take up embroidery.

Mrs. Linde Oh? Why?

Helmer It's much prettier. Watch me, now. You hold the embroidery in your left hand, like this, and then you take the needle in your right hand and go in and out in a slow, easy movement—like this. I am right, aren't I?

Mrs. Linde Yes, I'm sure —

Helmer But knitting, now—that's an ugly business—can't help it. Look—arms all huddled up—great clumsy needles going up and down—makes you looks like a damned Chinaman. I say, that really was a magnificent champagne they served us.

Mrs. Linde Well, good night, Nora. And stop being stubborn. Remember!

Helmer Quite right, Mrs. Linde!

Mrs. Linde Good night, Mr. Helmer

Helmer *(accompanies her to the door)* Good night, good night! I hope you'll manage to get home all right? I'd gladly—but you haven't far to go, have you? Good night, good night. *(She goes. He closes* *the door behind her and returns.)* Well, we've got rid of her at last. Dreadful bore that woman is!

Nora Aren't you very tired, Torvald?

Helmer No, not in the least.

Nora Aren't you sleepy?

Helmer Not a bit. On the contrary, I feel extraordinarily exhilarated. But what about you? Yes, you look very sleepy and tired.

Nora Yes, I am very tired. Soon I shall sleep.

Helmer You see, you see! How right I was not to let you stay longer!

Nora Oh, you're always right, whatever you do.

Helmer (*kisses her on the forehead*) Now my little songbird's talking just like a real big human being. I say, did you notice how cheerful Rank was this evening?

Nora Oh? Was he? I didn't have a chance to speak with him.

Helmer I hardly did. But I haven't seen him in such a jolly mood for ages. (*Looks at her for a moment, then comes closer.)* I say, it's nice to get back to one's home again, and be all alone with you. Upon my word, you're a distractingly beautiful young woman.

Nora Don't look at me like that, Torvald!

Helmer What, not look at my most treasured possession? At all this wonderful beauty that's mine, mine alone, all mine.

Nora (*goes round to the other side of the table*) You mustn't talk to me like that tonight.

Helmer (*follows her*) You've still the tarantella in your blood, I see. And that makes you even more desirable. Listen! Now the other guests are beginning to go. (*More quietly.*) Nora—soon the whole house will be absolutely quiet.

Nora Yes, I hope so.

Helmer Yes, my beloved Nora, of course you do! Do you know—when I'm out with you among other people like we were tonight, do you know why I say so little to you, why I keep so aloof from you, and just throw you an occasional glance? Do you know why I do that? It's because I pretend to myself that you're my secret mistress, my clandestine little sweetheart, and that nobody knows there's anything at all between us.

Nora Oh, yes, yes,yes—I know you never think of anything but me.

Helmer And then when we're about to go, and I wrap the shawl round your lovely young shoulders, over this wonderful curve of your neck—then I pretend to myself that you are my young bride, that we've just come from the wedding, that I'm taking you to my house for the first time—that, for the first time, I am alone with you—quite alone with you, and you stand there young and trembling and beautiful. All evening I've had no eyes for anyone but you. When I saw you dance the tarantella, like a huntress, a temptress, my blood grew hot, I couldn't stand it any longer! That was why I seized you and dragged you down here with me—

Nora Leave me, Torvald! Get away from me! I don't want all this.

Helmer What? Now, Nora, you're joking with me. Don't want, don't want—? Aren't I your husband—?

There is a knock at the front door.

Nora (*starts*) What was that?

Helmer (*goes towards the hall*) Who is it?

Rank (*outside*) It's me. May I come in for a moment?

Helmer (*quietly, annoyed*) Oh, what does he want now? (*Calls.*) Wait a moment. (*Walks over and opens the door.*) Well! Nice of you not to go by without looking in.

Rank I thought I heard your voice, so I felt I had to say goodbye. (*His eyes travel swiftly around the room.*) Ah, yes—these dear rooms, how well I know them. What a happy, peaceful home you two have.

Helmer You seemed to be having a pretty happy time yourself upstairs.

Rank Indeed I did. why not? Why shouldn't one make the most of this world? As much as one can, and for as long as one can. The wine was excellent—

Helmer Especially the champagne.

Helmer You noticed that too? It's almost incredible how much I managed to get down.

Nora Torvald drank a lot of champagne too, this evening.

Rank Oh?

Nora Yes. It always makes him merry afterwards.

Rank Well, why shouldn't a man have a merry evening after a well-spent day?

Helmer Well-spent? Oh, I don't know that I can claim that.

Rank (*slaps him across the back*) I can, though, my dear fellow!

Nora Yes, of course, Dr. Rank—you've been carrying out a scientific experiment today, haven't you?

Rank Exactly

Helmer Scientific experiment! Those are big words for my little Nora to use!

Nora And may I congratulate you on the finding?

Rank You may indeed.

Nora It was good, then?

Rank The best possible finding—both for the doctor and the patient. Certainty.

Nora (*quickly*) Certainty?

Rank Absolute certainty. So aren't I entitled to have a merry evening after that?

Nora Yes, Dr. Rank. You were quite right to.

Helmer I agree. Provided you don't have to regret it tomorrow.

Rank Well, you never get anything in this life without paying for it.

Nora Dr. Rank—you like the masquerades, don't you?

Rank Yes, if the disguises are sufficiently amusing.

Nora Tell me. What shall we two wear at the next masquerade?

Helmer You little gadabout? Are you thinking about the next one already?

Rank We two? Yes, I'll tell you. You must go the Spirit of Happiness—

Helmer You try to think of a costume that'll convey that.

Rank Your wife need only appear as her normal, everyday self—

Helmer Quite right! Well said! But what are you going to be? Have you decided that?

Rank Yes, my dear friend. I have decided that.

Helmer Well?

Rank At the next masquerade, I shall be invisible.

Helmer Well, that's a funny idea.

Rank There's a big, black hat—haven't you heard of the invisible hat? Once it's over your head, no one can see you any more.

Helmer *(represses a smile)* Ah yes, of course.

Rank But I'm forgetting what I came for. Helmer, give me a cigar. One of your black Havanas.

Helmer With the greatest pleasure. *(Offers him the box.)*

Rank *(takes one and cuts off the tip.)* Thank you.

Nora *(strikes a match)* Let me give you a light.

Rank Thank you. *(She holds out the match for him. He lights his cigar.)* And now—goodbye.

Helmer Goodbye, my dear chap, goodbye.

Nora Sleep well, Dr. Rank.

Rank Thank you for that kind wish.

Nora Wish me the same.

Rank You? Very well—since you ask. Sleep well. And thank you for the light. *(He nods to them both and goes.)*

Helmer *(quietly)* He's been drinking too much.

Nora *(abstractedly)* Perhaps.

Helmer takes his bunch of keys from his pocket and goes out into the hall.

Nora Torvald, what do you want out there?

Helmer I must empty the letter-box. It's absolutely full. There'll be no room for the newspapers in the morning.

Nora Are you going to work tonight?

Helmer You know very well I'm not. Hullo, what's this? Someone's been at the lock.

Nora At the lock—?

Helmer Yes, I'm sure of it. Who on earth—? Surely not one of the maids? Here's a broken hairpin. Nora, it's yours—

Nora *(quickly)* Then it must have been the children.

Helmer Well, you'll have to break them of that habit. Hm, hm. Ah, that's done it. *(Takes out the contents of the box and calls into the kitchen.)* Helen! Helen! Put out the light on the staircase. *(Comes back into the drawing room with the letters in his hand and closes the door to the hall.)* Look at this! You see how they've piled up? *(Glances through them.)* What on earth's this?

Nora *(at the window)* The letter! Oh, no, Torvald, no!

Helmer Two visiting cards—from Rank.

Nora From Dr. Rank?

Helmer *(looks at them)* Peter Rank, M.D. They were on top. He must have dropped them in as he left.

Nora Has he written anything on them?

Helmer There's a black cross above his name. Look. Rather gruesome, isn't it? It looks just as though he was announcing his death.

Nora He is.

Helmer What? Do you know something? Has he told you anything?

Nora Yes. When these cards come, it means he's said good-bye to us. He wants to shut himself up in his house and die.

Helmer Ah, poor fellow. I knew I wouldn't be seeing him for much longer. But so soon—! And now he's going to slink away and hide like a wounded beast.

Nora When the time comes, it's best to go silently. Don't you think so, Torvald?

Helmer *(walks up and down)* He was so much a part of our life. I can't realize that he's gone. His suffering and loneliness seemed to provide a kind of dark background to the happy sunlight of our marriage. Well, perhaps it's best this way. For him, anyway. *(Stops walking.)* And perhaps for us too, Nora. Now we have only each other. *(Embraces her.)* Oh, my beloved wife—I feel as though I could never hold you close enough. Do you know, Nora, often I wish some terrible danger might threaten you, so that I could offer my life and my blood, everything, for your sake.

Nora *(tears herself loose and says in a clear, firm voice)* Read your letters now, Torvald.

Helmer No, no. Not tonight. Tonight I want to be with you, my darling wife—

Nora When your friend is about to die—?

Helmer You're right. This news has upset us both. An ugliness has come between us; thoughts of death and dissolution. We must try to forget them. Until then— you go to your room; I shall go to mine.

Nora *(throws her arms around his neck.)* Good night, Torvald! Good night!

Helmer *(kisses her on the forehead)* Good night, my darling little song-bird. Sleep well, Nora. I'll go and read my letters.

He goes into the study with the letters in his hand, and closes the door.

Nora *(wild-eyed, fumbles around, seizes Helmer's cloak, throws it round herself and whispers quickly, hoarsely)* Never see him again. Never. Never. Never. *(Throws the shawl over her head.)* Never see the children again. Them too. Never. Never. Oh—the icy black water! Oh—that bottomless—that—! Oh, if only it were all over! Now he's got it—he's reading it. Oh, no, no! Goodbye, Torvald! Goodbye, my darlings!

Helmer Nora!

Nora *(screams)*. Oh—!

Helmer What is this? You know what's in this letter?

Nora Yes, I know. Let me go! Let me out!

Helmer *(holding her back)*. Where are you going?

Nora (*struggling to break loose*). You can't save me, Torvald!

Helmer (*slumping back*). True! Then it's true what he writes? How horrible! No, no, it's impossible—it can't be true.

Nora It *is* true. I've loved you more than all this world.

Helmer Ah, none of your slippery tricks.

Nora (*taking one step toward him*). Torvald—!

Helmer What *is* this you've blundered into!

Nora Just let me loose. You're not going to suffer for my sake. You're not going to take on my guilt.

Helmer No more playacting. (*Locks the hall door.*) You stay right here and give me a reckoning. You understand what you've done? Answer! You understand?

Nora (*looking squarely at him, her face hardening*). Yes. I'm beginning to understand everything now.

Helmer (*striding about*). Oh, what an awful awakening! In all these eight years—she who was my pride and joy—a hypocrite, a liar—worse, worse—a criminal! How infinitely disgusting it all is! The shame! (*Nora says nothing and goes on looking straight at him. He stops in front of her.*) I should have suspected something of the kind. I should have known. All your father's flimsy values—Be still! All your father's flimsy values have come out in you. No religion, no morals, no sense of duty—Oh, how I'm punished for letting him off! I did it for your sake, and you repay me like this.

Nora Yes, like this.

Helmer Now you've wrecked all my happiness—ruined my whole future. Oh, it's awful to think of. I'm in a cheap little grafter's hands; he can do anything he wants with me, ask for anything, play with me like a puppet—and I can't breathe a word. I'll be swept down miserably into the depths on account of a featherbrained woman.

Nora When I'm gone from this world, you'll be free.

Helmer Oh, quit posing. Your father had a mess of those speeches too. What good would that ever do me if you were gone from this world, as you say? Not the slightest. He can still make the whole thing known; and if he does, it could be falsely suspected as your accomplice. The might even think that I was behind it—that ! put you up to it. And all that I can thank you for—you that I've coddled the whole of our marriage. Can you see now what you've done to me?

Nora (*icily calm*). Yes

Helmer It's so incredible, I just can't grasp it. But we'll have to patch up whatever we can. Take off the shawl. I said, take it off! I've got to appease him somehow or other. The thing has to be hushed up at any cost. And as for you and me, it's got to seem like everything between us is just as it was—to the outside world, that is. You'll go right on living in this house, of course. But you can't be allowed to bring up the children; I don't dare trust you with them—Oh, to have to say this to someone I've loved so much! Well, that's done with. From now on happiness doesn't matter; all that matters is saving the bits and pieces, the appearance—(*The doorbell rings,* Helmer *starts.*) What's that? And so late. Maybe the worst—? You think he'd—? Hide, Nora! Say you're sick. (NORA *remains standing motionless.* HELMER *goes and opens the door.*)

Maid (*half dressed, in the hall*). A letter for Mrs. Helmer.

Helmer I'll take it. (Snatches the letter and shuts the door.) Yes, it's from him. You don't get it; I'm reading it myself.

Nora Then read it.

Helmer (*by the lamp*). I hardly dare. We may be ruined, you and I. But—I've got to know. (*Rips open the letter, skims through a few lines, glances at an enclosure, then cries out joyfully.*) Nora! (NORA *looks inquiringly at him.*) Nora? Wait—better check it again—Yes, yes, it's true. I'm saved. Nora, I'm saved!

Nora And I?

Helmer You to of course. We're both saved, both of us, Nora. He's sent back your note. He says he's sorry and ashamed—that a development in his life—oh, who cares what he says Nora, we're saved! No one can hurt you. Oh, Nora, Nora—but first, this ugliness all has to go. (*Takes look at the note.*) No, I don't want to see it, I want the whole thing to fade like a dream. (*Tears the note and both letters to pieces, throws them into the stove and watches them burn.*) There—now there's nothing left—He wrote that since Christmas Eve you—Oh, these must have been three terrible days for you, Nora.

Nora I fought a hard fight.

Helmer It must have been terrible—seeing no way out except—no, we'll forget the whole sordid business. We'll just be happy and go on telling ourselves over and over again: "It's over! It's over!" Listen to me, Nora. You don't seem to realize. It's over! Why are you looking so pale? Ah, my poor little Nora, I understand. You can't believe that I have forgiven you. But I have, Nora. I swear it to you. I have forgiven you everything. I know that what you did you did for your love of me.

Nora That is true.

Helmer You have loved me as a wife should love her husband. It was simply that in your inexperience you chose the wrong means. But do you think I love you any the less because you don't know how to act on your own initiative? No, no. Just lean on me. I shall counsel you. I shall guide you. I would not be a true man if your feminine helplessness did not make you doubly attractive in my eyes. You mustn't mind the hard words I said to you in those first dreadful moments when my whole world seemed to be tumbling about my ears. I have forgiven you, Nora. I swear it to you; I have forgiven you.

Nora Thank you for your forgiveness.

She goes out through the door, right.

Helmer No, don't go—*(Looks in.)* What are you doing, there?

Nora *(offstage)* Taking off my fancy dress.

Helmer *(by the open door)* Yes, do that. Try to calm yourself and get your balance again, my frightened little songbird. Don't be afraid. I have broad wings to shield you. *(Begins to walk around near the door.)* How lovely and peaceful this little home of our is, Nora. You are safe here; I shall watch over you like a hunted dove which I have snatched unharmed from the claws of the falcon. Your wildy beating little heart shall find peace with me. It will happen, Nora; it will take time, but it will happen, believe me. Tomorrow all this will seem quite different. Soon everything will be as it was before. I shall no longer need to remind you that I have forgiven you; your own heart will tell you that it is true. Do you really think I could ever bring myself to disown you, or even to reproach you? Ah, Nora, you don't understand what goes on in a husband's heart. There is something indescribably wonderful and satisfying for a husband in knowing that he has forgiven his wife—forgiven her unreservedly, from the bottom of his heart. It means that she has become his property in a double sense; he has, as it were, brought her into the world anew; she is now not only his wife but also his child. From now on that is what you shall be to me, my poor, helpless, bewildered little creature. Never be frightened of anything again, Nora. Just open your heart to me. I shall be both your will and your conscience. What's this? Not in bed? Have you changed?

Nora *(in her everyday dress)* Yes, Torvald. I've changed.

Helmer But why now—so late—?

Nora I shall not sleep tonight.

Helmer But, my dear Nora—

Nora *(looks at her watch)* It isn't that late. Sit down here, Torvald. You and I have a lot to talk about.

She sits down on one side of the table.

Helmer Nora, what does this mean? You look quite drawn—

Nora Sit down. It's going to take a long time. I've a lot to say to you.

Helmer *(sits down on the other side of the table)* You alarm me, Nora. I don't understand you.

Nora No, that's just it. You don't understand me. And I've never understood you—until this evening. No, don't interrupt me. Just listen to what I have to say. You and I have got to face facts, Torvald.

Helmer What do you mean by that?

Nora *(after a short silence)* Doesn't anything strike you about the way we're sitting here?

Helmer What do you mean by that?

Nora *(after a short silence)* Doesn't anything strike you about the way we're sitting here?

Helmer What?

Nora We've been married for eight years. Does it occur to you that this is the first time that we two, you and I, man and wife, have ever had a serious talk together?

Helmer Serious? What do you mean, serious?

Nora In eight whole years—no, longer—ever since we first met—we have never exchanged a serious word on a serious subject.

Helmer Did you expect me to drag you into all my worries—worries you couldn't possibly have helped me with?

Nora I'm not talking about worries. I'm simply saying that we have never sat down seriously to try to get to the bottom of anything.

Helmer But, my dear Nora, what on earth has that got to do with you?

Nora That's just the point. You have never understood me. A great wrong has been done to me, Torvald. First by Papa, and then by you.

Helmer What? But we two have loved you more than anyone in the world!

Nora *(shakes her head)* You have never loved me. You just thought it was fun to be in love with me.

Helmer Nora, what kind of a way is this to talk?

Nora It's the truth, Torvald. When I lived with Papa, he used to tell me what he thought about everything, so that I never had any opinions but his. And if I did have any of my own. I kept them quiet, because he wouldn't have liked them. He called me his little doll, and he played with me just the way I played with my dolls. Then I came here to live in your house—

Helmer What kind of a way is that to describe our marriage?

Nora *(undisturbed)* I mean, then I passed from Papa's hands into yours. You arranged everything the way you wanted it, so that I simply took over your taste in everything—or pretended I did—I don't really know—I think it was a little of both—first one and then the other. Now I look back on it, it's as if I've been living here like a pauper, from hand to mouth. I performed tricks for you, and you gave me food and drink. But that was how you wanted it. You and Papa have done me a great wrong. It's your fault that I have done nothing with my life.

Helmer Nora, how can you be so unreasonable and ungrateful? Haven't you been happy here?

Nora No; never. I used to think I was; but I haven't ever been happy.

Helmer Not—not happy?

Nora Not. I've just had fun. You've always been very kind to me. But our home has never been anything but a playroom. I've been your doll-wife, just as I used to be Papa's doll-child. And the children have been my dolls. I used to think it was fun when you came in and played with me, just as they think it's fun when I go in and play games with them. That's all our marriage has been, Torvald.

Helmer There may be a little truth in what you say, though you exaggerate and romanticize. But from now on it'll be different. Playtime is over. Now the time has come for education.

Nora Whose education? Mine or the children's?

Helmer Both yours and the children's, my dearest Nora.

Nora Oh, Torvald, you're not the man to educate me into being the right wife for you.

Helmer How can you say that?

Nora And what about me? Am I fit to educate the children?

Helmer Nora!

Nora Didn't you say yourself a few minutes ago that you dare not leave them in my charge?

Helmer In a moment of excitement. Surely you don't think I meant it, seriously?

Nora Yes. You were perfectly right. I'm not fitted to educate them. There's something else I must do first. I must educate myself. And you can't help me with that. It's something I must do by myself. That's why I'm leaving you.

Helmer *(jumps up)* What did you say?

Nora I must stand on my own feet if I am to find out the truth about myself and about life. So I can't go on living here with you any longer.

Helmer Nora, Nora!

Nora I'm leaving you now, at once. Christine will put me up for to-night—

Helmer You're out of your mind! You can't do this! I forbid you!

Nora It's no use your trying to forbid me any more. I shall take with me nothing but what is mine. I don't want anything from you, now or ever.

Helmer What kind of madness is this?

Nora Tomorrow I shall go home—I mean, to where I was born. It'll be easiest for me to find some kind of a job there.

Helmer But you're blind! You've no experience of the world—

Nora I must try to get some, Torvald.

Helmer But to leave your home, your husband, your children! Have you thought what people will say?

Nora I can't help that. I only know that I must do this.

Helmer But this is monstrous! Can you neglect your most sacred duties?

Nora What do you call my most sacred duties?

Helmer Do I have to tell you? Your duties towards your husband, and your children.

Nora I have another duty which is equally sacred.

Helmer You have not. What on earth could that be?

Nora My duty towards myself.

Helmer First and foremost you are a wife and a mother.

Nora I don't believe that any longer. I believe that I am first and foremost a human being, like you—or anyway, that I must try to become one. I know most people think as you do, Torvald, and I know there's something of the sort to be found in books. But I'm no longer prepared to accept what people say and what's written in books. I must think things out for myself, and try to find my own answer.

Helmer Do you need to ask where your duty lies in your own home? Haven't you an infallible guide in such matters—your religion?

Nora Oh, Torvald, I don't really know what religion means.

Helmer What are you saying?

Nora I only know what Pastor Hansen told me when I went to confirmation. He explained that religion meant this and that. When I get away from all this and can think things out on my own, that's one of the questions I want to look into. I want to find out whether what Pastor Hansen said was right—or anyway, whether it is right for me.

Helmer But it's unheard of for so young a woman to behave like this! If religion cannot guide you, let me at least appeal to your conscience. I presume you have some moral feelings left? Or—perhaps you haven't? Well, answer me.

Nora Oh, Torvald, that isn't an easy question to answer. I simply don't know. I don't know where I am in these matters. I only know that these things mean something quite different to me from what they do to you. I've learned now that certain laws are different from what I'd imagined them to be; but I can't accept that such laws can be right. Has a woman really not the right to spare her dying father pain, or save her husband's life? I can't believe that.

Helmer You're talking like a child. You don't understand how society works.

Nora No, I don't. But now I intend to learn. I must try to satisfy myself which is right, society or I.

Helmer Nora, you're ill; you're feverish. I almost believe you're out of your mind.

Nora I've never felt so sane and sure in my life.

Helmer You feel sure that it is right to leave your husband and your children?

Nora Yes, I do.

Helmer Then there is only one possible explanation.

Nora What?

Helmer That you don't love me any longer.

Nora No, that's exactly it.

Helmer Nora! How can you say this to me?

Nora Or, Torvald, it hurts me terribly to have to say it, because you've always been so kind to me. But I can't help it. I don't love you any longer.

Helmer *(controlling his emotions with difficulty)* And you feel quite sure about this too?

Nora Yes, absolutely sure. That's why I can't go on living here any longer.

Helmer Can you also explain why I have lost your love?

Nora Yes, I can. It happened this evening, when the miracle failed to happen. It was then that I realized you weren't the man I'd thought you to be.

Helmer Explain more clearly. I don't understand you.

Nora I've waited so patiently, for eight whole years—well, good heavens, I've not such a fool as to suppose that miracles occur every day. Then this dreadful thing happened to me, and then I knew: "Now the miracle will take place!" When Korgstad's letter was lying out there, it never occurred to me for a moment that you would let that man trample over you. I knew that you would say to him: "Publish the facts to the world." And when he had done this—

Helmer Yes, what then? When I'd exposed my wife's name to shame and scandal—

Nora Then I was certain that you would step forward and take all the blame on yourself, and say: "I am the one who is guilty!"

Helmer Nora!

Nora You're thinking I wouldn't have accepted such a sacrifice from you? No, of course I wouldn't! But what would my word have counted for against yours? That was the miracle I was hoping for, and dreading. And it was to prevent it happening that I wanted to end my life.

Helmer Nora, I would gladly work for you night and day, and endure sorrow and hardship for your sake. But no man can be expected to sacrifice his honor, even for the person he loves.

Nora Millions of women have done it.

Helmer Oh, you think and talk like a stupid child.

Nora That may be. But you neither think nor talk like the man I could share my life with. Once you'd got over your fright—and you weren't frightened of what might threaten me, but only of what threatened you—once the danger was past, then as far as you were concerned it was exactly as though nothing had happened. I was your little songbird just as before—your doll whom henceforth you would take particular care to protect from the world because she was so weak and fragile. *(Gets up.)* Torvald, in that moment I realized that for eight years I had been living here with a complete stranger, and had borne him three children—! Oh, I can't bear to think of it! I could tear myself to pieces!

Helmer *(sadly)* I see it, I see it. A gulf has indeed opened between us. Oh, but Nora—couldn't it be bridged?

Nora As I am now, I am no wife for you.

Helmer I have the strength to change.

Nora Perhaps—if your doll is taken from you.

Helmer But to be parted—to be parted from you! No, no, Nora. I can't conceive of it happening!

Nora *(goes into the room, right)* All the more necessary that it should happen

She comes back with her outdoor things and a small traveling-bag, which she puts down on a chair by the table.

Helmer Nora, Nora, not now! Wait till tomorrow!

Nora *(puts on her coat)* I can't spend the night in a strange man's house.

Helmer But can't we live here as brother and sister, then—?

Nora *(fastens her hat)* You know quite well it wouldn't last. (*Puts on her shawl.*) Goodbye, Torvald. I don't want to see the children. I know they're in better hands than mine. As I am now, I can be nothing to them.

Helmer But some time, Nora—some time—?

Nora How can I tell? I've no idea what will happen to me.

Helmer But you are my wife, both as you are and as you will be.

Nora Listen, Torvald. When a wife leaves her husband's house, as I'm doing now, I'm told that according to the law he is freed of any obligations towards her. In any case, I release you from any such obligations. You mustn't feel bound to me in any way, however small, just as I shall not feel bound to you. We must both be quite free. Here is your ring back. Give me mine.

Helmer That too?

Nora That too.

Helmer Here it is.

Nora Good. Well, now it's over. I'll leave the keys here. The servants know about everything to do with the house—much better than I do. Tomorrow, when I have left town, Christine will come to pack the things I brought here from home, I'll have them sent on after me.

Helmer This is the end then! Nora, will you never think of me any more?

Nora Yes, of course. I shall often think of you and the children and this house.

Helmer May I write to you, Nora?

Nora No. Never. You mustn't do that.

Helmer But at least you must let me send you—

Nora Nothing. Nothing

Helmer But if you should need help—?

Nora I tell you, no. I don't accept things from strangers.

Helmer Nora—can I never be anything but a stranger to you?

Nora *(picks up her bag)* Oh, Torvald! Then the miracle of miracles would have to happen.

Helmer The miracle of miracles?

Nora You and I would both have to change so much that—oh, Torvald, I don't believe in miracles any longer.

Helmer But I want to believe in them. Tell me. We should have to change so much that—?

Nora That life together between us two could become a marriage. Goodbye

She goes out through the hall.

Helmer *(sinks down on a chair by the door and buries his face in his hands.)* Nora! Nora! *(Looks round and gets up.)* Empty! She's gone! *(A hope strikes him.)* The miracle of miracles—?

The street door is slammed shut downstairs.

▼ ▼ ▼ ▼ ▼

Hamlet's Advice to the Players

William Shakespeare

Speak the speech, I pray you, as I pronounced it to you, trippingly on the tongue: but if you mouth it, as many of your players do, I had as lief the town-crier spoke my lines. Nor do not saw the air too much with your hand, thus; but use all gently: for in the very torrent, tempest, and, as I may say, whirlwind of your passion, you must acquire and beget a temperance that may give it smoothness. O, it offends me to the soul to hear a robustious periwig-pated fellow tear a passion to tatters, to very rags, to split the ears of the groundlings; who, for the most part, are capable of nothing but inexplicable dumbshows and noise. I would have such a fellow whipp'd for o'erdoing Termagant; it out-herods Herod: pray you, avoid it . . .

Be not too tame neither, but let your own discretion be your tutor: suit the action to the word, the word to the action; with this special observance, that you o'erstep not the modesty of nature: for anything so overdone is from the purpose of playing, whose end, both at the first and now, was and is, to hold, as 'twere, the mirror up to Nature; to show virtue her own feature, scorn her own image, and the very age and body of the time his form and pressure. But this overdone, or come tardy of, though it make the unskillful laugh, cannot but make the judicious grieve; the censure of the which one must, in your allowance, o'erweigh a whole theatre of others. O, there be players that I have seen play, and heard others praise, and that highly, not to speak it profanely, that , neither having the accent of Christians nor the gait of Christian, pagan nor man, have so strutted and bellowed, that I have thought some of Nature's journeymen had made men, and not made them well, they imitated humanity so abominably . . .

And let those that play your Clowns speak no more than is set down for them: for there be of them that will themselves laugh, to set on some quantity of barren spectators to laugh too; though, in the meantime, some necessary question of the play be then to be considered: that's villainous, and shows a most pitiful ambition in the Fool that uses it.

▼ ▼ ▼ ▼ ▼

Prose

Roselily

▼ *Alice Walker* ▼

Dearly Beloved,

She dreams; dragging herself across the world. A small girl in her mother's white robe and veil, knee raised waist high through a bowl of quicksand soup. The man who stands beside her is against this standing on the front porch of her house, being married to the sound of cars whizzing by on highway 61.

we are gathered here

Like cotton to be weighed. Her fingers at the last minute busily removing dry leaves and twigs. Aware it is a superficial sweep. She knows he blames Mississippi for the respectful way the men turn their heads up in the years, the women stand waiting and knowledgeable, their children held from mischief by teachings from the wrong God. He glares beyond them to the occupants of the cars, white faces glued to promises beyond a country wedding, noses thrust forward like dogs on a track. For him they usurp the wedding.

in the sight of God

Yes, open house. That is what country black folks like. She dreams she does not already have three children. A squeeze around the flowers in her hands chokes off three and four and five years of breath. Instantly she is ashamed and frightened in her superstition. She looks for the first time at the preacher, forces humility into her eyes, as if she believes he is, in fact, a man of God. She can imagine God, a small black boy, timidly pulling the preacher's coattail.

to join this man and this woman

She thinks of ropes, chains, handcuffs, his religion. His place of worship. Where she will be required to sit apart with covered head. In Chicago, a word she hears when thinking of smoke, from his description of what a cinder was, which they never had in Panther Burn. She sees hovering over the heads of the clean neighbors in her front yard black specks falling, clinging, from the sky. But in Chicago. Respect, a chance to build. Her children at last from underneath the detrimental wheel. A chance to be on top. What a relief, she thinks. What a vision, a view, from up so high.

in holy matrimony

Her fourth child she gave away to the child's father who had some money. Certainly a good job. Had gone to Harvard. Was a good man but weak because good language meant so much to him he could not live with Roselily. Could not abide TV in the living room, five beds in three rooms, no Bach except from four to six on Sunday afternoons. No chess at all. She does not forget to worry about her son among his father's people. She wonders if the New England climate will agree with him. If he will ever come down to Mississippi, as his father did, to try to right the country's wrongs. She wonders if he will be stronger than his father. His father cried off and on throughout her pregnancy. Went to skin and bones. Suffered nightmares, retching and falling out of bed. Tried to kill himself. Later told his wife he found the right baby through friends. Vouched for, the sterling qualities that would make up his character.

It is not her nature to blame. Still, she is not entirely thankful. She supposed New England, the North, to be quite different from what she knows. It seems right somehow to her that people who move there to live return home completely changed. She thinks of the air, the smoke, the cinders. Imagines cinders big as hailstones; heavy, weighing on the people. Wonders how this pressure finds its way into the veins, roping the springs of laughter.

If there's anybody here that knows a reason why

But of course they know no reason why beyond what they daily have come to know. She thinks of the man who will be her husband, feels shut away from him because of the still severity of his plain black suit. His religion. A lifetime of black and white. Of veils. Covered head. It is as if her children are already gone from her. Not dead, but exalted on a pedestal, a stalk that has no roots. She wonders how to make new roots. It is beyond her. She wonders what one does with memories in a brand-new life. This had seemed easy, until she thought of it. "The reason why . . . the people who" . . . she thinks, and does not wonder where the thought is from.

these two should not be joined

She thinks of her mother, who is dead. Dead, but still her mother. Joined. this is confusing. Of her father. A gray old man who sold wild mink, rabbit, fox skins to Sears, Roebuck. He stands in the yard, like a man waiting for a train. Her young sisters stand behind her in smooth green dresses, with flowers in their hands and hair. They giggle, she feels, at the absurdity of the wedding. They are ready for something new. She thinks the man beside her should marry one of them. She feels old. Yoked. An arm seems to reach out from behind her and snatch her backward. She thinks of cemeteries and the long sleep of grandparents mingling in the dirt. She believes that she believes in ghosts. In the soil giving back what it takes.

together,

In the city. He sees her in a new way. This she knows, and is grateful. But is it new enough? She cannot always be a bride and virgin, wearing robes and veil. Even now her body itches to be free of satin and voile, organdy and lily of the valley. Memories crash against her. Memories of being bare to the sun. She wonders what it will be like. Not to have to go to a job. Not to work in a sewing plant. Not to worry about learning to sew straight seams in workingmen's overalls, jeans and dress pants. Her place will be in the home, he has said, repeatedly, promising her rest she had prayed for. But now she wonders. When she is rested, what will she do? They will make babies—she thinks practically about her fine brown body, his strong black one. They will be inevitable. Her hands will be full. Full of what? Babies. She is not comforted.

let him speak

She wishes she had asked him to explain more of what he meant. But she was impatient. Impatient to be done with sewing. With doing everything for three children, alone. Impatient to leave the girls she had known since childhood, their children growing up, their husbands hanging around her, already old, seedy. Nothing about them that she wanted, or needed. The fathers of her children driving by, waving, not waving; reminders of times she would just as soon forget. Impatient to see the South Side, where they would live and build and be responsible and respected and free. Her husband would free her. A romantic hush. Proposal. Promises. A new life! Respectable, reclaimed, renewed. Free! In robe and veil.

or forever hold

She does not even know if she loves him. She loves his sobriety. His refusal to sing just because he knows the tune. She loves his pride. His blackness and his gray car. She loves his understanding of her condition. She thinks she loves the effort he will make to redo her into what he truly wants. His love of her makes her completely conscious of how unloved she was before. This is something; though it makes her unbearably sad. Melancholy. She blinks her eyes. Remembers she is finally being married, like other girls. Like other girls, women? Something strains upward behind her eyes. She thinks of the something as a rat trapped, cornered, scurrying to and fro in her head, peering through the windows of her eyes. She wants to live for once. But doesn't know quite what that means. Wonders if she has ever done it. If she ever will. The preacher is odious to her. She wants to strike him out of the way, out of her light, with the back of her hand. It seems to her he has always been standing in front of her, barring her way.

his peace.

The rest she does not hear. She feels a kiss, passionate, rousing, within the general pandemonium. Cars drive up blowing their horns. Firecrackers go off. Dogs come from under the house and begin to yelp and bark. Her husband's hand is like the clasp of an iron gate. People congratulate. Her children press against her. They look with awe and distaste mixed with hope at their new father. He stands curiously apart, in spite of the people crowding about to grasp his free hand. He smiles at them all but his eyes are as if turned inward. He knows they cannot understand that he is not a Christian. He will not explain himself. He feels different, he looks it. The old women thought he was like one of their sons except that he had somehow got away from them. Still a son, not a son. Changed.

She thinks how it will be later in the night in the silvery gray car. How they will spin through the darkness of Mississippi and in the morning be in Chicago, Illinois. She thinks of Lincoln, the president. That is all she knows about the place. She feels ignorant, wrong, backward. She presses her worried fingers into his palm. He is standing in front of her. In the crush of well-wishing people, he does not look back.

▼ ▼ ▼ ▼ ▼

From "Two Kinds" from The Joy Luck Club

Amy Tan

My mother believed you could be anything you wanted to be in America. You could open a restaurant. You could work for the government and get good retirement. You could buy a house with almost no money down. You could become rich. You could become instantly famous.

"Of course you can be prodigy, too," my mother told me when I was nine. "You can be best anything. What does Auntie Lindo know? Her daughter, she is only best tricky."

America was where all my mother's hopes lay. She had come here in 1949 after losing everything in China: her mother and father, her family home, her first husband, and two daughters, twin baby girls. But she never looked back with regret. There were so many ways for things to get better.

We didn't immediately pick the right kind of prodigy. At first my mother thought I could be a Chinese Shirley Temple. We'd watch Shirley's old movies on TV as though they were training films. My mother would poke my arm and say, *"Ni kan"*—You watch. And I would see Shirley tapping her feet, or singing a sailor song, or pursing her lips into a very round O while saying, "Oh my goodness."

"Ni kan," said my mother as Shirley's eyes flooded with tears. "You already know how. Don't need talent for crying!"

Soon after my mother got this idea about Shirley Temple, she took me to a beauty training school in the Mission district and put me in the hands of a student who could barely hold the scissors without shaking. Instead of getting big fat curls, I emerged with an uneven mass of crinkly black fuzz. My mother dragged me off to the bathroom and tried to wet down my hair.

"You look like Negro Chinese," she lamented, as if I had done this on purpose.

The instructor of the beauty training school had to lop off these soggy clumps to make my hair even again. "Peter Pan is very popular these days," the instructor assured by mother. I now had hair the length of a boy's, with straight-across bangs that hung at a slant two inches above my eyebrows. I liked the haircut and it made me actually look forward to my future fame.

In fact, in the beginning, I was just as excited as my mother, maybe even more so. I pictured this prodigy part of me as many different images, trying each one on for size. I was a dainty ballerina girl standing by the curtains, waiting to hear the right music that would send me floating on my tiptoes. I was like the Christ child lifted out of the straw manger, crying with holy indignity. I was Cinderella stepping from her pumpkin carriage with sparkly cartoon music filling the air.

In all of my imaginings, I was filled with a sense that I would soon become *perfect*. My mother and father would adore me. I would be beyond reproach. I would never feel the need to sulk for anything.

But sometimes the prodigy in me became impatient. "If you don't hurry up and get me out of here, I'm disappearing for good," it warned. "And then you'll always be nothing."

Every night after dinner, my mother and I would sit at the Formica kitchen table. She would present new tests, taking her examples from stories of amazing children she had read in *Ripley's Believe It or Not,* or *Good Housekeeping, Reader's Digest,* and a dozen other magazines she kept in a pile in our bathroom. My mother got these magazines from people whose houses she cleaned. And since she cleaned many houses each week, we had a great assortment. She would look through them all, searching for stories about remarkable children.

The first night she brought out a story about a three-year-old boy who knew the capitals of all the states and even most of the European counties. A teacher was quoted as saying the little boy could also pronounce the names of the foreign cities correctly.

"What's the capital of Finland?" my mother asked me, looking at the magazine story.

All I knew was the capital of California, because Sacramento was the name of the street we lived on in Chinatown. "Nairobi!" I guessed, saying the most foreign word I could think of. She checked to see if that was possibly one way to pronounce "Helsinki" before showing me the answer.

The tests got harder—multiplying numbers in my head, finding the queen of hearts in a deck of cards, trying to stand on my head without using my hands, predicting the daily temperatures in Los Angeles, New York, and London.

One night I had to look at a page from the Bible for three minutes and then report everything I could remember. "Now Jehoshaphat had riches and honor in abundance and . . . that's all I remember, Ma," I said.

And after seeing my mother's disappointed face once again, something inside of me began to die. I hated the tests, the raised hopes and failed expectations. Before going to bed that night, I looked in the mirror above the bathroom sink and when I saw only my face staring back—and that it would always be this ordinary face—I began to cry. Such a sad, ugly girl! I made high-pitched noises like a crazed animal, trying to scratch out the face in the mirror.

And then I saw what seemed to be the prodigy side of me—because I had never seen that face before. I looked at my reflection, blinking so I could see more clearly. The girl staring back at me was angry, powerful. This girl and I were the same. I had new thoughts, willful thoughts, or rather thoughts filled with lots of won'ts. I won't let her change me, I promised myself. I won't be what I'm not.

So now on nights when my mother presented her tests, I performed listlessly, my head propped on one arm. I pretended to be bored. And I was. I got so bored I started counting the bellows of the foghorns out on the bay while my mother drilled me in other areas. The sound was comforting and reminded me of the cow jumping over the moon. And the next day, I played a game with myself, seeing if my mother would give up on me before eight bellows. After a while I usually counted only one, maybe two bellows at most. At last she was beginning to give up hope.

Two or three months had gone by without any mention of my being a prodigy again. And then one day my mother was watching *The Ed Sullivan Show* on TV. The TV was old and the sound kept shorting out. Every time my mother got halfway up from the sofa to adjust the set, the sound would go back on and Ed would be talking. As soon as she sat down, Ed would go silent again. She got up, the TV broke into loud piano music. She sat down. Silence. Up and down, back and forth, quiet and loud. It was like a stiff embraceless dance between her and the TV set. Finally she stood by the set with her hand on the sound dial.

She seemed entranced by the music, a little frenzied piano piece with this mesmerizing quality, sort of quick passages and then teasing lilting ones before it returned to the quick playful parts.

"*Ni kan*," my mother said, calling me over with hurried hand gestures, "Look here."

I could see why my mother was fascinated by the music. It was being pounded out by a little Chinese girl, about nine years old, with a Peter Pan haircut. The girl had the sauciness of a Shirley Temple. She was proudly modest like a proper Chinese child. And she also did this fancy sweep of a curtsy, so that the fluffy skirt of her white dress cascaded slowly to the floor like the petals of a large carnation.

In spite of these warning signs, I wasn't worried. Our family had no piano and we couldn't afford to buy one, let alone reams of sheet music and piano lessons. So I could be generous in my comments when my mother bad-mouthed the little girl on TV.

"Play note right, but doesn't sound good! No singing sound," complained my mother.

"What are you picking on her for?" I said carelessly. "She's pretty good. Maybe she's not the best, but she's trying hard." I knew almost immediately I would be sorry I said that.

"Just like you," she said. "Not the best. Because you not trying." She gave a little huff as she let go of the sound dial and sat down on the sofa.

The little Chinese girl sat down also to play an encore of "Anitra's Dance" by Grieg. I remember the song, because later on I had to learn how to play it.

The Masque of the Red Death

Edgar Allan Poe

The "Red Death" had long devastated the country. No pestilence had ever been so fatal, or so hideous. Blood was its Avatar and its seal—the redness and the horror of blood. There were sharp pains, and sudden dizziness, and then profuse bleeding at the pores, with dissolution. The scarlet stains upon the body, and especially upon the face of the victim, were the pest ban which shut him out from the aid and from the sympathy of his fellow-men. And the whole seizure, progress, and termination of the disease were the incidents of half an hour.

But the Prince Prospero was happy and dauntless and sagacious. When his dominions were half depopulated, he summoned to his presence a thousand hale and light-hearted friends from among the knights and dames of his court, and with these retired to the deep seclusion of one of his castellated abbeys. This was an extensive and magnificent structure, the creation of the prince's own eccentric yet august taste. A strong and lofty wall girdled it in. This wall had gates of iron. The courtiers, having entered, brought furnaces and massy hammers and welded the bolts. They resolved to leave means neither of ingress nor egress to the sudden impulses of despair or of frenzy from within. The abbey was amply provisioned. With such precautions the courtiers might bid defiance to contagion. The external world would take care of itself. In the meantime it was folly to grieve, or to think. The prince had provided all the appliances of pleasure. There were buffoons, there were improvisatori, there were ballet dancers, there were musicians, there was Beauty, there was wine. All these and security were within. Without was the "Red Death."

It was toward the close of the fifth or sixth month of his seclusion, and while the pestilence raged most furiously abroad, that the Prince Prospero entertained his thousand friends at a masked ball of the most unusual magnificence.

It was a voluptuous scene, that masquerade. But first let me tell of the rooms in which it was held. There were seven—an imperial suite. In many palaces, however, such suites form a long and straight vista, while the folding doors slide back nearly to the walls on either hand, so that the view of the whole extent is scarcely impeded. Here the case was very different; as might have been expected from the duke's love of the *bizarre*. The apartments were so irregularly disposed that the vision embraced but little more than one at a time.

There was a sharp turn at every twenty or thirty yards, and at each turn a novel effect. To the right and left, in the middle of each wall, a tall and narrow Gothic window looked out upon a closed corridor which pursued the windings of the suite. These windows were of stained glass whose color varied in accordance with the prevailing hue of the decorations of the chamber into which it opened. That at the eastern extremity was hung, for example, in blue—and vividly blue were its windows. The second chamber was purple in its ornaments and tapestries, and here the panes were purple. The third was green throughout, and so were the casements. The fourth was furnished and lighted with orange—the fifth with white—the sixth with violet. The seventh apartment was closely shrouded in black velvet tapestries that hung all over the ceiling and down the walls, falling in heavy folds upon a carpet of the same material and hue. But in this chamber only, the color of the windows failed to correspond with the decorations. The panes here were scarlet—a deep blood color. Now, in no one of the seven apartments was there any lamp or candelabrum, amid the profusion of golden ornaments that lay scattered to and fro or depended from the roof. There was no light of any kind emanating from lamp or candle within the suite of chambers. But in the corridors that followed the suite, there stood, opposite to each window, a heavy tripod, bearing a brazier of fire, that projected its rays through the tinted glass and so glaringly illumined the room. And thus were produced a multitude of gaudy and fantastic appearances. But in the western or black chamber the effect of the firelight that streamed upon the dark hangings through the blood-tinted panes was ghastly in the extreme, and produced so wild a look upon the countenances of those who entered, that there were few of the company bold enough to set foot within its precincts at all.

It was in this apartment, also, that there stood against the western wall, a gigantic clock of ebony. Its pendulum swung to and fro with a dull, heavy, monotonous clang; and when the minute-hand made the circuit of the face, and the hour was to be stricken, there came from the brazen lungs of the clock a sound which was clear and loud and deep and exceedingly musical, but of so particular a note and emphasis that, at each lapse of an hour, the musicians of the orchestra were constrained to pause, momentarily, in their performance, to hearken to the sound; and thus the waltzers perforce ceased their evolutions; and there was a brief disconcert of the whole gay company; and, while the chimes of the clock yet rang, it was observed that the giddiest grew pale, and the more aged and sedate passed their hands over their brows as if in confused reverie or meditation. But when the echoes had fully ceased, a light laughter at once pervaded the assembly; the musicians looked at each other and smiled as if at their own nervousness and folly, and made whispering vows, each to the other, that the next chiming of the clock should produce in them no similar emotion; and then, after the lapse of sixty minutes (which embraced three thousand and six hundred seconds of the Time that flies), there came yet another chiming of the clock, and then were the same disconcert and tremulousness and meditation as before.

But, in spite of these things, it was a gay and magnificent revel. The tastes of the duke were peculiar. He had a fine eye for colors and effects. He disregarded the *decora* of mere fashion. His plans were bold and fiery, and his conceptions glowed with barbaric lustre. There are some who would have thought him mad. His followers felt that he was not. It was necessary to hear and see and touch him to be *sure* that he was not.

He had directed, in great part, the movable embellishments of the seven chambers, upon occasion of this great *fete*: and it was his own guiding taste which had given character to the masqueraders. Be sure they were grotesque. There were much glare and glitter and piquancy and phantasm—much of what has been since seen in "Hernani." There were arabesque figures with unsuited limbs and appointments. There were delirious fancies such as the madman fashions. There were much of the beautiful, much of the wanton, much of the *bizarre*, something of the terrible, and not a little of that which might have excited disgust. To and fro in the seven chambers there stalked, in fact, a multitude of dreams. And these—the dreams—writhed in and out taking hue from the rooms, and causing the wild music of the orchestra to seem as the echo of their steps. And, anon, there strikes the ebony clock which stands in the hall of the velvet. And just for a moment, all is still, and all is silent save the voice of the clock. The dreams are stiff-frozen as they stand. But the echoes of the chime die away and they have endured but an instant—and a light, half-subdued laughter floats after them as they depart. And now again the music swells, and the dreams live, and writhe to and fro more merrily than ever, taking hue from the many-tinted windows through which stream the rays from the tripods. But to the chamber which lies most westerly of the seven there are now none of the dreamers who venture; for the night is waning away; flows a ruddier light through the blood-red panes; and the blackness of the sable carpet appalls; and to him whose foot falls upon the sable carpet, there comes from the near clock of ebony a muffled peal more solemnly emphatic than any which reaches *their* ears who indulge in the more remote gayeties of the other apartments.

But these other apartments were densely crowded, and in them beat feverishly the heart of life. And the revel went whirlingly on, until at length there commenced the sounding of midnight upon the clock. And then the music ceased, as I have told; and the evolutions of the waltzers were quieted; and there was an uneasy cessation of all things as before. But now there were twelve strokes to be sounded by the bell of the clock; and thus it happened, perhaps, that more of thought crept, with more of time, into the meditations of the thoughtful among those who revelled. And thus, too, it happened, perhaps, that before the last echoes of the last chime had utterly sunk into silence, there were many individuals in the crowd who had found leisure to become aware of the presence of a masked figure which had arrested the attention of no single individual before. And the rumor of this new presence having spread itself whisperingly around, there arose at length from the whole company a buzz, or murmur, expressive of disapprobation and surprise—then, finally, of terror, of horror, and of disgust.

In an assembly of phantasms such as I have painted, it may well be supposed that no ordinary appearance could have excited such sensation. In truth the masquerade license of the night was nearly unlimited; but the figure in question had out-Heroded Herod, and gone beyond the bounds of even the prince's indefinite decorum. There are chords in the heart of the most reckless which cannot be touched without emotion. Even with the utterly lost, to whom life and death are equally jests, there are matters of which no jest can be made. The whole company, indeed, seemed now deeply to feel that in the costume and bearing of the stranger neither wit nor propriety existed. The figure was tall and gaunt, and shrouded from head to foot in the habiliments of the grave. The mask which concealed the visage was made so nearly to resemble the countenance of a stiffened corpse that the closest scrutiny must have had difficulty in detecting the cheat. And yet all this might have been endured, if not approved, by the mad revellers around. But the mummer had gone so far as to assume the type of the Red Death. His vesture was dabbled in *blood*—and his broad brow, with all the features of the face, was besprinkled with the scarlet horror.

When the eyes of Prince Prospero fell upon this spectral image (which, with a slow and solemn movement, as if more fully to sustain to *role*, stalked to and fro among the waltzers) he was seen to be convulsed, in the first moment with a strong shudder either of terror or distaste; but, in the next, his brow reddened with rage.

"Who dares"—he demanded hoarsely of the courtiers who stood near him—"who dares insult us with this blasphemous mockery? Seize him and unmask him—that we may know whom we have to hang, at sunrise, from the battlements!"

It was in the eastern or blue chamber in which stood the Prince Prospero as he uttered these words. They rang throughout the seven rooms loudly and clearly, for the prince was a bold and robust man, and the music had become hushed at the waving of his hand.

It was in the blue room where stood the prince, with a group of pale courtiers by his side. At first, as he spoke, there was a slight rushing movement of this group in the direction of the intruder, who, at the moment, was also near at hand, and now, with deliberate and stately step, made closer approach to the speaker. But from a certain nameless awe with which the mad assumptions of the mummer had inspired the whole party, there were found none who put forth hand to seize him; so that, unimpeded, he passed within a yard of the prince's person; and, while the vast assembly, as if with one impulse, shrank from the centres of the rooms to the walls, he made his way uninterruptedly, but with the same solemn and measured step which had distinguished him from the first, through the blue chamber to the purple—through the purple to the green—through the green to the orange—through this again to the white—and even thence to the violet, ere a decided movement had been to arrest him. It was him, however, that the Prince Prospero, maddening with rage and the shame of his own momentary cowardice, rushed hurriedly through the six chambers, while none followed him on account of a deadly terror that had seized upon all. He bore aloft a drawn dagger, and had approached, in rapid impetuosity, to within three or four feet of the retreating figure, when the latter, having attained the extremity of the velvet apartment, turned suddenly and confronted his pursuer. There was a sharp cry—and the dagger dropped gleaming upon the sable carpet, upon which, instantly afterward, fell prostrate in death the Prince Prospero. Then, summoning the wild courage of despair, a throng of the revellers at once threw themselves into the black apartment, and, seizing the mummer, whose tall figure stood erect and motionless within the shadow of the ebony clock, gasped in unutterable horror at finding the grave cerements and corpse-like masks, which they handled with so violent a rudeness, untenanted by any tangible form.

And now was acknowledged the presence of the Red Death. He had come like a thief in the night. And one by one dropped the revellers in the blood-bedewed halls of their revel, and died each in the despairing posture of his fall. And the life of the ebony clock went out with that of the last of the gay. And the flames of the tripods expired. And Darkness and Decay and the Red Death held illimitable dominion over all.

▼▼▼▼▼

The Grounded Aviator

Anais Nin

The next day we met at the beach. The grounded aviator was there. We were introduced. We took a walk along the beach. John began to talk: "I've had five years of war as a rear-gunner. Been to India a couple of years, to North Africa, slept in the desert, crashed several times, made about a hundred missions, saw all kinds of things. Men dying, men yelling when they're trapped in burning planes. Their arms charred, their hands like the claws of animals.

The first time I was sent to the field after a crash . . . the smell of burning flesh. It's sweet and sickening, and it sticks to you for days. You can't wash it off. You can't get rid of it. It haunts you. We had good laughs, though, laughs all the time. We laughed plenty. We would commandeer prostitutes and push them into the beds of the guys who didn't like women. We had drunks that lasted several days. I like that life. India. I'd like to go back. This life here, what people talk about, what they think, bores me. I liked sleeping in the desert. I saw a black woman giving birth. She worked in the fields carrying dirt for a new airfield. She stopped carrying dirt to give birth under the wing of a plane, just like that, and then bound the kid in some rags and went back to work. Funny to see the big plane, so modern, and this half-naked woman giving birth and then continuing to carry dirt in pails for an airfield. You know, only two of us came back alive of the bunch I started with. My buddies always warned me: 'Don't get grounded; once you're grounded, you're done for.' Well, they grounded me, too. Too many rear-gunners in the service. I didn't want to come home. What's a civilian life? Good for old maids. It's a rut. It's drab. Look at this: the young girls giggle, giggle at nothing, The boys are after me. Nothing ever happens. They don't laugh hard and they don't yell. They don't get hurt, and they don't die, and they don't laugh either."

There was a light in his eyes I could not read, something he had seen but would not talk about.

We walked tirelessly along the beach, until there were no more homes, no more cared-for-gardens, no more people, until the beach became wild.

"Some die silent," he continued, as if obsessed. "You know by the look in their eyes that they were going to die. Some die yelling, and you have to turn your face away and not look into their eyes. When I was being trained, you know, the first thing they told me: 'Never look into a dying man's eyes'."

"But you did," I said, suddenly understanding the expression of his eyes, I could see him clearly at seventeen, not yet a man, with the delicate skin of a girl, the finely carved features, the small straight nose, the mouth of a woman, a shy laugh, something very tender about the face and body, looking into the eyes of the dying.

I saw him two or three times and then he disappeared. He was in the hospital with a bout of malaria.

I returned to New York. The sea at East Hampton had not renewed me. It was not the same sea.

▼ ▼ ▼ ▼ ▼

Papa's Ring

▼ *Barbara Pasternack* ▼

Mama lay in the hospital bed, a sheet half covering her tiny, withered body. Sometimes she would convulse so badly that the nurse had to tie her arms to the sides of the bed. Her once beautiful features were disguised by involuntary facial contortions. Her parched mouth moved continuously, as if she wanted to speak, but she could only emit incomprehensible sounds.

She was unaware of Papa's presence. She didn't know that he sat in a chair near the window of the hospital room every day, staring at the bed, waiting for a response of any kind. He sat quietly, from time to time touching the ring on his finger.

There were three other beds in the room. They contained similar figures: old women too sick and weak to respond to the visitors who brought flowers that would soon wither in the stale air of the hospital. Papa was one of those hopeless, wordless visitors who sat silently in that dying room, staring at the beds, waiting and praying to some distant God, a God that never answered their prayers.

When a new visitor entered the room, Papa would take a worn photograph from his shirt pocket and hold it up saying, "This was my wife, Nina. This is what she used to look like. Wasn't she beautiful? Look what can happen to a person!"

The other women in the room were wives and mothers; Nina had been a star. Her admirers used to say, "She looks like Vilma Banky, the silent movie actress."

Papa wanted every stranger to know that she was different. He wanted them to know that this shriveled creature in the bed was not the woman he had married over fifty years earlier. He couldn't understand the mysteries of illness and old age, or didn't want to understand. How could this have happened to her?

After all, he was 90 years old, still proud and strong, still able to work. She was 10 years younger than he; how could she have allowed this to happen?

He rarely touched her. Only when the attendant brought food did he go close to Mama's bed. He tried to coerce her to eat, but the twitching and convulsing never stopped long enough for her to take more than a few bites. Papa usually gave up trying to feed her and ate the meal himself. Food shouldn't go to waste. Even if he wasn't hungry, it was important that nothing should be left. There had been too many hungry days in his life to allow it to go uneaten.

Papa hungered for other things as well as food: for the love that should have been his when he and Mama were young. He hungered for the years when they were in the Russian and Yiddish theatres. How talented Mama had been! She had had the lead role in Tolstoy's *Resurrection*, at the Amphion Theatre in Brooklyn. There had been many curtain calls. Flowers had filled the dressing room, and Mama's "admirers" had waited at the stage door to pay her homage. Papa always knew that, even though she called them "admirerers," they were in reality her lovers. He chose to ignore them. It was the only way their marriage could survive.

Papa rubbed the gold ring with the blue stone. It was on the middle finger of his left hand, and it was too tight. It made the flesh of his finger swell. Sasha, Mama's special admirerer had given it to him. He was the only one who presented a threat to Papa. The ring was a token, an apology for the many years of deception. Papa had accepted it silently and graciously. He was able to avoid unpleasant feelings, especially when they concerned Mama's indiscretions. At some level, Papa was aware that she would never leave him. They had been through too much together. He had even written a play about their married life. He called it *Forty Years on the Fourth Floor*.

Papa never took the ring off his finger. It became a part of him. In a strange way, it was his hold on Mama. It was all that was left of her relationship with Sasha, and now it was Papa's to keep, as she was his to keep.

Sasha was a merchant seaman. He used to disappear on long seagoing trips for months, sometimes years. On the day he gave Papa the ring, Sasha had just returned from one of his voyages. He arrived at their door unannounced. He had aged considerably; his once lean body was no longer firm; his clothes hung loosely around him. He had been drinking and his hands shook, but he still retained some of the charm that Mama had found so attractive.

Sasha brought many gifts that Papa accepted as if they were owed to him. "Thank you, Sashinka," he said.

They shared a bottle of Vodka while Mama played the role of coquette, serving tea and cake and flirting like a 16 year old. Papa became slightly drunk and animated. He made little jokes and claimed all of Sasha's attention, never giving Mama a chance to renew her relationship with him.

Before he left, Sasha impulsively took the gold ring with the blue stone off his finger and presented it to Papa. "Here Mischa, this is for you to remember me by," he said. They never saw him again.

In the glare of the hospital room, Sasha was no longer a threat, no longer real. The reality was the small figure in the bed, clinging to life, unaware of the old man sitting in the chair waiting. Papa waited and hoped. He hoped she would die, and at the same time hoped she would live. He hoped for a miracle that he knew would never materialize. He touched the ring lightly. His eyes filled with tears. The ring was meaningless now, connected to another time. Sitting back in the chair, he closed his eyes. He ignored the sun shining through the window, warming his neck and giving an angelic glow to his white hair. Maybe he could get Mama to eat a little something before he went home.

The Yellow Wallpaper
Charlotte Perkins Gilman

We shall sleep downstairs tonight, and take the boat home tomorrow.

I quite enjoy the room, now it is bare again.

How those children did tear about here!

This bedstead is fairly gnawed!

But I must get to work.

I have locked the door and thrown the key down into the front path.

I don't want to go out, and I don't want to have anybody come in, till John comes.

I want to astonish him.

I've got a rope up here that even Jennie did not find. If that woman does get out, and tries to get away, I can tie her!

But I forgot I could not reach far without anything to stand on!

This bed will *not* move!

I tried to lift and push it until I was lame, and then I got so angry I bit off a little piece at one corner—but it hurt my teeth.

Then I peeled off all the paper I could reach standing on the floor. It sticks horribly and the pattern just enjoys it! All those strangled heads and bulbous eyes and waddling fungus growths just shriek with derision!

I am getting angry enough to do something desperate. To jump out of the window would be admirable exercise, but the bars are too strong even to try.

Besides, I wouldn't do it. Of course not. I know well enough that a step like that is improper and might be misconstrued.

I don't like to *look* out of the windows even—there are so many of those creeping women, and they creep so fast.

I wonder if they all come out of that wallpaper, as I did?

But I am securely fastened now by my well-hidden rope—you don't get *me* out in the road there!

I suppose I shall have to to get back behind the pattern when it comes night, and that is hard!

It is so pleasant to be out in this great room and creep around as I please!

I don't want to go outside. I won't, even if Jennie asks me to.

For outside you have to creep on the ground, and everything is green instead of yellow.

But here I can creep smoothly on the floor, and my shoulder just fits in that long smooch around the wall, so I cannot lose my way.

Why, there's John at the door!

It is no use, young man, you can't open it!

How he does call and pound!

Now he's crying for an axe.

It would be a shame to break down that beautiful door!

"John, dear!" said I in the gentlest voice, "the key is down by the front steps, under a plantain leaf!"

That silenced him for a few moments.

Then he said—very quietly indeed, "Open the door, my darling!"

"I can't," said I. "The key is down by the front door, under a plantain leaf!"

And then I said it again, several times, very gently and slowly, and said it so often that he had to go and see, and he got it, of course, and came in. He stopped short by the door.

"What is the matter?" he cried. "For God's sake, what are you doing?"

I kept on creeping just the same, but I looked at him over my shoulder.

"I've got out at last," said I, "in spite of you and Jennie! And I've pulled off most of the paper, so you can't put me back!"

Now why should that man have fainted? But he did, and right across my path by the wall, so that I had to creep over him every time!

▼ ▼ ▼ ▼ ▼

Speeches

A Vindication of the Rights of Woman
Mary Wollstonecraft

... Women are, therefore, to be considered either as moral beings, or so weal that they must be entirely subjected to the superior faculties of men.

Let us examine this question. Rousseau declares, that a woman should never, for a moment feel herself independent, that she should be governed by fear to exercise her *natural* cunning, and made a coquettish slave in order to render her a more alluring object of desire, a *sweeter* companion to man, whenever he chooses to relax himself. He carries the arguments, which he pretends to draw from the indications of nature, still further, and insinuates that truth and fortitude the cornerstones of all human virtue, shall be cultivated with certain restrictions, because with respect to the female character, obedience is the grand lesson which ought to be impressed with unrelenting rigor.

What nonsense! When will a great man arise with sufficient strength of mind to puff away the fumes which pride and sensuality have thus spread over the subject! If women are by nature inferior to men, their virtues must be the same in quality, if not in degree, or virtue is a relative idea; consequently, their conduct should be founded on the same principles and have the same aim.

Connected with man as daughters, wives, and mothers, their moral character may be estimated by their manner of fulfilling those simple duties; but the end, the grand end of their exertions should be to unfold their own faculties, and acquire the dignity of conscious virtue. They may try to render their road pleasant; but ought never to forget, in common with man, that life yields not the felicity which can satisfy an immortal soul. I do not mean to insinuate, that either sex should be so lost, in abstract reflections or distant views, as to forget the affections and duties that lie before them, and are in truth, the means appointed to produce the fruit of life; on the contrary, I would warmly recommend them, even while I assert, that they afford most satisfaction when they are considered in their true subordinate light.

▼ ▼ ▼ ▼ ▼

On His Condemnation to Death
Socrates

There are many reasons why I am not grieved, O men of Athens, at the vote of condemnation. I expected this, and am only surprised that the votes are so nearly equal, for I had thought that the majority against me would have been much larger; but now, had thirty votes gone over to the other side, I should have been acquitted. And I may say, I think, that I have escaped Meletus. And I may say something more; for without the assistance of Amytus and Lycon, he would not have had one fifth of the votes, as the law requires, in which case he would have incurred a fine of a thousand drachmae.

And so he proposes death to be the penalty. And what shall I propose on my part, O men of Athens? Clearly that which is my due. And what then is my due? What shall be done to the man who has never had the wit to be idle in his whole life—but has been careless of what concerns many—wealth, family interests, and military offices, and speaking in the assembly, and magistracies, and plots, and parties. Reflecting that I was really too honest a man to follow in this way and live, I did not go where I could do no good to you or to myself; but where I could do the greatest good privately to everyone of you, thither I went, and sought to persuade every man among you that he must look to himself, and seek virtue and wisdom before he looks to his private interests, and that this should be the order which he observes in all his actions. What shall be done to such a man? Doubtless some good things, O men of Athens, if he has his reward. What would be a reward suitable to a poor man who is your benefactor, who desires leisure that he may instruct you? There can be no reward so fitting as maintenance in the Prytaneum, O men of Athens, a reward which he deserves far more than the citizen who has won the prize at Olympia in the horse or chariot race, whether the chariots were drawn by two horses or by many. For I am in want, and he has enough; and he only gives you the appearance of happiness, and I give you the reality. And if I am to estimate the penalty justly, I say that maintenance in the Prytaneum is the just return.

Someone will say: Yes, Socrates, but cannot you hold your tongue, and then you may go into a foreign city to live on in exile, and no one will interfere with you. Now I have great difficulty in making you understand my answer to this. For if I tell you that to do as you say would be disobedient to the God, and therefore I cannot hold my tongue, you will not believe that I am serious; and if I say again that daily to talk about virtue, and of those other things about which you hear me examining myself and others, is the greatest good of man, and that the unexamined life is not worth living, you are still less likely to believe me. But as it is, I might have estimated the offence at what I could pay, for money I have none; and therefore I must ask you to proportion the fine according to my means. Well, perhaps I could afford a mina [approximately fifty dollars] and therefore I propose that penalty: Plato, Crito, Critobulus, and Apollodorus, my friends here, bid me say thirty minae, and they will be ample security to you.

Not much time will be gained, O men of Athens, in return for the evil name which you will get the detractors of the city, who will say that you killed Socrates, a wise man; for when they want to reproach you, they will call me wise, even though I am not wise. If you had waited a little longer, your desire would have been fulfilled in the course of nature. For I am very advanced in years, as you may perceive, and near death. But I say this not to you all, but to those only who have condemned me to die. And I say this too to the same persons. Perhaps you think, O men of Athens, that I have been convicted through the want of arguments, by which I might have escaped punishment. Far otherwise: I have been convicted through want indeed, yet not of arguments, but of audacity and impudence, and of the inclination to say such things to you as would have been most agreeable to hear, had I lamented and bewailed and done and said many things unworthy of me, as I affirm, but such as you are accustomed to hear from others.

Neither did I then think that I ought, for the sake of avoiding danger, to do anything unworthy of a freeman, nor do I now repent of having so defended myself; but I should rather choose to die having so defended myself than to live in that way. For neither in a trial nor in battle is it right that I or anyone else should employ every possible means whereby he may avoid death; for in battle it is frequently evident that a man might escape death by laying down his arms and throwing himself on the mercy of his pursuers. And there are many other devices in every danger, by which to avoid death, if a man dares to do and say everything.

But this is not difficult, O men of Athens, to escape death, but it is much more difficult to avoid depravity, for it flies faster than death. And now I, being slow and aged, am overtaken by the slower of the two; but my accusers, being strong and active, have been overtaken by the swifter, wickedness. And now I depart, condemned by you to death; but they are condemned by truth, as guilty of iniquity and injustice: and I abide my sentence and so do they. These things, perhaps, ought so to be, and I think that they are for the best.

In the next place, I wish to predict to you who have condemned me, what your fate will be: for I am now in that condition in which men most frequently prophesy, namely, when they are about to die. I say then to you, O Athenians, who have condemned me to death, that immediately after my death a punishment will overtake you, far more severe, by Zeus, than that which you have inflicted on me. For you have done this thinking that you should be freed from the necessity of giving account of your life. The very contrary, however, as I declare, will happen to you. Your accusers will be greater in number whom I have restrained, though you did not perceive it; and they will be more severe, inasmuch as they are younger and you will be more indignant. For, if you think that by putting men to death you will restrain anyone from upbraiding you because you do not live well, you are much mistaken; for this method of escape is neither possible nor honorable, but that other is most honorable and most easy, not to put a check upon others, but for a man to take heed to himself, how he may be most perfect. Having predicted this much to those of you who have condemned me, I take my leave of you.

But with you who have voted for my acquittal, I would gladly hold converse about what has taken place, while the officials are busy [preparing the formal record] and I am not yet taken to the place where I must die. Stay with me then, so long, O Athenians, for nothing hinders our conversing with each other, while we are permitted to do so; because I wish to make known to you, as being my friends, the meaning of that which has just now befallen me. To me then, O my judges—and in calling you judges I call you rightly—a strange thing has happened. For the accustomed prophetic voice of my guardian diety, on every former occasion, even in the most trifling affairs, opposed me, if I was about to do anything wrong; but now, that has befallen me which you yourselves behold, and which anyone would think, and which is supposed to be, the extremity of evil; yet neither when I departed from home in the morning did the warning of the god oppose me, nor when I came up here to the place of trial, nor in my address when I was about to say anything; yet on other occasions it has frequently restrained me in the midst of speaking. But now it has never throughout this proceeding opposed me, either in what I did or said. What then do I suppose to be the cause of this? I will tell you: what has happened to me appears to be a blessing; and it is impossible that we think rightly who suppose that death is an evil. A great proof of this to me is the fact that it is impossible but that the accustomed signal from the god should have opposed me, unless I had been about to meet with some good.

Moreover, we may hence conclude that there is greater hope that death is a blessing. For to die is one of two things; to be dead is as to be nothing and have no sensation of anything whatever; or, as it is said, there is a certain change and passage of the soul from one place to another. And if it is a privation of all sensation, as it were, as sleep in which the sleeper has no dream, death would be a wonderful gain. For I think that if anyone, having selected a night in which he slept so soundly as not to have had a dream, and having compared this night with all the other nights and days of his life, should be required on consideration to say how many days and nights he had passed better and more pleasantly than this night throughout his life, I think that not only a private person, but even a great king himself would find them easy to number in comparison with other days and nights. If, therefore, death is a thing of this kind, I say it is a gain; for thus all futurity appears to be nothing more than one night.

But if, on the other hand, death is a removal from hence to another place, and what is said to be true, that all the dead are there, what greater blessing can there be than this, my judges? For if, on arriving at Hades, released from these who pretend to be judges, one shall find those who are true judges, and who are said to judge there, Minos, and Rhadamanthus, Aeacus, and Triptolemus, and such others of the demigods as were just during their own life, would this be a sad removal? At what price would you estimate a conference with Orpheus and Museaus, Hesoid and Homer? I indeed should be willing to die often, if this be true. For to me, the sojourn there would be admirable when I should meet with Palamedes, and Ajax, son of Telamon, and any other of the ancients who has died by an unjust sentence. The comparing of my sufferings with theirs would, I think, be no unpleasing occupation. But the greatest pleasure would be to spend my time in questioning and examining the people there as I have done those here, and discovering who among them is wise, and who fancies himself to be so but is not. At what price, my judges, would not anyone estimate the opportunity of questioning him who led that mighty army against Troy, or Ulysses, or Sisyphus, or ten thousand others, whom one might mention, both men and women? With whom to converse and associate, and to question them, would be an inconceivable happiness! In any event I am sure that they put no man to death there; in other respects those who live there are more happy than those that are here, and are henceforth immortal, if at lest what is said be true.

You, therefore, O my judges, ought to enjoy good hopes as to death, and to think upon this one truth that to a good many nothing is evil, neither while he lives nor when he is dead, nor are that man's concerns neglected by the gods. And what has befallen me is not the effect of chance; but this is clear to me that now must die, and, thus freed from my cares, that this is better for me. On this account the warning in no way turned me aside; and I bear no resentment toward those who condemned me, or against my accusers, although they did not condemn and accuse me with this intention, but thinking to injure me: in this they deserved to be blamed.

Thus much, however, I beg of them. Punish my sons, when they grow up, O judges, paining them as I have pained you, if they appear to you to care for riches or anything else before virtue, and if they think themselves to be something when they are nothing, reproach them as I have done you, for not attending to what they ought, and for conceiving themselves something when they are worth nothing. If you do this both I and my sons shall have met with just treatment from your hands.

It is now time to depart—for me to die, for you to live. But which of us is going to a better state is unknown to everyone but God.

▼ ▼ ▼ ▼ ▼

On Being Sentenced to Death

John Brown

John Brown of Ossawatomie, Kansas, became one of the most famous figures in the fight against slavery during the years preceding the Civil War. His methods were militant. He was for the immediate liberation of slaves. On the night of October 16, 1859, leading a small band of supporters, Brown seized the arsenal at Harpers Ferry, now in West Virginia. He was captured, tried and convicted. On being sentenced to death, on November 2, 1859, Brown made this extemporaneous speech to the court.

I have, may it please the Court, a few words to say.

In the first place, I deny everything but what I have all along admitted: of a design on my part to free slaves. I intended certainly to have made a clean thing of that matter, as I did last winter, when I went into Missouri and there took slaves without the snapping of a gun on either side, moving them through the country, and finally leaving them in Canada. I designed to have done the same thing again on a larger scale. That was all I intended. I never did intend murder, or treason, or the destruction of property, or to excite or incite slaves to rebellion, or to make insurrection.

I have another objection, and that is that it is unjust that I should suffer such a penalty. Had I interfered in the manner which I admit, and which I admit has been fairly proved—for I admire the truthfulness and candor of the greater portion of the witnesses who have testified in this case—had I so interfered in behalf of the rich, the powerful, the intelligent, the so-called great, or in behalf of any of their friends, either father, mother, brother, sister, wife or children, or any of that class, and suffered and sacrificed what I have in this interference, it would have been all right. Every man in this Court would have deemed it an act worthy of reward rather than punishment.

This Court acknowledges, too, as I suppose, the validity of the law of God. I see a book kissed, which I supposed to be the Bible, or at least the New Testament, which teaches me that all things whatsoever I would that men should do to me, I should do even so to them. It teaches me, further, to remember them that are in bonds as bound with them. I endeavored to act up to that instruction.

I say I am yet too young to understand that God is any respecter of persons. I believe that to have interfered as I have done, as I have always freely admitted I have done, in behalf of His despised poor, I did no wrong, but right. Now, if it is deemed necessary that I should forfeit my life for the furtherance of the ends of justice, and mingle my blood further with the blood of my children and with the blood of millions in this slave country whose rights are disregarded by wicked, cruel, and unjust enactments, I say, let it be done.

Let me say one word further. I feel entirely satisfied with the treatment I have received on my trial. Considering all the circumstances, it has been more generous than I expected. But I feel no consciousness of guilt. I have stated from the first what was my intention, and what was not. I never had any design against the liberty of any person, nor any deposition to commit treason or incite slaves to rebel or make any general insurrection. I never encouraged any man to do so, but always discouraged any idea of that kind.

Let me say, also, in regard to the statements made by some of those who were connected with me, I hear it has been stated by some of them that I have induced them to join me. But the contrary is true. I do not say this to injure them, but as regretting their weakness. Not one but joined me of his own accord, and never had a word of conversation with, till the day they came to me, and that was for the purpose I have stated.

Now, I have done.

▼▼▼▼▼

Address at Gettysburg
Abraham Lincoln

This great speech of President Lincoln was, according to one story, written on his railroad trip from Washington to Gettysburg. According to Andrew Carnegie, who worked on the road as a young man, he supplied Lincoln with the pencil which he used to compose the speech on the back of an envelope.

But whatever means, in whatever restricted space, President Lincoln created a lasting literary monument. It was written with the whole of his reading in the Bible and Shakespeare in his mind. It is condensed with a sense of great style. He gave the speech November 19, 1863.

The audience at Gettysburg had been greatly impressed by the speaker who preceded the President; he was Senator Edward Everett from Massachusetts, whose roaring voice was heard at the very edge of the crowd. Everett's speech is now forgotten. Lincoln spoke with a small voice and was heard by few in the great gathering. His speech passed almost unnoticed in the newspapers the next day, but it is a speech that Americans have long remembered.

Fourscore and seven years ago our fathers brought forth upon this continent a new nation, conceived in liberty, and dedicated to the proposition that all men are created equal.

Now we are engaged in a great civil war, testing whether that nation, or any nation so conceived and so dedicated, can long endure. We are met on a great battlefield of that war. We have come to dedicate a portion of that field as a final resting place for those who here gave their lives that that nation might live. It is altogether fitting and proper that we should do this.

But in a larger sense, we cannot dedicate, we cannot consecrate, we cannot hallow this ground. The brave men, living and dead, who struggled here, have consecrated it far above our poor power to add or detract. The world will little note nor long remember what we say here; but it can never forget what they did here. It is for us, the living, rather to be dedicated here to the unfinished work which they who fought here have thus far so nobly advanced. It is rather for us to be here dedicated to the great task remaining before us: that from these honored dead we take increased devotion to that cause for which they gave the last full measure of devotion; that we here highly resolve that these dead shall not have died in vain; that this nation, under God, shall have a new birth of freedom; and that government of the people, by the people, for the people, shall not perish from the earth.

▼▼▼▼▼

Oral Testimony of a Former Slave

Anonymous

My mother was the smartest black woman in Eden. She was as quick as a flash of lightning, and whatever she did could not be done better. She could do anything. She cooked, washed, ironed, spun, nursed and labored in the field. She made as good a field hand as she did a cook. I have heard Master Jennings say to his wife, "Fannie has her faults, but she can outwork any nigger in the country. I'd bet my life on that."

The one doctrine of my mother's teaching which was branded upon my senses was that I should never let anyone abuse me. "I'll kill you, gal, if you don't stand up for yourself," she would say. "Fight, and if you can't fight, kick; if you can't kick, then bite." Ma was generally willing to work, but if she didn't feel like doing something, none could make her do it. At least, the Jennings couldn't' make, or didn't make her.

On the day my mother died, she called pa and said . . . "Go tell Master Jennings to come in, and get all the slaves too."

Pa went and returned in five minutes with old master.

"Fannie, are you any worse?" said old master.

"No, no, Master Jennings, no worse, but I'm going to leave you at eight o'clock."

"Where are you going, Fannie," Master Jennings asked as if he didn't know that ma was talking about dying.

Ma shook her head slowly and answered, "I'm going where there ain't no fighting and cussing and damning."

"Is there anything that you want me to do for you, Fannie?"

Ma told him that she reckoned there wasn't much of anything that anybody could do for her now. "But I would like for you to take Puss . . . she always called me Puss . . . and hire her out among ladies, so she can be raised right. She will never be any good here, Master Jennings."

A funny look came over Master Jennings' face, and he bowed his head up and down. All the hands had come in and were standing around with him.

My mother died just about eight o'clock.

The Meaning of July Fourth for the Negro

Frederick Douglass

Frederick Douglass, the foremost Negro leader in nineteenth-century America, was born a slave on the Eastern Shore of Maryland. Upon his escape to the North in 1838, he dedicated his energies to the destruction of the system of slavery and rapidly became the outstanding Black Abolitionist. During and after the Civil War, he played a distinguished role as leader of and spokesman for his people. He ranks with the greatest of nineteenth-century orators.

In 1847, Douglass moved to Rochester, New York, where he began publication of his newspaper, *The North Star*. He was requested to address the citizens of Rochester on the Fourth of July celebration in 1852. The speech was delivered under the title, "The Meaning of July Fourth for the Negro."

Fellow citizens: pardon me, and allow me to ask, why am I called upon to speak here today? What have I or those I represent to do with your national independence? Are the great principles of political freedom and of natural justice, embodied in that Declaration of Independence, extended to us? And am I, therefore, called upon to bring our humble offering to the national altar, and to confess the benefits, and express devout gratitude for the blessings resulting from your independence to us?

Would to God, both for your sakes and ours, that an affirmative answer could be truthfully returned to these questions. Then would my task be light, and my burden easy and delightful. For who is there so cold that a nation's sympathy could not warm him? Who so obdurate and dead to the claims of gratitude, that would not thankfully acknowledge such priceless benefits? Who so stolid and selfish that would not give his voice to swell the hallelujahs of a nation's jubilee, when the chains of servitude had been torn from his limbs? I am not that man. In a case like that, the dumb might eloquently speak, and the "lame man leap as a hart."

But such is not the state of the case. I say it with a sad sense of disparity between us. I am not included within the pale of this glorious anniversary! Your high independence only reveals the immeasurable distance between us. The blessings in which you this day rejoice are not enjoyed in common. The rich inheritance of justice, liberty, prosperity, and independence bequeathed by your fathers is shared by you, not by me. The sunlight that brought life and healing to you has brought stripes and death to me. This Fourth of July is *yours*, nor *mine*. *You* may rejoice, *I* must mourn. To drag a man in fetters into the grand illuminated temple of liberty, and call upon him to join you in joyous anthems, were inhuman mockery and sacrilegious irony. Do you mean, citizens, to mock me, by asking me to speak today? If so, there is a parallel to your conduct. And let me warn you, that it is dangerous to copy the example of a nation whose crimes, towering up to heaven, were thrown down by the breath of the Almighty, burying that nation in irrecoverable ruin. I can today take up the lament of a peeled and woe-smitten people.

"By the rivers of Babylon, there we sat down. Yes! We wept when we remembered Zion. We hanged our harps upon the willows in the midst thereof. For there they that carried us away captive, required of us a song; and they who wasted us, required of us mirth, saying, Sing us one of the songs of Zion. How can we sing the Lord's song in a strange land? If I forget thee, O Jerusalem, let my right hand forget her cunning. If I do not remember thee, let my tongue cleave to the roof of my mouth."

Fellow citizens, above your national, tumultuous joy, I hear the mournful wail of millions, whose chains, heavy and grievous yesterday, are today rendered more intolerable by the jubilant shouts that reach them. If I do forget, if I do not remember those bleeding children of sorrow this day, "may my right hand forget her cunning, and may my tongue cleave to the roof of my mouth!" To forget them, to pass lightly over their wrongs, and to chime in with the popular theme, would be treason most scandalous and shocking, and would make me a reproach before God and the world. My subject, then, fellow citizens, is "American Slavery." I shall see this day and its popular characteristics from the slave's point of view. Standing here, identified with the American bondman, making his wrongs mine, I do not hesitate to declare, with all my soul, that the character and conduct of this nation never looked blacker to me than on this Fourth of July. Whether we turn to the declarations of the past, or to the professions of the present, the conduct of the nation seems equally hideous and revolting. America is false to the past, false to the present, and solemnly binds herself to be false to the future. Standing with God and the crushed and bleeding slave on this occasion, I will, in the name of humanity, which is outraged, in the name of liberty, which is fettered, in the name of the Constitution and the Bible, which are disregarded and trampled upon, dare to call in question and to denounce, with all the emphasis I can command, everything that serves to perpetuate slavery—the great sin and shame of America! "I will not equivocate; I will not excuse," I will use the severest language I can command, and yet not one word shall escape me that any man, whose judgment is not blinded by prejudice, or who is not at heart a slave-holder, shall not confess to be right and just.

But I fancy I hear some of my audience say it is just in this circumstance that you and your brother Abolitionists fail to make a favorable impression on the public mind. Would you argue more and denounce less, would you persuade more and rebuke less, your cause would be much more likely to succeed. But, I submit, where all is plain there is nothing to be argued. What point in the anti-slavery creed would you have me argue? On what branch of the subject do the people of this country need light? Must I undertake to prove that the slave is a man? That point is conceded already. Nobody doubts it. The slave-holders themselves acknowledge it in the enactment of laws for their government. They acknowledge it when they punish disobedience on the part of the slave. There are seventy-two crimes in the State of Virginia, which, if committed by a black man (no matter how ignorant he be), subject him to the punishment of death; while only two of these same crimes will subject a white man to like punishment. What is this but the acknowledgment that the slave is a moral, intellectual, and responsible being? The manhood of the slave is conceded. It is admitted in the fact that Southern statute-books are covered with enactments, forbidding, under severe fines and penalties, the teaching of the slave to read and write. When you can point to any such laws in reference to the beasts of the field, then I may consent to argue the manhood of the slave. When the dogs in your streets, when the fowls of the air, when the cattle on your hills, when the fish of the sea, and the reptiles that crawl, shall be unable to distinguish the slave from a brute, then I will argue with you that the slave is a man!

For the present it is enough to affirm the equal manhood of the Negro race. It is not astonishing that, while we are plowing, planting, and reaping, using all kinds of mechanical tools, erecting houses, constructing bridges, building ships, working in metals of brass, iron, copper, silver, and gold; that while we are reading, writing, and cyphering, acting as clerks, merchants, and secretaries, having among us lawyers, doctors, ministers, poets, authors, editors, orators, and teachers; that while we are engaged in all the enterprises common to other men—digging gold in California, capturing the whale in the Pacific, feeding sheep and cattle on the hillside, living, moving, acting, thinking, planning, living in families as husbands, wives, and children, and above all, confessing and worshipping the Christian God, and looking hopefully for life and immortality beyond the grave—we are called upon to prove that we are men?

Would you have me argue that man is entitled to liberty? That he is the rightful owner of his own body? You have already declared it. Must I argue the wrongfulness of slavery? Is that a question for republicans? Is it to be settled by the rules of logic and argumentation, as a matter beset with great difficulty, involving a doubtful application of the principle of justice, hard to understand? How should I look today in the presence of Americans, dividing and subdividing a discourse, to show that men have a natural right to freedom, speaking of it relatively and positively, negatively and affirmatively? To do so would be to make myself ridiculous, and to offer an insult to your understanding. There is not a man beneath the canopy of heaven who does not know that slavery is wrong *for him*.

What! Am I to argue that it is wrong to make men brutes, to rob them of their liberty, to work them without wages, to keep them ignorant of their relations to their fellow men, to beat them with sticks, to flay their flesh with the lash, to load their limbs with irons, to hunt them with dogs, to sell them at auction, to sunder their families, to knock out their teeth, to burn their flesh, to starve them into obedience and submission to their masters? Must I argue that a system thus marked with blood and stained with pollution is wrong? No; I will not. I have better employment for my time and strength than such arguments would imply.

What, then, remains to be argued? Is it that slavery is not divine; that God did not establish it; that our doctors of divinity are mistaken? There is blasphemy in the thought. That which is inhuman cannot be divine. Who can reason on such a proposition? They that can, may; I cannot. The time for such argument is past.

At a time like this, scorching irony, not convincing argument, is needed. Oh! had I the ability, and could I reach the nation's ear, I would today pour out a fiery stream of biting ridicule, blasting reproach, withering sarcasm, and stern rebuke. For it is not light that is needed, but fire; it is not the gentle shower, but thunder. We need the storm, the whirlwind, and the earthquake. The feeling of the nation must be quickened; the conscious of the nation must be roused; the propriety of the nation must be startled; the hypocrisy of the nation must be exposed; and its crimes against God and man must be denounced.

What to the American slave is your Fourth of July? I answer, a day that reveals to him more than all other days of the year, the gross injustice and cruelty to which he is the constant victim. To him your celebration is a sham; your boasted liberty an unholy license; your national greatness, swelling vanity; your sounds of rejoicing are empty and heartless; your denunciation of tryants, brass-fronted impudence; your shouts of liberty and equality, hollow mockery; your prayers and hymns, your sermons and thanksgivings, with all your religious parade and solemnity, are to him mere bombast, fraud, deception, impiety, and hypocrisy—a thin veil to cover up crimes which would disgrace a nation of savages. There is not a nation of the earth guilty of practices more shocking and bloody than are the people of these United States at this very hour.

Go where you may, search where you will, roam through all the monarchies and despotisms of the Old World, travel through South America, search out every abuse and when you have found the last, lay your facts by the side of the every-day practices of this nation, and you will say with me that, for revolting barbarity and shameless hypocrisy, America reigns without a rival.

Red Jacket

Friend and Brother:—It was the will of the Great Spirit that we should meet together this day. He orders all things and has given us a fine day for our council. He has taken His garment from before the sun and caused it to shine with brightness upon us. Our eyes are opened that we see clearly; our ears are unstopped that we have been able to hear distinctly the words you have spoken. For all these favors we thank the Great Spirit, and Him only.

Brother, this council fire was kindled by you. It was at your request that we came together at this time. We have listened with attention to what you have said. You requested us to speak our minds freely. This gives us great joy; for we now consider that we stand upright before you and can speak what we think. All have heard our voice and all speak to you now as one man. Our minds are agreed.

Brother, you say you want an answer to your talk before you leave this place. It is right you should have one, as you are a great distance from home and we do not wish to detain you. But first we will look back a little and tell you what our fathers have told us and what we have heard from the white people.

Brother, listen to what we say. There was a time when our forefathers owned this great island. Their seats extended from the rising to the setting sun. The Great Spirit had made it for the use of Indians. He had created the buffalo, the deer, and other animals for food. He had made the bear and the beaver. Their skins served us for clothing. He had scattered them over the country and taught us how to take them. He had caused the earth to produce corn for bread. All this He had done for His red children because He loved them. If we had some disputes about our hunting-ground they were generally settled without the shedding of much blood.

But an evil day came upon us. Your forefathers crossed the great water and landed on this island. Their numbers were small. They found friends and not enemies. They told us they had fled from their own country for fear of wicked men and had come here to enjoy their religion. They asked for a small seat. We took pity on them, granted their request, and they sat down among us. We gave them corn and meat; they gave us poison in return.

The white people, brother, had found our country. Tidings were carried back and more came among us. Yet we did not fear them. We took them to be friends. They called us brothers. We believed them and gave them a larger seat. At length their numbers had greatly increased. They wanted more land; they wanted our country. Our eyes were opened and our minds became uneasy. Wars took place, Indians were hired to fight against Indians, and many of our people were destroyed. They also brought strong liquor among us. It was strong and powerful, and has slain thousands.

Brother, our seats were once large and yours were small. You have now become a great people, and we have scarcely a place left to spread our blankets. You have got our country, but are not satisfied; you want to force your religion upon us.

Brother, continue to listen. You say that you are sent to instruct us how to worship the Great Spirit agreeable to His mind; and, if we do not take hold of the religion which you white people teach we shall be unhappy hereafter. You say that you are right and we are lost. How do we know this to be true? We understand that your religion is written in a Book. If it was intended for us, as well as you, why has not the Great Spirit given to us, and not only to us, but why did He not give to our forefathers the knowledge of the Book, with the means of understanding it rightly. We only know what you tell us about it. How shall we know when to believe, being so often deceived by the white people?

Brother, you say there is but one way to worship and serve the Great Spirit. If there is but one religion, why do you white people differ so much about it? Why not all agreed, as you can all read the Book?

Brother, we do not understand these things. We are told that your religion was given to your forefathers and has been handed down from father to son. We also have a religion which was given to our forefathers and has been handed down to us, their children. We worship in that way. It teaches us to be thankful for all the favors we receive, to love each other, and to be united. We never quarrel about religion.

Brother, the Great Spirit has made us all, but He has made a great difference between His white and His red children. He has given us different complexions and different customs. To you He has given the arts. To these He has not opened our eyes. We know these things to be true. Since He has made so great a difference between us in other things, why may we not conclude that He has given us a different religion according to our understanding? The Great Spirit does right. He knows what is best for His children; we are satisfied.

Brother, we do not wish to destroy your religion or take it from you. We only want to enjoy our own.

Brother, you say you have not come to get our land or our money, but to enlighten our minds. I will now tell you that I have been at your meetings and saw you collect money from the meeting. I can not tell what this money was intended for, but supposed that it was for your minister; and, if we should conform to your way of thinking, perhaps you may want some from us.

Brother, we are told that you have been preaching to the white people in this place. These people are our neighbors. We are acquainted with them. We will wait a little while and see what effect your preaching has upon them. If we find it does them good, makes them honest, and less disposed to cheat Indians, we will then consider again of what you have said.

Brother, you have now heard our answer to your talk, and this is all we have to say at present. As we are going to part, we will come and take you by the hand, and hope the Great Spirit will protect you on your journey and return you safe to your friends.

Tecumseh

It is true I am a Shawanee. My forefathers were warriors. Their son is a warrior. From them I only take my existence; from my tribe I take nothing. I am the maker of my own fortune; and oh! that I could make that of my red people, and of my country, as great as the conceptions of my mind, when I think of the Spirit that rules the universe. I would not then come to Governor Harrison, to ask him to tear the treaty and to obliterate the landmark; but I would say to him: Sir, you have liberty to return to your own country. The being within, community with past ages, tells me that once, nor until lately, there was no white man on this continent. That it then all belonged to red men, children of the same parents, placed on it by the Great Spirit that made them, to keep it, to traverse it, to enjoy its productions, and to fill it with the same race. Once a happy race. Since made miserable by the white people, who are never contented, but always encroaching. The way, and the only way, to check and to stop this evil, is for all the red men of unite in claiming a common and equal right in the land, as it was at first, and should be yet; for it never was divided, but belongs to all for the use of each. That no part has a right to sell, even to each other, much less to strangers; those who want all, and will not do with less.

The white people have no right to take the land from the Indians, because they had it first; it is theirs. They may sell, but all must join. Any sale not made by all is not valid. The late sale is bad. It was made by a part only. Part do not know how to sell. It requires all to make a bargain for all. All red men have equal rights to the unoccupied land. The right of occupancy is as good in one place as in another. There cannot be two occupations in the same place. The first excludes all others. It is not so in hunting or traveling; for there the same ground will serve many, as they may follow each other all day; but the camp is stationary, and that is occupancy. It belongs to the first who sits down on his blanket or skins which he has thrown upon the ground; and till he leaves it no other has a right.

▼ ▼ ▼ ▼ ▼

On Woman's Right to Suffrage

Susan B. Anthony

Friends and fellow citizens:—I stand before you to-night under indictment for the alleged crime of having voted at the last presidential election, without having a lawful right to vote. It shall be my work this evening to prove to you that in thus voting, I not only committed no crime, but, instead, simply exercised my *citizen's rights*, guaranteed to me and all United States citizens by the National Constitution, beyond the power of any State to deny.

The preamble of the Federal Constitution says:

"We, the people of the United States, in order to form a more perfect union, establish justice, insure *domestic* tranquility, provide for the common defense, promote the general welfare, and secure the blessings of liberty to ourselves and our posterity, do ordain and establish this Constitution for the United States of America."

It was we, the people; not we, the white male citizens; nor yet we, the male citizens; but we, the whole people, who formed the Union. And we formed it, not to give the blessings of liberty, but to secure them; not to the half of ourselves and the half of our posterity, but to the whole people—women as well as men. And it is a downright mockery to talk to women of their enjoyment of the blessings of liberty while they are denied the use of the only means of securing them provided by this democratic republican government—the ballot.

For any State to make sex a qualification that must ever result in the disenfranchisement of one entire half of the people is to pass a bill of attainder, or an *ex post facto* law, and is therefore a violation of the supreme law of the land. By it the blessings of liberty are for ever withheld from women and their female posterity. To them this government has no just powers derived from the consent of the governed. To them this government is not a democracy. It is not a republic. It is an odious aristocracy; a hateful oligarchy of sex; the most hateful aristocracy every established on the face of the globe; an oligarchy of wealth, where the rich govern the poor. An oligarchy of learning, where the educated govern the ignorant, or even an oligarchy of race, where the Saxon rules the African, might be endured, but this oligarchy of sex, which makes father, brothers, husband, sons, the oligarchs over the mother and sisters, the wife and daughters of every household—which ordains all men sovereigns, all women subjects, carries dissension, discord and rebellion into every home of the nation.

Webster, Worcester and Bouvier all define a citizen to be a person in the United States, entitled to vote and hold office.

The only question left to be settled now is: Are women persons? And I hardily believe any of our opponents will have the hardihood to say they are not. Being persons, then, women are citizens; and no State has the right to make any law, or to enforce any old law, that shall abridge their privileges or immunities. Hence, every discrimination against women in the constitutions and laws of the several States is to-day null and void, precisely as is every one against negroes.

▼ ▼ ▼ ▼ ▼

What If I Am a Woman?

Maria W. Stewart

What if I am a woman; is not the God of ancient times the God of these modern days? Did he not raise up Deborah to be a mother and a judge of Israel?

Did not Queen Esther save the lives of the Jews? And Mary Magdalene first declare the resurrection of Christ from the dead? Come, said the woman of Samaria, and see a man that hath told me all things that ever I did; is not this the Christ? St. Paul declared that it was a shame for a woman to speak in public, yet our great High Priest and Advocate did not condemn the woman for a more notorious offense than this; neither will he condemn this worthless worm . . . Did St. Paul but know of our wrongs and deprivations, I presume he would make no objection to our pleading in public for our rights . . .

Among the Greeks, women delivered the oracles. The respect the Romans paid to the Sybils is well known. The Jews had their prophetesses. The prediction of the Egyptian woman obtained much credit at Rome, even unto the emperors. And in most barbarous nations all things that have the appearance of being supernatural, the mysteries of religion, the secrets of physic, and the rities of magic, were in the possession of women.

If such women as are here described have once existed, be no longer astonished, then, my brethern and friends, that God at this eventful period should raise up your own females to strive by their example, both in public and private, to assist those who are endeavoring to stop the strong current of prejudice that flows so profusely against us at present. No longer ridicule their efforts, it will be counted for sin. For God makes use of feeble means sometimes to bring about his most exalted purposes.

In the fifteenth century, the general spirit of this period is worthy of observation. We might then have seen women preaching and mixing themselves in controversies. Women occupying the chairs of Philosophy and Justice; women haranguing in Latin before the Pope; women writing in Greek and studying in Hebrew; nuns were poetresses and women of quality divines; and younger girls who had studied eloquence would, with the sweetest countenances and the most plaintiff voices, pathetically exhort the Pope and the Christian princes to declare war against the Turks. Women in those days devoted their leisure hours to contemplation and study. The religious spirit which has animated women in all ages showed itself at this time. It has made them, by turns, martyrs, apostles, warriors, and concluded in making them divines and scholars. . . .

What if such women as are here described should rise among our sable race? And it is not impossible; for it is not the color of the skin that makes the man or the woman, but the principle formed in the soul. Brilliant wit will shine, come from whence it will; and genius and talent will not hide the brightness of its lustre. . . .

Men of eminence have mostly risen from obscurity; nor will I, although a female of a darker hue, and far more obscure than they, bend my head or hang my harp upon willows; for though poor, I will virtuous prove. And if it is the will of my Heavenly Father to reduce me to penury and want, I am ready to say: Amen, even so be it.

▼ ▼ ▼ ▼ ▼

Woman in the Nineteenth Century
Education of Women
Margaret Fuller

Another sign of the times is furnished by the triumphs of Female Authorship. These have been great, and are constantly increasing. Women have taken possession of so many provinces for which men had pronounced them unfit, that, though these still declare there are some inaccessible to them, it is difficult to say just *where* they must stop.

The shining names of famous women have cast light upon the path of the sex, and many obstructions have been removed. When a Montague could learn better than her brother, and use her lore afterwards to such purpose as an observer, it seemed amiss to hinder women from preparing themselves to see, or from seeing all they could, when prepared. Since Somerville has achieved so much, will any young girl be prevented from seeking a knowledge of the physical sciences, if she wishes it? De Stael's name was not so clear of offence; she could not forget the Woman in the thought; while she was instructing you as a mind, she wished to be admired as a Woman; sentimental tears often dimmed the eagle glance. Her intellect, too, with all its splendor, trained in a drawing-room, fed on flattery, was tainted and flawed; yet its beams make the obscurest school-house in New England warmer and lighter to the little rugged girls who are gathered together on its wooden bench. They may never through life hear her name, but she is not the less their benefactress.

The influence has been such, that the air certainly is, now, in arranging school instruction for girls, to give them as fair a field as boys. As yet, indeed, these arrangements are made with little judgment or reflection; just as the tutors of Lady Jane Grey, and other distinguished women of her time, taught them Latin and Greek, because they knew nothing else themselves, so now the improvement in the education of girls is to be made by giving them young men as teachers, who only teach what has been taught themselves at college, while methods and topics need revision for these new subjects, which could better be made by those who had experienced the same wants. Women are, often, at the head of these institutions; but they have, as yet, seldom, been thinking women, capable of organizing a new whole for the wants of the time, and choosing persons to officiate in the departments. And when some portion of instruction of a good sort is got from the school, the far greater proportion which is infused from the general atmosphere of society contradicts its purport. Yet books and a little elementary instruction are not furnished in vain. Women are better aware how great and rich the universe is, not so easily blinded by narrowness or partial views of a home circle. "Her mother did so before her" is no longer a sufficient excuse. Indeed, it was never received as an excuse to mitigate the severity of censure, but as adduced as a reason, rather, why there should be no effort made for reformation.

Whether much or little has been done, or will be done,—whether women will add to the talent of narration the power or systematizing,—whether they will carve marble, as well as draw and paint,—is not important. But that it should be acknowledged that they have intellect which needs developing—that they should not be considered complete, if beings of affection and habit alone—is important.

Yet even this acknowledgment, rather conquered by Woman than preferred by Man, has been sullied by the usual selfishness. Too much is said of women being better educated, that they may become better companions and mothers for *men*. The should be fit for such companionship, and we have mentioned, with satisfaction, instances where it has been established. Earth knows no fairer, holier relation than that of a mother. It is one which, rightly understood, must both promote and require the highest attainments. But a being of infinite scope must be treated with an exclusive view to any one relation, give the soul free course, let the organization, both of body and mind, be freely developed, and the being will be fit for any and every relation to which it may be called. The intellect, no more than the sense of hearing, is to be cultivated not merely that Women may be a more valuable companion to Man, but because the Power who gave a power, by its mere existence signifies that it must be brought out toward perfection.

In this regard of self-dependence, and a greater simplicity and fullness of being, we must hail as a preliminary the increase of the class contemptuously designated as "old maids."

We cannot wonder at the aversion with which old bachelors and old maids have been regarded. Marriage is the natural means of forming a sphere, of taking root in the earth; it requires more strength to do this without such an opening; very many have failed, and their imperfections have been in every one's way. They have been more partial, more harsh, more officious and impertinent, than those compelled by severer friction to render themselves endurable. Those who have a more full experience of the instincts have a distrust as to whether the unmarried can be thoroughly human and humane, such as is hinted in the saying, "Old maids' and bachelors' children are well cared for," which derides at once their ignorance and their presumption.

Yet the business of society has become so complex, that it could now scarcely be carried on without the presence of these despised auxiliaries; and detachments from the army of aunts and uncles are wanted to stop gaps in every hedge. They rove about, mental and moral Israelites, pitching their tents amid the fixed and ornamented homes of men.

In a striking variety of forms, genius of late, both at home and abroad, has paid its tribute to the character of the Aunt and the Uncle, recognizing in these personages the spiritual parents, who have supplied defects in the treatment of the busy or careless actual parents.

They also gain a wider, if not so deep experience. Those who are not intimately and permanently linked with others, are thrown upon themselves; and, if they do not there find peace and incessant life, there is none to flatter them that they are not very poor, and very mean.

A position which so constantly admonishes, may be of inestimable benefit. The person may gain, undistracted by other relationships, a closer communion with the one. Such a use is made of it by saints and sibyls. Or she may be one of the lay sisters of charity, a canoness, bound by an inward vow,—or the useful drudge of all men, the Martha, much sought, little prized,—or the intellectual interpreter of the varied life she sees; the Urania of a half-formed world's twilight.

Or she may combine all these. Not "needing to care that she may please a husband," a frail and limited being, her thoughts may turn to the centre, and she may, by steadfast contemplation entering into the secret of truth and love, use it for the good of all men, instead of a chosen few, and interpret through it all the forms of life. It is possible, perhaps, to be at once a priestly servant and a loving nurse.

Saints and geniuses have often chosen a lonely position, in the faith that if, undisturbed by the pressure of near ties, they would give themselves up to the inspiring spirit, it would enable them to understand and reproduce life better than actual experience could.

How many "old maids" take this high stand we cannot say: it is an unhappy fact that too many who have come before the eye are gossips rather, and not always good-natured gossips. But if these abuse, and none make the best of their vocation, yet it has not failed to produce some good results. It has been seen by others, if not by themselves, that beings, likely to be left alone, need to be fortified and furnished within themselves; and education and thought have tended more and more to regard these beings as related to absolute Being, as well as to others. It has been seen that, as the breaking of no bond ought to destroy a man, so ought the missing of none to hinder him from growing. And thus a circumstance of the time, which springs rather from its luxury than its purity, has helped to place women on the true platform.

Perhaps the next generation, looking deeper into this matter, will find that contempt is put upon old maids, or old women, at all, merely because they do not use the elixir which would keep them always young. Under its influence, a gem brightens yearly which is only seen to more advantage through the fissures Time makes in the casket. No one thinks of Michael Angelo, Persican Sibyl, or St. Theresa, or Tasso's Leonora, or the Greek Electra, as an old maid, more than of Michael Angelo or Canova as old bachelors, though all had reached the period in life's course appointed to take that degree.

▼ ▼ ▼ Chapter VI Key Terms

Internal life of the character	Manuscript
External life of the character	Poetry
Introspective	Prose
Scanning	Drama

VII

Informative Speaking

- Speeches of Personal Experience
- Speeches about Processes or Demonstration Speeches
- Student Sample Demonstration Speeches
- Speeches about Objects
- Speeches about Events
- Speeches about Concepts
- Entertaining Speeches
- Types of Outlines
- Sentence Outline
- Short Phrase Outline
- Word Outline
- Student Sample Informative Speeches
- Speech Evaluation Forms

VII

Informative Speaking

How many times have you heard someone say: "The speaker was good, I guess, but I didn't really get the point he was trying to make." Or, "My professor is an expert in her field but somehow she can't get the material across to the class. We're all so confused."

Unfortunately, statements like these are all too common. Although imparting information to others is something we all do in our everyday lives, instructions are often unclear because giving information accurately is not as easy as it may appear. Our lives would probably be a lot easier if we could make ourselves understood all of the time.

One of the most important assignments in your speech class will be the speech to inform. The primary purpose of this speech is to communicate your information clearly so that it will be easily understood by your listeners.

As with any type of presentation, your first job is to know to whom you are speaking, that is, to analyze your listeners. The type of presentation you give will depend upon the age, background, and size of your audience. The style is extemporaneous. Once you know the general make-up of your audience, you can then determine the topic, purpose, and pattern of organization and style of presentation.

There are several ways to classify informative speeches but no matter which one you choose, the goal is to tell the audience something they don't know.

Speeches of Personal Experience

A good ice-breaker speech uses an event in a person's life to create a speech. Here are two examples:

Example 1

Introduction

A/G When you look at others there are differences about them you could tell right away, and there are others that may not be so obvious. Just by looking at me there is something about me you wouldn't know.

S/P To inform my audience of how being adopted gave me a chance at life.

C/I The advantages of being adopted.

V/S Thousands of children need a home and a chance to grow up in a loving household.

Transition

Let me explain how two individuals gave me that chance.

Body

I. Early childhood
   1. Heroin addicted mother
   2. Constantly on the move

II. Being born addicted
   1. A "child junkie"
   2. Constant hospital visits
   3. Cold turkey withdrawal

III. Life in a foster home

IV. Permanent placement in a new home
   1. Life with my new family
   2. My new brothers and sisters

Transition

Statistically, I am not supposed to have survived and reached this point in my life. But I made it!

Conclusion

As you can see, adoption is a benefit that will help a child grow and develop into an individual that she may not otherwise become. If you give a child a chance at life, she will be forever grateful and repay 1,000 fold with love.

Shantee Whaley, Student

Example 2

Introduction

Why do people immigrate?

I. Religious, economical, and political reasons
   A. Russia — political, religious
   B. Latin America — economical
II. Immigration is a very complicated, time-consuming process

S/P To inform my class about my immigration to America
C/I Immigration is a very painful, long, and hard process

Transition

Let's start from the beginning

Body

I. Russia
   1. Permission
   2. Selling your things
      a. Books
      b. Empty apartment
II. Austria
   1. Fairy tale
   2. Streets
      a. Old houses
      b. History in every building
III. Italy
   1. Looking for an apartment
   2. American counselor
      a. Fear
      b. Uncertainty
      c. Responsibility
IV. America.
   1 Arrival
      a. NAYANA representative
      b. Money
      c. Welcoming
   2. Father — new profession
   3. Mother — Midtown Business School

Transition
Let me tell you about my life now

Conclusion

1. Our life now
    a. Father — working
    b. Mother — looking for a job, working part-time
2. Process of immigration
    a. Series of events
        1. You control
        2. Others control
    b. Painful
        1. Leave everything behind
        2. Go to unknown
    c. Depend on hope at first
    d. Work hard to overcome difficulties

Tatyana Sulkin — Student

Speeches about Processes or Demonstration Speeches

Speeches about processes teach the audience how to do something or to understand the process. This is sometimes called a "how to" or a demonstration speech. You are providing your listeners with instructions or directions. This type of informative speech can have entertaining aspects, like how to dance the Mambo, or it can be a useful teaching tool such as how to fill out a financial aid form, taking it step-by-step and using visual aids.

In one of our classes the students had a wonderful time teaching the class how to do something related to their cultural backgrounds. One topic chosen by the class was how to cook exotic dishes from their culture using step-by-step instructions. This provided the class the opportunity to taste new foods. The usual pattern of organization for the process speech is chronological.

Here is an evaluation sheet used to analyze the demonstration speech. Looking it over might help you to understand the criteria used to grade your presentation.

Demonstration Speech

Check all items that were accomplished effectively.

Introduction

_____ 1. Were the purpose and central idea clear?
_____ 2. Were they appropriate for this assignment?
_____ 3. Was the topic interesting?
_____ 4. Was there an attention getter?

Body

_____ 1. Did the speaker have the necessary materials to demonstrate the process?
_____ 2. Were the materials used in the demonstration large enough to be seen clearly by everyone in the audience?
_____ 3. Did the speaker show expertise with the process?
_____ 4. Did the speech follow a time order?
_____ 5. If not, was the order appropriate for a process demonstration?
_____ 6. Were there at least 10-12 steps in the process?
_____ 7. Was the language _____clear? _____vivid? _____emphatic? _____appropriate?
_____ 8. Was the speech delivered _____enthusiastically? _____with good eye contact? _____extemporaneously? _____with appropriate vocal variety and emphasis? _____with effective bodily action?

Conclusion

_____ 1. Did the conclusion tie the speech together and restate the specific purpose and central idea?
_____ 2. Evaluate the speech as (check one) _____excellent, _____ good, _____average, _____fair, _____poor.

Here are a few student sample Demonstration Speeches:

Demonstration Speech #1
Cornrowing

Introduction

A/G Have you ever heard the term, "your hair is your crowning glory," well it's true. Most people take this statement very seriously and spend lots of time and money making sure their hair has a certain look. Many women feel that only straight hair can look good, however; women have worn their hair in variations without it being straight. Hair texture does not limit the style of your crowning glory. In reflection of my culture I will present a style and method of hair grooming worn by many men and women.

S/P Today I will demonstrate African Cornrowing in 10 steps.

C/I To perform this demonstration I will need a fine tooth comb, brush, pick, hairpins, rubber bands, beads (cowrie shells), and hair softener: Lanolin (the fat from sheep.)

V/S Hair, referred to as the crowning glory should be presented with pride by all women.

Transition

Let's begin.

Body

1. The *scalp is oiled* to prevent dryness of the hair. Prepare the hair by massaging from front to back to promote hair growth.
2. *Brushing* then combing the hair from front to back.
3. *Parting the hair*: A science done by the use of the teeth of the comb.
4. *Process of braiding the hair*: Each separated section of the hair is then parted evenly by the fingers to make three separate sections of one braid.
5. *The hair is braided firmly* on the surface of the scalp.
6. Starting at the roots of the hair to pick up all short hair from the front/back of the head and *weaving it into each strand of hair*.
7. This method is continued until the completion of the hairdo. To ensure that the neighboring hair does not get intertwined, *rubber bands are placed to keep the hair secure*.

8. Forming a basket or beehive style as it is called in some parts of the world *(completion of the hairdo).*
9. *Place rubber band around the hair* to keep it together at the crown of the head.
10. It is optional to *add beads or other decorations* for an attractive look.

Transition

Now that I have shown you how easy it is to Cornrow your hair you should be able to do it yourself.

Conclusion

In conclusion, cultural hair styles can be your crowning glory to take pride in having your hair worn in its natural coarse state.

Cheryl Mabry — Student

Demonstration Speech #2

I. **Introduction:** Good evening, my name is Helen Walker.

Attention Getter: Have you ever had to do something very important, but when it came to doing this task, you didn't have the nerve to do so?

Specific Purpose: Today I will demonstrate how to give an Insulin injection.

Central Idea: The things you need to administer the Insulin are:

1. Needle
2. Insulin
3. Alcohol swab
4. Patient (tonight an orange)
5. Disposal bottle

Value Statement: The injection must be given properly, and in a timely manner, or there can be problems later.

Transition: So now, let me show you what I was so nervous about.

II. **Body**

A Main point — show setup

1. Show how to mix Insulin properly
2. Pull air into needle

3. Wipe bottle
4. Push needle into bottle and inject air
5. Turn bottle upside down
6. Pull Insulin into needle
7. Check for air bubbles in the needle's neck
8. Now push plunger with Insulin to the right amount needed
9. Grab skin between forefinger and thumb
   a. Show areas where patient may be injected
   b. Pinching of skin, patient doesn't feel needle being inserted
10. Wipe patient's body area to be injected. (Downward motion)
11. Insert needle on a slant
    a. Avoid muscle (muscle won't allow Insulin to be injected)
    b. Avoid lumps

Transition

So as you can see, there was really nothing for me to be nervous about. I was just injecting an inanimate object. But when it came time to perform the same procedure on my mother, there is where the nervousness kicked in (horse of a different color).

III. Conclusion

A. Disposal of needle (UNIVERSAL)
   1. Explain mixture in bottle
      a. Water, bleach, and alcohol
      b. Can't get AIDs (explain)
      c. When bottle is full
         i. Tape bottle.
         ii. Put in plastic bag, and dispose of in trash

B. Thought I would not be able to stick my mom
   1. Giving her Insulin for the past 24 years
   2. My children can give mother Insulin
   3. So if and when you have to give any member of your family an injection, you will be nervous at first, but eventually it all becomes routine.

Helen Walker — Student

Demonstration Speech #3
A Helping Hand

Introduction

A/G What would you do if a family member or friend suddenly clutches his throat, turns blue, cannot speak/breathe and/or collapses? These are the universal signs of a choking victim.

S/P Today I will demonstrate a method to counteract — the Heimlich Maneuver.

C/I To perform the Heimlich Maneuver a choking victim and a helping hand are needed.

V/S After tonight, you may one day prevent an unnecessary death.

Transition

Let me demonstrate the Heimlich Maneuver for you.

Body

I. Victim — Standing/Sitting
  A. First — 4 quick sharp blows to back, between shoulder blades
  B. No success — stand behind victim
  C. Wrap arms around waist
  D. Place thumb side of fist against abdomen (above navel, below rib cage)
  E. Grasp fist with other hand
  F. Press with quick upward thrusts (repeat if necessary).

II. Victim — Collapsed/Unconscious
  A. Lay victim on back
  B. Kneel down over — victim's legs between yours
  C. Place one hand on top of the other
  D. Place heel of bottom hand on abdomen (above navel, below rib cage)
  E. Press with quick upward thrusts (repeat if necessary)
  F. Vomit — place victim on side and clear out mouth (prevents aspiration)

Transition

Either procedure — only when life threatening — follow with a doctor's visit.

Conclusion

This demonstration of the Heimlich Maneuver showed you that your hand can be transformed into a helping hand for a choking victim.

Learning this and other first-aid techniques can mean the difference between life and death.

Tamatha Hines — Student

Demonstration Speech #4

Attention Getter How many of you are nature lovers? Plants are nature's lifeline. Providing the proper care, we become the beneficiaries of clean air.

Specific Purpose Today I will show you how to repot a plant.

Central Idea Breathing, eating, and drinking are the three requirements of a plant's survival. Needed for this demonstration are a plant and a new pot, soil, water, and plant food.

Value Statement The life of a plant is very essential to human beings because it serves as a daily supplier of oxygen.

Transition Here are a few steps on how to nourish a plant for growth:

Body

1. Cut a stem from another plant.
2. Get a plant pot.
3. Insert half the soil in the pot.
4. Using your finger or a stick, make a hole in the soil deep enough to insert the stem.
5. Place plant stem in the hole, then close it.
6. Insert remaining soil around plant.
7. Pour water all around the soil and water every three weeks. Also supply sun or lamp light for food energy.
8. Plants like you to talk to them, for oxygen (ex. "Good morning").
9. Once a month, add 3 or 4 drops of plant food so that it grows and stays green. Transition: As the plant grows, you can then take a piece of it and begin growing a whole new plant.

Conclusion

So, the next time your companion wants to buy you some flowers, say "That's okay baby, I can grow my own."

Natasha Rowe — Student

Demonstration Speech #5

Introduction

A/G As summer fun in the sun fast approaches so do the excuses for not being able to fit into that dress or bathing suit you've been longing for. You start saying "Diets don't work for me." or "I don't have time to work out." All you need is fifteen minutes, a comfortable outfit, and a set of 3-10 lb dumbell weights.

S/P To inform audience how you can work out at home.

C/I Exercise can help one feel better about oneself. The tools needed are:

a. Dumbells

b. Comfortable clothing

c. Gloves (optional)

d. Chair or bench

e. Towel

V/S Exercise not only keeps one's body looking good but you also feel better about yourself.

Transition

Now let's get fit.

Body

I. Arms
   A. Biceps — front curls
   B. Triceps — curls behind head
   C. Shoulders — military press behind head
II. Chest
   A. Bench press — front chest
   B. Forward press — lower chest

III. Back
   A. Lats — Shoulder shrugs
   B. Kneel pulls — wings
IV. Abdominals — sit-up
V. Legs — leg lifts

Transition

You see that you don't need to pay for that $2,000 Jack LaLane membership.

Conclusion

Exercise is an important part of our everyday lives. It helps us to look good as well as feel good. You begin to realize that it isn't necessary to go to the gym in order to have that perfect body. So get off that couch and begin that home workout.

Shantee Whaley — Student

Demonstration Speech #6

Introduction

A/G How many of you have really gone out of your way to set a formal table for no special occasion? Let me tell you a secret, if you want something from your spouse or friend, try preparing his or her favorite meal and use a formal table setting. How many of you know the correct way to set a table formally?

S/P Pretty table setting can be the perfect invitation to dining at home. I'd like to inform you of the proper procedure in setting a formal table.

C/I

1. Dinner Plate
2. Salad Plate
3. Soup Spoon
4. Coffee Spoon
5. Dinner Knife
6. Salad Fork
7. Dinner Fork
8. Dessert Fork
9. Napkin
10. Waterglass
11. Wine Glass
12. Bread Plate
13. Soup Bowl

V/S Half the fun of preparing a delicious meal lies in planning a pretty table setting.

Transition

Let's begin to set a table for a formal dinner.

Body

1. Dinner Plate — Center
2. Salad Plate — On dinner plate
3. Soup Bowl — On salad plate
4. Soup Spoon — Extreme right
5. Coffee Spoon — Center right
6. Dinner Knife — Right of plate
7. Salad Fork — Left of plate
8. Dinner Fork — Center left
9. Dessert Fork — Extreme left
10. Napkin — Far left/Glass
11. Waterglass — Tip of knife
12. Wine Glass — Right of water glass
13. Bread Plate — Above fork

Conclusion

As you can see, setting a table is easy if you follow these steps. Finally, to obtain any effect on any table, brighten your table with a cheerful centerpiece. Your table should look balanced. Food tastes better and conversation flows more freely when the scene has been set with a bit of attention. It does not matter what you serve, it is how you serve it.

Earnestine Norman — Student

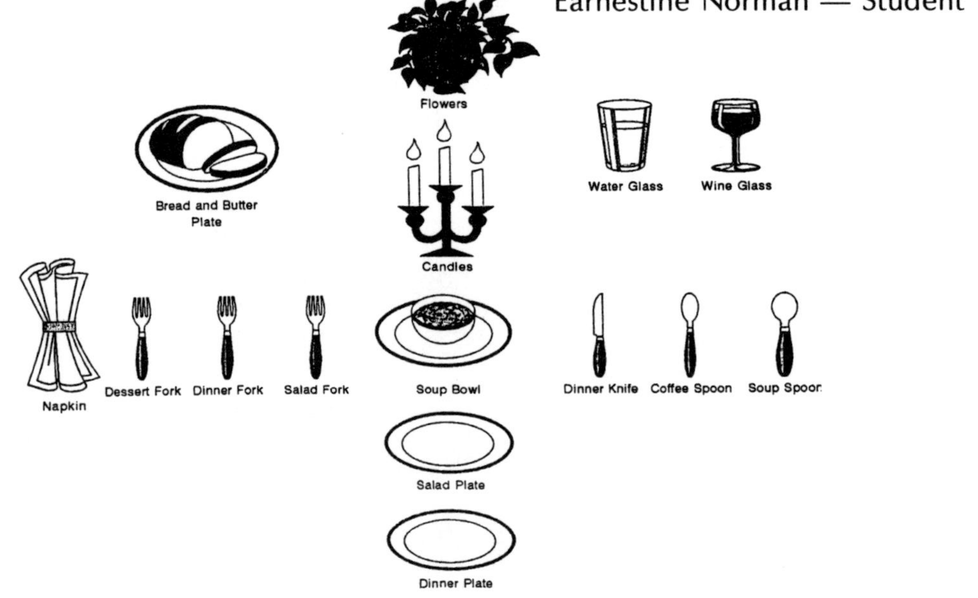

Speeches about Objects

A speech centered about an object describes the object in detail. The object may be anything you can see or touch such as a place, person, animal, or machine. If you decide to choose a famous person such as Malcolm X, obviously you cannot attempt to relate his entire life story. Instead, you might choose an aspect of his fascinating life such as his trip to Mecca. Or if you are talking about an inanimate object such as a compact disc player, you might tell the audience what to look for when buying the newest model.

Your pattern of organization for this speech about an object is dependent upon your specific purpose and central idea.

Speeches about Events

A speech centered around an event may be about something that is going on right now, something historical, or something that might happen in the future. If you choose an historical topic such as the beginnings of the Civil Rights Movement in America you might develop it using a chronological pattern. Or you might want to use a topical pattern showing, for example, the similarities and differences between the American and French revolutions.

Speeches about Concepts

Concepts are abstracts such as beliefs, ideas, and theories. Here care must be taken to clarify the topic of your speech and define terms in language that is appropriate for the audience you are addressing. The method of organization for a concept speech is most often topical. Speeches about "isms" such as communism, fascism, and socialism are general topics for concept speeches. Of course they must be narrowed down to more specific purposes such as "the major principles of communism in Cuba."

Here are some interesting specific purpose statements for speeches about concepts: "To inform my audience of the basic beliefs of Confucianism" or "To inform my audience about the major theories of Feminism."

Entertaining Speeches

This speech type is designed to inform with a primary focus to entertain. There is usually no real expectation that people will recall what they have heard. However, this speech consists of a group of humorous references developed around a central theme. This is the kind of speech you would hear at a dinner or a social gathering. These speeches use humor to make strong points.

Types of Outlines

The following is a professor's model of an informative outline which shows a sentence, short phrase, and word outline.

Living in New York

Introduction

A/G As Frank Sinatra sings, "If you can make it there, you can make make it anywhere."

S/P To inform the audience what it is like to live in New York.

C/I Living in New York involves a special life style, diverse recreation, serious social problems, and an interesting multicultural population.

V/S To give a deeper understanding of one of the greatest cities in the United States. Transition: Let's begin by looking at....

Sentence Outline

I. New York City has a special life-style.
   A. There are 7,000 miles of subways for transportation.
   B. Air pollution and noise pollution are serious problems.
   C. Summers are very humid.
   D. Winters are usually long and cold.
II. Recreation in New York City is varied and exciting.
   A. There are many Broadway theatres, off-Broadway theatres, dance, and music performances.
   B. Private health clubs and spas are available in many areas of the city for those who can afford them.
   C. New York City is famous for its art and science museums.
   D. There are historical sites to visit including buildings, churches, etc.
III. There are social problems in New York City that may deter visitors and present difficulties for city dwellers.
   A. Homelessness is prevalent and men and women can be seen sleeping in doorways and on park benches.
   B. Due to high-rise buildings and over-crowdedness, there is a limited sense of community in New York City.

   C. Crime is rampant in certain neighborhoods.
   D. Poverty in New York City is a contributing factor in the selling and use of illegal drugs.

IV. New York City has a diverse population due to the influx of people from many lands.
   A. There is a large Russian emigrant community, especially in the Brighton Beach section of Brooklyn.
   B. Many people from the Caribbean countries have settled in the New York area.
   C. Indian and Pakistani people have opened interesting shops and restaurants in New York.
   D. Interesting food marts and restaurants have been opened by Chinese, Vietnamese, Korean, and Japanese people.

Short Phrase Outline

Living in New York

I. New York City's special life-style
  A. 7,000 miles of subways for transportation.
  B. Air and noise pollution a problem.
  C. Humid summers.
  D. Long cold winters.

II. Recreation.
  A. Theatre, dance, and music.
  B. Private health clubs.
  C. Science and art museums.
  D. Historic places.

III. New York City's social problems.
  A. Homeless on the streets.
  B. Limited sense of community.
  C. Rampant crime.
  D. Illegal drugs.

IV. Multicultural population.
  A. Russian immigrant community.
  B. Caribbean community.
  C. Indian, Pakistani.
  D. Chinese, Vietnamese, Korean, and Japanese.

Word Outline

Living in New York

I. Life-style
   A. Transportation
   B. Pollution
   C. Humidity
   D. Cold
II. Recreation
   A. Entertainment
   B. Health clubs
   C. Museums
   D. History
III. Problems
   A. Homeless
   B. Community
   C. Crime
   D. Drugs
IV. Population
   A. Russian
   B. Caribbean
   C. Indian
   D. Asian

Conclusion

The special life-style, various recreation possibilities, multicultural population, and the many social problems all contribute to a city that is a fascinating place to visit or to live. Frank Sinatra summed it all up when he sang, "It's up to you New York, New York."

Student Sample Informative Speeches

Example 1—Amyotrophic Lateral Sclerosis

A/G In the medical world, there are many motor neuron diseases which are being discovered, analyzed, and cured. Two weeks ago I heard in the news that a cure was being found for a certain motor neuron disease. The disease they spoke about is called Amyotrophic Lateral Sclerosis (ALS), otherwise known as Lou Gehrig's disease.

S/P To inform the audience of what ALS (Lou Gehrig's disease) is.

C/I In this speech I will present the types of this disease, its symptoms, and treatments.

Transition

Here is my speech on the deadly and incurable disease known as Lou Gehrig's disease.

Body

I. Definition and Explanation
   A. Motor Neuron Disease — A group of rare disorders in which the nerves that control muscular activity degenerate within the brain and the spinal cord.
   B. Explanation — Person loses all control of voluntary muscles, muscles which allow you to walk, lift arms and legs.

II. Amyotrophic Lateral Sclerosis (ALS)
   A. Disease in which muscles of the body become weak and begin to waste away slowly due to the breakdown of the nerves which control muscle movement.
      1. Types of Disease:
         a. Classic ALS — Nerve breakdown begins in the extremities
         b. Progressive Muscular Atrophy — Nerve breakdown mostly seen in the spinal cord
         c. Progressive Bulbar Palsy — Nerve breakdown is centered on the neurons of the cranial nerves and brainstem

2. Symptoms:
   a. Classic ALS
      i. Weakness of the hands with atrophy
      ii. Lower extremities become weak and spastic
      iii. Fibrillation — rapid twitching; always present
      iv. Death usually from atrophy of lung and diaphragm nerves
   b. Progressive Muscular Atrophy
      i. Same as above except atrophy and weakness of muscles present instead of spasticity.
      ii. A longer life span than classic ALS.
   c. Progressive Bulbar Palsy
      i. Loss of chewing, talking, and swallowing ability.
      ii. Involuntary outcry of laughter and crying.
      iii. Fibrillation of tongue and atrophy.
      iv. Short life span; death occurs in 1 to 3 years of outbreak.
3. Treatment and Outlook:
   a. Physical therapy
   b. Wheelchairs, walkers, and other aids
   c. Feeding tubes and ventilators
   d. No known treatment

Transition

Now that I have informed you of what ALS is and its types, symptoms, and treatment, I would like to conclude by saying...

Conclusion

Amyotrophic Lateral Sclerosis (Lou Gehrig's Disease) is a crippling disease which eats away at the body's nervous system just like any kind of cancer that destroys body tissues. This disease is a rare one and is hardly seen in the medical world. It is deadly and we need to find something that will either stop or kill the disease, but in the meantime all we can do is pray for the recovery of the people who already have this critical disease known as Lou Gehrig's Disease.

Frank Morales — Student

Example 2—Popular Club Plan

Introduction

A/G Wouldn't it be nice to earn something, for every time someone else spends money?

S/P To inform my audience how to sell merchandise for the Popular Club Plan.

C/I I am going to show you how to begin your club, to place orders, to assist your members with problems and to collect payment for merchandise.

Transition

Let me start by telling you first how to...

Body

I. Begin your club
  A. Show off catalog — "The President of the Popular Club Plan states that shopping clubs are made through friendships.
    1. Begin with family and friends
      a. Feel more comfortable
      b. Have contact with...
    2. Next — co-workers
      a. While having a conversation
        1. Ask them to see the catalog
        2. Gesture to see the catalog
      b. Work on sales pitch
  B. Convince people to buy; tell of advantages
    1. Easy payment plan — "The catalog says the payment plan is a practical way to keep up payments and to avoid bills from piling up."
      a. 20-week plan (used for all merchandise)
      b. 44-week plan (used for merchandise over $200)
    2. Member dividends — Earn $2 dividend for every $10 spent
    3. Fast delivery — UPS delivers in 3 to 4 days
II. Place orders
  A. Complete order forms
    1. Merchandise/address correct
    2. Tell breakdown of their bill
  B. 2 ways to place orders
    1. By mail
    2. By phone

C. Wait for payment book
D. Member receives merchandise
1. Merchandise is satisfactory
a. Clothes/shoes right size
b. Leather/fabric good quality
2. All parts are included

III. Assist members
A. General inquiries
1. Catalog
2. Change of address
3. Using dividends
a. Need $40 to use them
b. Can't use them on sale items
B. Replace damaged merchandise
C. Returning merchandise
1. Mail by UPS
2. 3rd class insured mail

IV. Collect payment
A. Work out payments
1. More convenient for members
2. Collect weekly
3. Collect bi-weekly
B. Prepare to mail out
1. Detach stubs
2. Collect money
3. Complete remittance form
C. When order is completed
1. Show members pleasure
2. Shop again

Transition

In closing...

Conclusion

I. I have told you everything you need to know.
II. A guaranteed way of earning.
III. For those of you interested.
IV. "Join over the half million people who are already enjoying the benefits of the Popular Club Plan."

Kishawn Wise — Student

Example 3—Fear of Flying

Introduction

A/G If you had the opportunity to travel from New York to Chicago, Florida, or California, with all expenses paid, would you go by car? Would you go by train? Or, would you go by plane?

S/P The event that has changed/affected my life is the high percentage of plane casualties each year.

C/I Some bad experiences on air planes. My emotional feelings when traveling by plane. The amount of plane casualties. My fear of getting on a plane.

V/S Without the luxury of traveling by plane, we would miss out on many things, vacations, interstate, and overseas travel.

Transition

In addition to the many fatal plane crashes each year, millions of people all over the world travel by plane at least 12 to 20 times a year.

Body

I. Some bad experiences on air planes
  A. Bad weather
  B. Trip to Chicago
  C. Trip to South Carolina
II. My emotional feelings on planes
  A. No control over my life
  B. Pilot's decision
  C. 95% of plane crashes are fatal
III. My fear of getting on planes

Conclusion

I hope that I've not put my fear of flying into you, but when you look at the number of plane crashes and the percentage of survivors, you may want to change your mind about flying also. There's no question that flying is the most enjoyable, relaxing, and fastest way to travel, but if you have a fear of flying, why put yourself through all the pressure, pain, stress, and tension. I eliminated my fear of flying, I get aboard AMTRAK.

Ernestine Norman — Student

Example 4—Reggae

Introduction

A/G "The dance music today just makes you want to do crazy things but long after it is forgotten people will be listening to Bob because he brings culture." Frederick Hibbert — singer - coined the name reggae in the 1960s hit with group Maytals.

S/P Today, I would like to inform you about Bob Marley's major influence on reggae music.

C/I First, I will talk about how Bob Marley got started and who influenced him. Since he has passed away, I will then focus on where his music is today.

V/S Hopefully, you will see that you can't talk about reggae without talking about Bob Marley.

Transition

Let's begin...

Body

I. Robert Nesta Marley
  - A. Singer, songwriter, guitarist
  - B. Born 1945, St. Ann's Parish, Jamaica
  - C. Began singing at the age of 6
    1. Spent one year in Kingston
    2. Moved there permanently in 1957
    3. Grew up in tough slum Trench Town
    4. Spent whole evenings
       - a. Listening to Blues and R&B
       - b. Broadcast — Miami
       - c. Transistor radio

II. Bob began playing and singing
  - A. 1960
  - B. Two men — Bunny Livingston and Peter McIntosh
  - C. Influenced by
    1. Sam Cooke
    2. Brook Benton
    3. Fats Domino
    4. Elvis Presley
    5. Also native music developing at time

- D. Three took lessons — Joe Higgs
  1. Jamaican duo Higgs and Wilson
  2. Higgs an influence
     a. Insisted on correct harmonies
     b. Wrote songs — marijuana, Rastafarianism became fashionable
- E. Marley
  1. First record 1962 — *Judge Not*
  2. Trio expands — several members
     a. Singers
     b. Musicians
  3. Called the Wailers
- F. Marley and the Wailers
  1. Bring reggae international prominence 1970s
  2. Marley
     a. Outspoken champion of racial equality and social justice
     b. Tireless promoter of Rastafarianism
- G. Pro-African sect
  1. Followers grow hair long, matted dreadlocks
  2. Smoke marijuana as part of religious rite
- H. Timothy White, author of *Catch a Fire: The Life of Bob Marley* said Marley: "Gave the poor a voice in the arena of ideas. Marley's message was that the individual has intrinsic dignity"

III. Bob Marley
- A. Died of cancer 1981
- B. Continues — top record seller throughout world
- C. Compilation of greatest hits, "Legend"
  1. Sold 7 million copies
  2. Worldwide sales
- D. Compact Disc box set, "Songs of Freedom." — Sold a million copies
- E. With 2 posthumous albums
  1. Still listed on Billboard charts
  2. Bootleg versions sold third world
  3. Thought by many music industry experts
     a. Top contender
     b. Title — biggest selling record artist of all time

Conclusion

Again, I hope I've shown Bob Marley's major influence on reggae with illustrations how he got started, who influenced him, where his music is today. Bob Marley and reggae continue to influence the music community, linguistic and cultural boundaries.

Brooke Young — Student

Here are some possible topics for the Speech to Inform:

Events

- Battle of Gettysburg
- Attack on Pearl Harbor
- Assassination of Malcolm X
- The Cuban Missile Crisis
- The Celebration of Kwanza

Concepts

- Feminism
- Buddhism
- Astrology
- Witchcraft
- Confucianism

Processes

- How a Bill Becomes a Law
- How Beer Is Made
- The Birth Process

- Photosynthesis
- Playing an Instrument

Places

- Disneyland
- Las Vegas
- Niagara Falls
- Grand Canyon
- Yosemite National Park

People

- Martin Luther King
- Arthur Ashe
- Gandhi
- Tito Puento
- Boris Pasternak

Objects

- Model Trains
- Video Games
- Movies
- Art

Here are two Informative Speech grading evaluations. Review them.

Speech Evaluation Form

Title ______________________ Student's Name ______________

	Poor	Fair	Average	Good	Excellent
Choice of Subject					
Clarity of Specific Purpose and Central Ideas					
Organization of Material					
Language					
Diction					
Voice					
Bodily Control					
Audience Feedback					

Comments:

Date ______________________ Instructor's Name ______________

Speech Evaluation Form

Rate the speaker on each point

5	4	3	2	1
Excellent	good	average	fair	poor

Speaker

Topic

Comments

Introduction

_____ gained attention and interest

_____ introduced specific purpose and central idea topic clearly

_____ established credibility

_____ previewed body of speech

Body

_____ main points clear

_____ main points fully supported

_____ organization well planned

_____ language accurate, clear, and appropriate

_____ transitions effective

Conclusion

_____ prepared audience for ending

_____ reinforced central idea

Delivery

_____ eye contact

_____ voice effective

_____ used nonverbal communication	
_____ seemed truly interested in communicating ideas	
_____ used outlines effectively	
_____ appeared poised and confident	
_____ gestured	
_____ spoke at a good rate	
_____ voice was animated, voice was conversational and easy to listen to	
_____ spoke clearly and loud enough for everyone to hear	
_____ used no distracting mannerisms	
_____ avoided verbal crutches (uh, um, er, ah, okay, ya know)	
Overall Evaluation	
_____ topic interesting	
_____ visual aids well chosen	
_____ speech adapted to audience	
_____ speech completed in time limit	

▼ ▼ ▼ Chapter VII Key Terms

Personal experience speech
Demonstration speech
Process speech
Concept speech

VIII

The Speech to Persuade

- Types of Persuasive Speeches
- Monroe's Motivated Sequence
- Student's Speeches Using Monroe's Motivated Sequence
- Monroe's Motivated Sequence Evaluation Form
- Credibility
- Evidence Through Reasoning
- Guidelines for Persuasive Speaking
- Topics for the Speech to Persuade

VIII

The Speech to Persuade

"If only I could convince him to change his ways!" — familiar? All of us at one time or another have tried to persuade or convince someone to do something our way. Mothers and fathers often tend to say to their children: "I know what's best for you so listen to me and follow my advice." Friends try to influence by giving their opinions as to how to solve a problem. Sales people ring your door bell and try to convince you to buy their products. What then makes one vacuum cleaner better than another? The answer lies with the ability of the sales person to make it so believable that the customer is convinced his product is the best.

Everywhere you look there are advertisements, posters, and leaflets telling you what to buy and how marvelous something is in comparison to something else. Just look around you on the subway or bus, in magazines and newspapers, or every time a commercial interrupts a television program you are watching. The people who are responsible for these persuasive devices know just how to get the general public to follow their advice. Stop for a moment and think "Why did I buy this soap and not the other brands?" or "Why am I so taken with a label on a pair of jeans even though they are terribly overpriced?" The answer is that persuasive techniques have influenced you to choose one product over another.

Persuasive speech making is very similar to persuasive advertising. Whereas the goal of the informative speech is to teach, clarify, or merely share ideas, the persuasive speech is organized to effect a change in the listener's beliefs, behavior, or attitude. It may take different forms such as trying to get the listeners to join an organization, donate blood, or vote for a particular candidate, in other words a speech to bring about action. Or it might be to influence the audience to change their viewpoints on a certain issue. For example, trying to convince a somewhat hostile audience to the concept that busing children to integrate schools is beneficial to all concerned. Persuasive speeches are organized according to either questions of fact, policy, or value.

Types of Persuasive Speeches

A speech on a *question of fact* means that the speaker is trying to prove or disprove whether something really exists. Look at the following examples:

- Crime is declining in New York City.
- Secondhand smoke causes lung cancer.
- Lee Harvey Oswald was the sole assassin of President Kennedy.

A speech based on a *policy question* centers around whether or not to do something. Assuming the audience disagrees as to whether or not to follow a particular course of action, the speaker defends his or her position. Proposals such as the following are examples of questions of policy:

- Cigarette smoking should be banned in all public institutions.
- X-rated films should not be allowed in video stores.
- Should the United States send troops to help countries solve their internal problems?

Questions of value deal with the speaker's judgments, his or her personal beliefs of what is right or wrong, justifiable or not. The following are illustrations of questions of value:

- There is too much violence in prime time television.
- Abortion is morally and legally wrong.
- Capital punishment is definitely a deterrent to crime.

Monroe's Motivated Sequence

The pattern of organization you choose for your persuasive speech depends upon your topic and your goal. If you want to motivate your audience to take a course of action, an excellent method is "Monroe's Motivated Sequence" which is based on the psychology of persuasion. It is important to keep in mind that all good persuasive speeches contain fact, value, and policy. Monroe's method contains the following five steps:

1. **Attention.** This step occurs in the introduction of your speech and is designed to gain the attention of your audience.
2. **Need.** This step begins the body of your speech and makes your audience realize there is a serious issue affecting their lives.
3. **Satisfaction.** This is the step that provides a solution to the problem by presenting your plan and how it works.
4. **Visualization.** This is the final step of the body which uses vivid imagery showing your audience the benefit of your plan.
5. **Action.** This occurs in the conclusion and asks the audience to act on your plan.

Attention (Introduction)	Are you aware of the amount of high fat foods you consume daily — foods that have no nutritional value?
Need (Body)	I. The American high fat diet is dangerous to your health. A. If you eat too many foods that are high in fat content you may gain unnecessary pounds. B. The food you eat may cause high cholesterol content in your blood.
Satisfaction	II. You should reduce the amount of fat in your diet. A. Substitute foods that have low fat content such as grains, fruits, vegetables, and carbohydrates. B. Many kinds of foods you are accustomed to eating now are reduced in fat content such as fat free cakes or low fat margarine.
Visualization	III. If you continue to eat high fat foods you run the risk of a heart attack. Use your imagination! Picture yourself unable to do things you like because of a heart condition caused by clogged arteries and you are bound to rethink the way you live.
Action (Conclusion)	IV. Change your diet today! Learn to enjoy foods low in fat and you'll be on your way to a long and happy life.

Here is an instructor's example of a speech that follows the motivated sequence:

Homelessness

A/G How many of us step right over a homeless person in the street and don't really ever notice him?

S/P To persuade my audience that the government should change their policies and take action to help the homeless of New York City.

C/I The problem of homelessness can be solved by studying these reasons for homelessness: Providing more money to organizations that handle these individuals, and by caring personally and giving time to this unfortunate situation.

V/S It could happen to anyone...

Transition

So listen to me further.

Need

I. In New York City, in 1992, 24,151 people were in public shelters.
   A. There are reasons why people are homeless.
      1. Drugs
      2. Natural disasters to homes
      3. Fires in homes
      4. Loss of jobs — therefore no money
   B. Understanding reasons allows you to care for these individuals and to make changes to resolve some of the reasons.
   C. These people are unsanitary and deserve better than this ignored treatment.

Satisfaction

II. The government could provide to allow for
   A. More public, low-cost housing complexes
   B. Creation of more shelters
   C. More free food/clothing programs
   D. Better health care for the poor
   E. Need job development for the homeless

III. The government could also provide more to organizations like UHO (United Homeless Organization) and HELP (Housing Enterprise for the Less Privileged).

A. UHO — formed by Steve Riley, a homeless person.
   1. There are 5,000 registered members
   2. Provides free food and clothing
   3. More money could allow this organization to service more people.

B. HELP — founded by Andrew Cuomo
   1. Built temporary housing for people moving from shelters and Welfare hotels to their permanent apartments.
   2. Built 1,000 housing units in New York State in its first five years of existence.
   3. Besides providing housing this organization works to change the behavior of the homeless.
   4. It also provides child day care and treatment for drug addiction.

IV. Personally you can help the homeless by
   A. Volunteering to work in shelters
   B. Donating money and old clothes
   C. Writing to your government officials expressing your concerns

Visualization

V. Picture This...
A family, 2 children, a mother and a father, right next door to you. They are good neighbors and suddenly the father lost his job. Well, now they are homeless.

Action

Conclusion

VI. Don't ignore this situation. Be concerned. Put yourself in their place. Write your congressman for action to provide money to organizations. Devote your time and energy to this cause because the homeless are people too.

Student's Speeches Using Monroe's Motivated Sequence

Example 1

Introduction

Do you think about your health? And do you think about becoming old?

S/P I hope you will soon agree that New York is not a suitable place for the elderly.

C/I The elderly are usually weakened by age and sometimes become sickly. In New York their health is at risk. However, I think they would benefit by living in warmer climates as in the Caribbean.

V/S Imagine yourself being elderly, do you think New York would be suitable for you health?

Body (Need)

I. New York winters affect elders mental and physical health
   A. New York cold half the year
   B. Don't get out much
   C None/few activities in home
   D. Grouchy, naggy, bored
   E. No exercise —> unhealthy weight, fat
   F. Medical research —> fat —> cause heart diseases
   G. Likely to suffer high blood pressure, heart attacks

II. Winter in New York can also be dangerous for elderly
   A. Ice and snow cause falls
   B. Break, fracture bones
   C. Older bones, slow painful healing process
   D. Falls can be life threatening, crippling
   E. Can you imagine? Ice cause such trauma?

III. We also have to remember that their immune systems are weak
   A. Higher risk getting sick often
   B. More likely to catch colds and flu
   C. Did you know cold contributes to arthritis?
   D. Pollution of air (incinerators)

Satisfaction (Benefits)

IV. Many of these problems can be reduced or prevented by:
  A Living in a warmer climate
    1. Warm all year round
    2. Catch less flu and colds
    3. Outdoor hobbies, add pleasure (gardening, etc.)
    4. Get more exercise.
  B. Result
    1. Better physical health
    2. Better mental health

V. Less hazards
  A. On islands no snow or ice
  B. Less chance of falls, injuries
  C. Every one has accidents, but some can be prevented

VI. Some may bring up the question of hurricanes on islands
  A. Out of our hands
    1. Mother nature's doing
    2. Act of God
  B. Natural disasters happen any where
    1. Example Florida
    2. Even New York recently hit
  C. If one occurs, safety precautions are taken

Visualization

VII. Now can you imagine what the elderly go through? Do you have grandparents living with you?
  A. Mine live with me and are sick
  B. Suffering from a stroke
  C. Very cranky
  D. He wants to live in St. Croix
  E. Although around grand children
  F. Often complains, type that wants to be active
  G. In the house nothing for him to do
  H. It is too cold
  I. Doctors advise not to travel as yet.

Conclusion

I'm sure every one in this room would prefer to be healthy when older. Rather than suffering, being unhappy and frustrated with health problems. I urge you to think about your future health. Action: Conclusion: Start making plans now and help others to do the same. And remember that Caribbean sunshine, health, and happiness is the right way to live.

Angeline Lewis — Student

Example 2

I. **Introduction**

Good evening, my name is Helen T. Walker.

A/G How many of you get high? Now let's be honest. Well, I'm here to tell you that I will get high every chance I get. There are six places I like to go to in particular to get high. I don't hide in dark hallways, under cellar stairs, or on the roof. I get high where there are lots of people. I don't really care who sees me, I just want to get high. My places in particular are Newark Airport, Kennedy Airport, LaGuardia Airport, Pier 52 (New York), Port San Juan (Puerto Rico), and Port Orlando (Florida).

S/P Tonight, I will try to persuade you about the high of travelling, or the joy of travelling just because its fun.

C/I Travelling is fun, enjoyable, inexpensive, a learning experience, relaxing, and unforgettable. You can obtain all of this from one or many trips.

V/S By travelling you get to see other places, new faces, make new friends, and have fun, fun, fun, fun.

Transition

Let's begin

II. Need
   A. Inexpensive
      1. Travel for little or nothing
      2. Plan in advance
      3. Good travel agency & agent (Liberty)
      4. Lay away plan

B. Enjoyable!!!!!!!:
    1. Go with friends/husband/lover/kids
    2. Visiting new cities/natives of the land
    3. Lazing in the sun
    4. Taking lots of pictures
    5. Cozy
C. Relaxing/Unforgettable
    1. No work
    2. No hassles
    3. No phones
    4. No boss/children
    5. No housework/cooking or cleaning
    6. Can get very spoiled
D. Learning Experiences
    1. Learn about different cultures
    2. Meet new people
    3. Learn about different parts of the world
E. Fun, Fun, Fun
    1. Swimming
    2. Horseback riding
    3. Lying on beach/sunning
    4. Strolling through the various cities/towns

III. Satisfaction from Travelling
A. Different cities
B. Get away from home/work
C. Getting high and enjoying it
    1. No drugs
    2. 35,000 to 40,000 feet in the air or cruising on a ship
D. Feel good/want to go again and again
E. Places to visit
    1. Islands/Disney
    2. Cruise/Hawaii
    3. Las Vegas/Upstate New York
    4. Virginia Beach/Carolinas

IV. Visualization (Set up pictures to show)
A. Plenty of sun
B. Huge mountains
C. Blue skies/water

D. White sandy beaches
E. Driving a car through a tree (Redwood forest)
F. Camping out at the bottom of the Grand Canyon
G. Swishing down a snowy hill

Transition

Travelling can be what you make it.

So what I suggest to you is to try getting high my way. My drug agent is Liberty Travel and my substance of drugs are Piedmont, Delta, American, BWIA, Pan Am, and U.S. Air just to name a few.

Conclusion

So as you can see, travelling is fun; and I recommend that you try it once, maybe twice before the end (death). Now that you know travelling is fun, enjoyable, inexpensive, a learning experience, relaxing, and unforgettable, why not give it a try soon? So in closing, all I have to say is: There is a great big world out there waiting for you to explore its wonders. You will never experience getting high at 35 (thousand feet) the way I often do if you don't like to travel (getting high).

Helen T. Walker — Student

Example 3

Introduction (Attention)

Suppose we imagine for a moment that I am your dentist, and have walked into the room dressed as I am, ready to treat you. Would this safety gear make you feel safe and sure that I would be giving you only treatment, and not a transmittable disease?

Well if you answered yes, you could possibly be dead wrong. For you see, this barrier is only assuring me protection, from possibly being infected by you. If you answered no, you are right, but do you know why?

S/P To persuade my audience that there is a real need for them to become aware of the dangers they face in a dental chair and to take action to insure themselves the safest dental treatment they deserve.

C/I Universal precautions which have been around since 1986, were finally enacted into a law after a tragedy occurred in Florida and much debate, not only for the safety of the Health Care Worker (HCW), but also for the safety of the patients. Are you in the habit of sitting in the dental chair and allowing treatment without observing what is happening around you, either because you fear the dental treatment, trust the dentist, or are just unaware of exactly what it is that you should observe. I see this attitude and behavior almost every day at work. I also see the mistakes which are done by us in the office, sometimes by accident, and sometimes not. These accidents can be harmful and deadly to both you and me. Such was the case of Kimberly Bergalis, a young woman that went to her dentist for an extraction, and left with a deadly disease. Kimberly died of AIDS last year. I also know for a fact that AIDS is not the only disease which can be contracted in a dental chair. Five years ago, while I was assisting, I did not wear a mask and contracted a severe throat infection, which hospitalized me for almost a week with massive doses of intravenous antibiotics and was almost given a tracheotomy. Transmission can occur from me to you, from you to me, and from you to the next person in the dental chair, by crosscontamination. Your safety is not guaranteed unless I have taken the Universal Precautions needed to protect you from this cross- contamination. You are now probably wondering what are Universal Precautions? Why are they so important for your safety? And what is it that you can do to assure yourself that these precautions are being observed. I will now speak to you about Universal Precautions, why they became a law, and what are the things you should look for, so that you can make sure that your treatment is safe. My hope is that with this knowledge, I will be able to persuade you to change from being a fearful passive patient, into a fearless aggressive one, by asking questions and insisting on the things which by law are now owed to you.

Main Points: (Need)

I. Since 1986 Universal Precautions have been recommended by the Centers of Disease Control (CDC), but only as advice.

A. The recommendations consisted of various procedures which were to be observed by the HCW with all patients.

1. Two of the most important procedures were proper hand washing before and after being gloved, and the wearing of protective barriers, like these (demonstrate).

   a. In 1987 the CDC reported that three HCWs were infected with the AIDS virus when blood splashed into the face of one.
   b. The other two did not wear gloves when they were exposed to infected blood.
  2. The next procedures are the proper care and sterilization of instruments, along with the proper handling and disposal of needles and other sharp instrument.
   a. The CDC also reported on the case of a doctor who be came infected.
   b. She stuck her finger with a needle which was left uncovered.

 B. The problem with the recommendations was that they were not regulated and compliance was left up to the individual to either observe, neglect, or modify.
  1. I know from experience that the option which was adopted by many health facilities was modification, since adherence was costly and time consuming.
  2. In order to compensate for this, many cuts were made.
  3. This resulted in cases where gloves were being washed in between patients because of their shortage.

C. Before it became a law, a report from the CDC about a dentist in Florida who infected five of his patients with the AIDS virus, reinforced the need for Universal Precaution adherence.
 1. They reported that the dentist possibly injured himself during an invasive procedure, but that there was no documentation of any such injuries.
 2. They also reported that infection control in the office was not always observed or consistent with the Universal Precautions.

D. This tragedy triggered a controversy between the HCWs and Congress.
 1. Congress was trying to pass a Bill which required that all HCWs be tested on a mandatory basis, for the purpose of preventing any HCW from performing invasive procedures on any patients, without first informing them of their health status.
 2. Testimonies were given in many states by those who favored and those opposing the Bill, which was named after Kimberly Bergalis, who was dying of AIDS at the time.

3. I myself gave a testimony in 1991 at City Hall opposing the new Bill which Congress introduced, but I was in favor of a law which would ensure the compliance of Universal Precautions, by all.
   a. The purpose of my testimony was not fear for my position, but that as a HCW I knew that it would not protect the public, it would only cause other problems, such as fear which would lead to discrimination and a shortage of HCWs.
   b. I described to the House Committee on Health and Environment, that the law would just be treating the HCWs as disposable commodities, such as these gloves and masks that I am required to wear.
   c. We use them, when they are contaminated, we remove them and throw them away.

Satisfaction

II. After many years, the CDCs recommendations of Universal Precautions, were finally enacted into a law in 1992.
   A. Now the law mandates that Universal Precautions be observed by everyone, or they risk the punishment of fines and or imprisonment if they are negligent.
   B. Many steps have now been taken to insure the HCW's compliance, by giving them the skills, knowledge and equipment they need.
      1. The regulations now state that the employer must supply the employees with the protective gear they need and the employee must use them with every patient.
      2. Employees must be given in-house training and seminars yearly, on infection control techniques.

Visualization

III. Unfortunately, for you as the patient no such training is available.
   A. You are still dependent on our compliance for your safety.
      1. Many of us will do everything that is possible to maintain a safe environment for our patients.
      2. But others will resist change, especially if for years they have been doing it the old way, without an incident.
      3. While others will not be able to afford the new requirements, since as I stated before they are costly and time consuming.

B. So, the next time you sit in a dental chair, don't assume that we are doing the right thing, make it your business to make sure that we are.

Conclusion:

There are a few things which you can do to assure yourself the safest dental treatment.

A. The first thing is, learn to observe and question the maintenance of the office.
   1. Is the office clean and organized, and is there a sink in the treatment room.
   2. Do you see a sterilization room and are the instruments wrapped and sealed.

B. Then you should observe the steps which your dentist and his assistant take before they begin your treatment.
   1. Do they wash their hands before putting on their gloves, and do they remove them and wash their hands when they leave the room, answer the phone, write on charts, or reach into cabinets.
   2. Do they prepare the necessary instruments and equipment and put on their safety equipment in your presence.

C. Finally, do not let your fear of dental treatment allow you to overlook the real danger.
   1. The pain that you fear from this needle, should not be the only thing you fear.
   2. Don't be afraid to ask if it is new, if you are still not satisfied ask for a new needle.
   3. Do the same with any instruments that are being used.
   4. If you see that your safety is being neglected, you should report it to OSHA, as I would.
   5. At work I am on the Health and Safety Committee, one of my duties is to go around making sure that the guidelines are being followed by the employer and employees, for your sake and theirs.

Marta Alvarado — Student

Example 4

A/G Do you deserve rest at least once a year? Don't you want your chosen place of rest to meet certain standards? At least beautiful weather and picturesque diverse scenery?

S/P I'm going to convince you to visit the small country in the Mediterranean that happened to be my birth place — Greece. The land of Alexander the Great, Aristotle, and Hipocrates to name a few, should be considered for vacation.

C/I Greece is an ideal place for a vacation not only because it has beautiful weather and picturesque diverse scenery but also has many ancient sites, recreational facilities, and hospitality. I love and know every inch of Greece. I go every year to relive magical moments.

V/S Because I didn't want to present you a speech based solely on my own experience and beliefs, I consulted the National Organization of Greek Tourism. After I finish, I hope you'll plan to go at least once in your life to Greece. I'm sure that you'll have such a great time that you'll revisit and you'll persuade others to go. Our best advertisement comes from people like you (open minded, full of energy, and appreciative of the best).

T Let me start my speech concentrating on why you should consider going to Greece.

Body

I. Weather

   A. Importance of good weather while vacationing.

      1. We spend money to enjoy our carefree days under the sun and not being bound in a hotel room.
      2. Summer is hot and dry, always accompanied by cool seasonal breezes called "meltemia."

   3. Rain is almost nonexistent in the summer time and that is why all of the movie theaters in summer are outdoors.
   4. The sunshine is ample.
   5. According to world statistics, there are 3000 hours per year of sunshine and according to the environmental almanac, Greece has the largest area of solar collectors installed in Europe.

II. Diversity in natural scenery
   A. Greece has numerous islands; 20% of the country consists of islands.
   B. Resorts
      1. Greece has mountain resorts
      2. Sea resorts
      3. Spas near picturesque parts where you can combine hydrotherapy for many ailments
      4. Summer resorts
   C. Greece has the bluest sea water and sky you can see
   D. Beaches
      1. Golden sandy beaches
      2. Pebbled beaches
      3. Nude beaches
   E. Fields of color from red poppies, yellow chrysanthemums, and white daisies
   F. Magical sunrises and mystical sunsets
   G. There is also a mixture of fragrances from orange blossoms, louren, and thyme.

III. Numerous ancient sites from different eras
   A. Greece is famous for Olympia, where the Olympic games started
   B. The Parthenon where you can admire architecture at its finest
   C. The many archaeological museums in Crete, Athens, and Thessaloniki
   D. Medieval castles on the island of Rhodes
   E. Byzantine churches in Mystra
   F. Monasteries, with their Icons, hidden on treacherous mountain tops like Meteora
   G. Neoclassical mansions with their Venetian architecture mark many of the foreign civilizations that make up Greece (Roman, Frankish, Gothic, etc.). Greece is a blend of different eras, a blend of ancient and modern.

IV. Greece's entertainment and tourist facilities
   A. There are many night clubs with Bouzouki (Greek music organ) and breaking plates (Greek custom)
   B. Fancy restaurants for familiar dishes or Greek specialties, small cafes in Plaka, casinos in Corju, Athens, and Rhodes.

C. Yearly wine festivals in Dafni and Athens where the National Organization of Greek Tourism organizes free tastings with dancing and singing contests.
D. There are also expensive tourist facilities with golf courses, ski runs, yachting, sailing, fishing, tennis, horse back riding, and bird watching in the forest of Rhodope in Thrace where you can find some of the rarest birds of prey in Europe.
E. Greek hospitality: the people are friendly and anxious to help people and many residents speak English. You'll agree that this is indeed the country of "Xenioos" — the god Zeus, to whom everyone was treated as a guest.

C In conclusion I would like you to picture yourself in a beautiful, comfortable and affordable hotel. You wake up to the finest weather, surrounded by aromatic trees and colorful perfumed flowers. The scenery is great and you can enjoy the blue sea water and warm inviting sun. At midday you go sightseeing and at night you get dressed up to enjoy the good food and night life that Greece has to offer. Greece is a place of diversion and choices. Greece is where you can find the good weather and beautiful scenery and you can combine entertainment and excellent tourist facilities. Greece is for you because, as individuals, you have choices. Greece flourishes on good advertisement. That's why, according to the World Almanac, more than 8.5 million tourists visit Greece each year. Greece is the land where one of the greatest civilizations began. Under those clear blue skies and by its inviting water you can definitely enjoy and be inspired in the land of the gods. I hope, now that we are approaching our humid summer, I have persuaded you to pay a visit to your travel agent to arrange for your lifetime experience, vacationing in Greece.

Joanna Iliopoulos — Student

The following is an example of an evaluation form from Stephen Lucas' *"The Art of Public Speaking"* on how to grade Monroe's Motivated Sequence:

Monroe's Motivated Sequence Evaluation Form

Rate the speaker on each point 5 Excellent — 4 good — 3 average — 2 fair — 1 poor	Speaker Topic
Attention Step _____ gained attention of listeners _____ introduced topic clearly _____ showed importance of topic to this audience	Comments
Need step _____ need clearly explained _____ need demonstrated with evidence _____ need related to audience **Satisfaction step** _____ plan clearly explained _____ plan well thought out	
Visualization step _____ practicality of plan shown _____ benefits of plan related to audience	
Action step _____ call for specific action by audience _____ vivid concluding appeal	

Delivery	Comments
_____ maintained eye contact _____ extemporaneous and conversational _____ showed importance of topic to this audience _____ poised, confident presentation _____ words articulated clearly _____ nonverbal communication effective _____ communicated enthusiasm for topic	
Overall evaluation _____ language clear, concise _____ connectives effective _____ completed in time limit _____ speaker's purpose achieved	

Credibility

To be effectively persuasive you must have credibility. The ancient Greeks called this "estras." This refers to an audience's acceptance of the speaker's authority. To enhance credibility use good organization, clear and vivid language, strong delivery, effective evidence and reasoning.

One way to achieve credibility is to be an expert in your field, but since you are not experts, you have to quote people who are in order to substantiate your point of view.

In a persuasive speech it is important to differentiate between what constitutes a fact and what constitutes opinion. A fact (logos) is something you can prove, whereas an opinion is a judgment made by you. To deliver a persuasive speech effectively you have to use both fact and opinion. In an informative speech you use only fact.

Look at the following statements:

1. **Fact** The Japanese attacked Pearl Harbor on December 7, 1941.
2. **Opinion** Men look more attractive with short hair.

Regardless of how much *factual* information you have in your speech or how credible you may appear, to be powerfully persuasive you must also appeal to the emotions (pathos) of your audience. Consider, for example, President Kennedy's appeal to the patriotic feelings of his audience when he said: "Ask not what your country can do for you, but rather what you can do for your country!" Susan B. Anthony's courageous words when she fought for the rights of women to vote: "It was we, the people, not we, the white male citizens, not we, the male citizens, but we, the whole people, who formed this union."

Evidence through Reasoning

It is important to use evidence to prove your point of view. Evidence can consist of examples, statistics, or testimonials. Make sure your evidence is meaningful to your audience.

Although your evidence may be strong, you will not be persuasive unless you can tap into the audience's reasoning abilities.

Several methods of reasoning are as follows:

- Deductive
- Inductive
- Causal

Deductive reasoning is a syllogism that moves from a general premise to the specific (Syllogisms consist of three statements; the major premise, the minor premise, and the conclusion that follows from them):

- People who don't smoke cigarettes live longer.
- You want to live longer.
- Therefore, you should not smoke cigarettes.

Inductive reasoning is the opposite of deductive. It moves from the specific to the general, progressing from several facts to a general conclusion:

- My speech class last semester was motivating.
- My friend's speech class was motivating.
- My brother's speech class was motivating.

Conclusion Therefore all speech classes are motivating.

Causal reasoning is the type of logic that shows the cause of a situation and its effects. For example: Engaging in sex without protection can result in sexually transmitted diseases or AIDS.

Speaking in public is never easy without a lot of hard work, but, it is a tool needed by most adults in our society. Understanding the different types of oral presentations—oral interpretation; informative; entertaining; and persuasive speaking—used in communicating a message allows you to be heard and understood by your peers. Remember: don't be afraid of the challenge. Conquer it and feel its power! This skill will benefit you in the future.

Guidelines for Persuasive Speaking

- Decide on your subject and position. Ideally it should be something you feel strongly about: a cause you advocate, a change you believe in, a behavior you want to alter.
- Analyze yourself as a speaker — your ethos. What are your credentials? In the body of your speech, research findings attributed to their sources constitute credentials. By referring to them, you demonstrate to your audience that you have investigated your topic and know what you are

talking about. Give some thought to how you can heighten your appeal to your audience so they will respond positively to your appeal. We grant you trustworthiness.

- Analyze your audience. What kind of people are in it? What is it you want them to do as a result of your speech? What kinds of appeals can they be counted on to respond to?
- Assemble evidence. Research your topic (using a minimum of three sources) to give you the factual ammunition you need. Remember to attribute facts to appropriate sources.
- Organize information. Identify issues involved. Treat each issue individually using tools of logic to arrive at a convincing conclusion. (For example: inductively you can supply the audience with a collection of data and draw a conclusion from it; deductively you can begin with a shared theory, present your information relative to it and draw a conclusion.) Link various issues to one another so that your speech has an appealing flow (transitions). Give some thought to placement of issues (strongest argument first or last?) and whether to deal with both sides of your message — the logos.
- Prepare an effective, attention-getting introduction and a powerful conclusion. Remember pathos is an important aspect of persuasion, reaching your audience on an emotional level.
- Use index cards, speak from notes, rehearse!

Final note: The three components of persuasion: Ethos, Logos, and Pathos are all connected. We identify each separately for purpose of clarification. Your address is a unity of the three. Keeping in mind who you are as speaker, the composition of the audience, and what your goal is will help focus your presentation.

Topics for the Speech to Persuade

1. Gay men and lesbians should (should not) be allowed to serve in the Armed Forces.
2. Haitian men and women infected with the HIV virus should (should not) be allowed into the United States.
3. Cigarette smoking should (should not) be banned in public buildings.
4. Nuclear testing should (should not) be permanently banned.

5. The electoral college should (should not) be the determining factor in the presidential vote.
6. Our prison system needs a complete overhaul.
7. Child care in the United States must be improved.
8. Prayer does (does not) belong in our schools.
9. The Vietnam War was (was not) a mistake.
10. It is important to teach young children how to protect themselves against sexual abuse by adults.
11. Assault weapons should (should not) be banned.
12. Affirmative action must be taken into consideration in hiring University Professors.
13. We should (should not) have a national health care system.
14. A woman's place is no longer in the home.
15. Professors who espouse racist theories do not belong in our Universities.
16. Animals have rights too!
17. Children should (should not) be allowed to testify in court.
18. Has "political correctness" gone too far?
19. Our homeless must be helped.
20. The American Civil Liberties Union should (should not) protect the rights of Neo-Nazis.
21. Capital punishment is not a deterrent to murder.
22. The school year should (should not) be made longer.
23. Support for public radio and television.
24. Children should (should not) be allowed to watch violent programs on television.

▼▼▼ Chapter VIII Key Terms

Persuasive speaking	Attention
Questions of fact	Need
Questions of value	Satisfaction
Questions of policy	Visualization
Monroe's Motivated Sequence	Action

IX

Group Discussion

- Brainstorming
- Working in a Group
- Maslow's Hierarchy of Needs
- Practice Examples for Group Discussion
- Characteristics of Group Discussion
- Roles of the Leader
- Styles of Leadership
- Roles of Members in a Group Discussion
- The Subject Problem
- Six Steps Used in the Problem-Solving Process
- Problem-Solving Practice Sheet
- The Panel
- Duties of Panel Members
- The Chairman's Duties in a Panel Discussion
- The Symposium
- The Forum
- The Colloquium
- The Round Table
- Class Discussion
- Performance Tips for a Discussion
- Strategies to Use While Contributing to a Discussion
- Topic Selection
- Suggested Topics for Public Group Discussion
- Helpful Tips for Group Members in Discussions
- Group Discussion Grading and Evaluation Sheets
- Remember!

IX

Group Discussion

During the sixties the "rap session" was very popular. People sat around and engaged in a spontaneous, casual type of conversation for a number of reasons. Either they were releasing their tensions and hostilities, or they were simply exchanging points of view on any subject which came up. It is important to remember that these discussion sessions had no real scheme or plan, with few exceptions they were spur-of-the-moment conversations.

All conversation is like that. It is unplanned, spontaneous and usually without any special purpose or specific end. If you meet your friends or neighbors and the conversation remains for an extended period on the subject of condom distribution in schools or the Rainbow Coalition, it might become apparent that as a group, you should meet together for a more planned and purposeful session in which these issues can be more effectively studied. You agree to look into the matter, and to meet.

When that meeting takes place, and is specifically purposeful, you are shaping a discussion. If six or eight of your neighbors have done some investigating, have gathered some facts and statistics, if they have come prepared with more authoritative information than merely their own opinions, if they are eager to come up with alternate programs relevant to the issues, then you are involved in a group discussion. In fact, you might just turn out to be the chairman or leader of that discussion, if only to maintain some sense of order as you exchange views and information. You are seeking, in this instance, alternative solutions to the problems.

Whatever it is you may be worried about, it is a matter which will lend itself to discussion. No matter how complex the problems, how deeply divided the community, how confused the subject may appear to be, it will lend itself to discussion.

"I know you believe you understand what you think I said, but I am not sure you realize what you heard is not what I meant." Confusing? Read it again! Is it clearer now? We hope so. At first reading, it is at least mildly amusing, but it resounds with truth when you have been teaching this subject for so long. People do not hear each other accurately because they really do not listen to each other with more care. They are too busy composing what they want to say, and this kind of poor listening will cause barriers in communication. Elliot Seiden, Professor Emeritus, of Long Island University stated: "'But that is not what I said at all' is so common a reply in this modern world, that such errors in how we think we hear what others say seem to be the rule rather than the exception." Here is an example of poor listening.

Group discussion is guided conversation during which the participants, with the effective direction of an informed leader or chairperson, discuss issues and viable solutions for the problems. They use empirical factual data, explore the available resources, and propose possible avenues of solutions. This approach to problem solving created by John Dewey in 1910 is called reflective thinking, whereby a reasonable hypothesis may lead to a useful solution, even if only in theory.

Discussion occurs when a group interacts orally for knowledge or policy-determination. If the aim is informative, members systematically *define*, *analyze*, and *exchange information*. When the end is problem-solving, members systematically *define, analyze, evaluate possible solutions, and attempt to agree upon a high-quality decision to which all or the majority will be committed* then they *test and implement the solution*. Casual social conversation and idle talk are never considered discussion.

Brainstorming

Brainstorming is a technique sometimes used when it is desirable to produce a large number of creative ideas in a short period of time. Like group discussion, brainstorming usually involves three or more people who meet to solve a problem or to share information. A brainstorming session, however, consists of rapidly throwing ideas out on the table, without taking time to evaluate each idea as it is spoken. Since the purpose is only to generate ideas, criticism of any ideas presented is not allowed during a brainstorming session. Group members are encouraged to mention any idea about the topic that occurs to them, even if it seems unusual. The purpose is for each member's idea to trigger additional ideas in other members. Brainstorming, however, is only a first step in solving a problem or reaching a decision. The ideas are recorded, but not evaluated during the brainstorming session. Evaluating and sorting through the ideas occurs during a later group discussion session.

Working in a Group

People need groups to help satisfy interpersonal needs. Although people differ in the reasons they join groups, all people need to belong.

Working with your classmates in a group to exchange ideas, information, and opinions is an exercise which pays careful attention to each others' statements creating the best form of interpersonal communication. It is imperative that you pay attention to what the other group members say, as well as to their support materials, such as quoted authorities, in order to determine your own response. It is often necessary to disagree with your colleagues in the group, not only to agree. And herein lies the value of discussion.

Research involving small groups has shown that five is an excellent number for a work group. Members of groups with fewer than five people usually complain that their groups are too small. Groups composed of an even number of people are not as efficient as odd-numbered groups. Larger groups change character and have different patterns of communication.

In smaller groups all participants speak to one another, even those people who speak very little usually contribute. In groups of seven or more, the shier members are silent, usually only speaking to the leader. As groups get even larger, this problem increases and interaction falls off. In permanent working groups larger than thirteen members, forming smaller groups within the larger group is advisable.

Most groups need to socialize as well as work. When several people come together to share ideas, a whole social dimension can exist. A major question people have while working in a new work group is: "How do I relate to these other people?" Every member asks this question.

You cannot ignore the social aspect of your work group. Talking about hobbies, reading habits, sports, travels, family, and friends is important to the social well being of a group. Take a few minutes at the beginning of the session for this kind of communication.

Maslow's Hierarchy of Needs

What makes people tick? Why do they join groups? Many of us are puzzled by human interpersonal behavior. Explanations of people's motives in behavior were studied by scientists A.H. Maslow and G.W. Allport. Here is an adaptation of Maslow and Allport's ideas by Professor William S. Howell, a leading authority in persuasion at the University of Minnesota.

A good explanation of human motivation is shown through Sequential Arrangement of Basic Needs. Some needs take priority over others, and these more basic needs have to be satisfied before the higher level needs emerge. If you picture the motives as rungs on a ladder you can visualize priorities.

1. **Physiological Needs**. The first and most important rung of the ladder consists of the universal physiological needs. These needs include such things as food, drink, activity, sleep, and sex. A tired man thinks only of sleep. When he has sleep he begins to climb the ladder. Unsatisfied needs are motivators of behavior. When basic needs are satisfied and the first rung is reached, the unsatisfied needs of the next rung begin to gain the individual's attention and actions.
2. **Security Needs**. Human beings want security, predictability, and an organized life. We want to look ahead and know what will happen to us.
3. **Social Needs**. When the security is taken care of the social needs begin to develop. These are extremely important in developing a cohesive work group because they are the needs the group must meet. They include the need to belong to a group through giving and receiving acceptance.
4. **Prestige and Esteem Needs**. When the social needs are met, the desire for status and esteem emerge. We need to feel that we stand high in the eyes of others. We want a good reputation and career. Associated with the need for prestige is the desire for esteem. There are two sides to this motive. They are a public side and a private side. Our public side demands that we be recognized, respected, and appreciated by our peers. However, this is not the same as status. For example, we could have status because of our reputations or because we inherited great wealth, no matter what type of person we are to others. Esteem

is earned by our association with others. Our private side demands we need to like ourselves.

Having a good image of ourselves, and feelings of self-confidence, are really important to us. Wealthy people often find their physiological and security needs largely met, but they seldom have all of the status and esteem they want. Most of us are struggling to climb the upper rungs of the ladder. Groups can provide some of their most powerful rewards because of this struggle.

You can use this theory to help to determine where you are on the ladder and to analyze how this will affect your ability to work in a group.

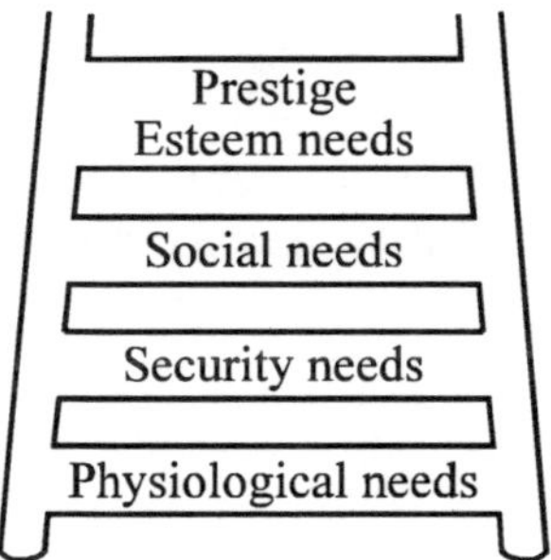

Figure 1 illustrates the deficit ladder of human motivations. These motives are basic universals common to everyone, and they can be thought of as minimum essentials. A lack at any level is usually sufficient to trigger a person's energy resources and make him seek out rewards that will satisfy the need.[1]

Practice Examples for Group Discussion

Here are some examples to practice when you begin to work together.

Example #1
Whom Would You Pick to Start a New World?

What are your values? Even if you've never clearly defined your personal philosophy, and if you don't even know you have one, you do. Your values affect what you do, what you like. They decide your emotions, your actions, and your reactions. Everything you do is directly related to your values. Dr. Melvin Jones, Professor of Education at a major university offers a "test" to help you determine your own values. There is no score. There are no right or wrong answers. You might even be surprised by your own answers. Your choices will reflect the values that you consider important in a society.

The world is in the throes of a nuclear war. There is only one fallout shelter available, and it can sustain only six people. You must choose the six.

1. A 16-year-old girl of questionable IQ, who is a high school drop-out and is pregnant.
2. A 28-year-old former policeman, who was thrown off the police force for brutality, and who always carries his gun with him.
3. A 75-year-old clergyman.
4. A 36-year-old female physician, who has recently had an operation and is now unable to have children.
5. A 46-year-old male violinist, who is a suspected homosexual.
6. A 20-year-old black militant, who has no skills.
7. A 39-year-old former prostitute, who has been retired for four years.
8. A 26-year-old male law student. Note: If you select the law student, you must also take his wife. They refuse to be separated. Either keep both or drop both.
9. The law student's 25-year-old wife, who has an incurable blood disease which is hereditary.
10. An architect, who is an ex-convict. He had served seven years for pushing narcotics and has been out of jail for six months.

Example #2
The Candidate

The Department of Speech, Communication Sciences, and Theatre at Long Island University has been interviewing applicants to fill a vacancy. As members of the Appointments Committee, your decision must be made among these final candidates.

Ms. Franks	Outstanding scholastic credentials including a Ph.D. Highly respected by colleagues and by high-achieving students. Has little patience with average students. Is well organized; spends little time with students.
Mr. George	Adequate scholastic qualifications. Very popular with students. Courses are enjoyable. Academic standards are not high. Uses innovative methods. Has an unconventional life style — lives in a commune. Bearded, smokes marijuana, wears jeans to class.

Mr. Henry	Good scholastic qualifications. Well organized. Has reasonable academic standards. Relates well with all students — low and high achievers. Is a member of the Gay Liberation Front.
Ms. June	Good scholastic qualifications. Maintains high academic standards but relates well to all types of students. Is a member of the Communist Party and believes that revolution is inevitable. Tends to be popular with faculty and administrators.

Example #3
The Toy Corporation

As a member of the executive board of this corporation, you must select a new president from among three people who are currently in charge of three subsidiary corporate divisions of the company.

The corporation is presently concerned with averting an impending strike, locating new suppliers of low-cost materials, and filling large back orders for newly designed toys.

The applicants and their qualifications are:

- Miss Snow is 30. Her division experienced several strikes in the past 3 years. Although her sales have decreased, she has managed to pay less for materials over the past 5 years. -
- Mr. Worth is 32. His division increased sales during the past 5 years; he has had to pay more for materials over the past 2 years. But there have been no strikes for the past 4 years. -
- Mr. Smith is 42. His division produced fewer sales over the past 2 years, paid less for materials over the past 5 years and had no strikes in the past 3 years.

The Executive Board has been asked to develop specific criteria which would most benefit the need of the corporation before making its selection.

Example #4
The Financial Crisis

Mercy Hospital is facing a financial crisis. Rather than close its doors to the public, the Board of Directors has decided to lay off one nurse from each department. As a representative advisory panel, you are involved in making this decision.

- Mrs. Adams — 50-year-old woman whose work is mediocre. She is married and has two children who are no longer at home.
- Mrs. Battle — a 34-year-old woman whose work has been described as efficient. She is divorced with one child to support. She leads an irregular life and often arrives late for work.
- Mrs. Calloway — a 23-year-old woman whose work has been described as average. She has made a poor impression on her superiors because of her critical comments. She is married with one child.

Example #5 A
Scholarship Determination

Your committee has raised money to provide a college scholarship for a deserving student. The scholarship consists of $5,000 per year, renewable for four years as long as academic progress is satisfactory.

Candidates

- John — 19, finished high school in three years because "I couldn't have stood another year." His average in high school was 90. His mother can provide almost nothing for his college education but hopes that he will become a physician. He hasn't made up his mind about his career and he has had emotional difficulties; his psychiatrist says he needs an "intellectual challenge."
- Susan — 18, has very high recommendations from her high school where she had a 95 average. In her senior year, she became engaged to a local truck driver who wants her to forget about college. She thinks she wants to become a social worker and "help young people in big cities." Her pastor says she's very bright but predicts that she will marry and drop out.

- Robert — 21, earned the Silver Star and lost his right hand in the war. In high school, he earned an 80 average. His family wants him to work to help support the five younger children. He is eager to attend college so that he can major in business in order "to make enough money so that I can have a better life than my parents have." A high school counselor recommended that he train as an automobile mechanic since he "is not college material."

After working with these examples, you should have begun to experience the complexity of problem solving.

Characteristics of Group Discussion

- Discussion involves a group whose members have interdependent objectives. This group must operate as a whole and not as individuals or cliques.
- Through words and nonverbal language group members communicate.
- Discussion involves all members of the group participating. Each person in the group must be permitted to interact freely with the others.
- The experience must be cooperative. There may be disagreement and argument during a discussion, but all members of a discussion group must search for a solution that will be as satisfactory as possible to all involved.
- Discussion should have a clear, specific purpose which brings the group together on a particular occasion.
- It should proceed systematically with the clarification of a limited question and move in problem-solving through analysis, evaluation of alternatives to a decision. It is in providing systematic forward movement that leadership is necessary.
- In discussion, members must work cohesively and use their interpersonal perception. Members must be aware of the group.

Roles of the Leader

1. To open the discussion, the leader introduces all group members and the problem.
2. The purpose of the group, the procedure, and time limit are explained. Audience interest can be created by relating the problem to the experiences of the audience.

3. The leader helps guide the group's thinking along the problem-solving process and when one step has been discussed, provide a summary of the points agreed upon.
4. The next step is a transition.
5. Help the group to think clearly by asking for specific examples and support sources. Material must be logical and relate to the subject problem. Use questions such as "Can you give the group an example?" "Who said this?" Or, "Is there evidence to support this idea?" Be careful of questions that require a "yes" or "no" response.
6. Secure the participation of everyone, even shy members. If certain group members monopolize the discussion, firmly break in and say, "Now we need to hear from someone else on this subject."
7. Close the discussion by summarizing the agreements reached and the further aspects to be investigated at a later date.

Prior to discussions, the leader notifies all members of the time and place for all meetings. These meetings usually are conducted in committee style in the classroom as the professor moves from group to group to assist with problems.

Since the leader is either appointed or elected by the group, there should be courtesy and consideration for his or her ability to guide the group through the discussion and to familiarize the members with their responsibilities in the discussion.

During the discussion, the leader introduces the topic and the speakers, delivers to the professor a copy of the agenda, defines the terms, and carefully guides the group through the use of questions. The leader utilizes opportunities to bridge the elements of the agenda with summations leading from question to question until the discussion ends, at which point he or she delivers an appropriate summation. It is the leader's task to keep within time limits, encourage participation from all, avoid off-the-topic matters, and maintain a balanced role for participants.

Styles of Leadership

Students studying leadership always question whether there is an ideal style of leadership. Authoritarian, democratic, and laissez-faire (hands off) styles of leadership are possibilities for how to run a group. Morale and productivity are usually high in a democratic style of leadership. However, some groups do well with a more directive or authoritarian style and some people need the freedom of laissez-faire. Clearly, the purpose of the group and the kind of work it has to do plays a part in determining the best style of leadership for that particular group.

Roles of Members of a Group Discussion

Members' contributions to a group are presented in the forms of verbal or nonverbal behavior which may be analyzed according to their purpose or function. Verbal behaviors have been classified as group task functions, group maintenance functions, and self-centered or self-oriented functions.

A particular comment produced by a member of a group discussion may be related to helping the group accomplish its task. Or the comment may help members to function together socially as a group. Such maintenance functions or roles help the group to improve and to satisfy interpersonal relationships. A comment which serves only individual needs at the expense of the group is viewed as self-centered and often is destructive to the group.

I. **Task roles or functions**
   A. Initiating. Proposing tasks or goals; defining a group problem; suggesting a procedure or ideas for solving a problem.
   B. Seeking information or opinions. Requesting facts or clarification, seeking relevant information about group concerns, asking for expressions of feeling, values, suggestions or ideas.
   C. Giving information or opinions. Offering facts, providing relevant information about group concerns.
   D. Clarifying and elaborating. Interpreting ideas or suggestions, clearing up confusions, defining terms, expanding ideas, indicating alternatives and issues before the group.
   E. Summarizing. Pulling together related ideas, restating suggestions after the group has discussed them, offering a decision or a conclusion for the group to accept or reject.
   F. Consensus testing. Asking to see if a group is nearing a decision, sending up a trial balloon to test the group's possible agreement or conclusion.
   G. Recording. Keeping written records of actions taken.

II. **Maintenance or support roles/functions**
   A. Harmonizing. Attempting to reconcile disagreements, reducing tension, getting people to explore differences.
   B. Gatekeeping. Helping to keep communication channels open; facilitating the participation of others, suggesting procedures that enable others to share.
   C. Encouraging. Being friendly, warm, and responsive to others, indicating by facial expression or statements the acceptance of others' contributions.

D. Compromising. When your own idea or status is involved in a conflict offering a compromise which yields status, or admiting the error; modifying your position in the interest of group cohesion or growth.

E. Standard testing and setting. Testing whether the group is satisfied with its procedures, pointing out explicit or implicit norms which have been set — which may or may not be helpful.

III. **Self-centered or self-oriented roles/functions**

A. Blocking. Constantly raising objections, repeatedly bringing up the same topic or issue after the group has considered it or rejected it.

B. Attacking. Attacking the competence of another, name calling, impugning the motive of another instead of describing your own feeling, joking at the expense of another, attempting to destroy the "face" of another.

C. Recognition seeking. Boasting, calling attention to one's own expertise or experience when it is not necessary or relevant, relating irrelevant experiences, game playing to elicit sympathy or pity.

D. Dominating. Giving orders, interrupting and cutting off, flattering to get one's own way, insisting on own way.

E. Advocating. Playing the advocate for the interests of a different group, thus acting as its representative, apologist or advocate, counter to the best interests or consensus of the current group; developing a "hidden agenda."

F. Horseplaying. Making tangential jokes, engaging in horseplay that takes the group away from serious work or maintenance behavior.

IV. **Other kinds of behavior which interfere with effective group functioning**

A. Dependency-counterdependency. Leaning on or resisting anyone in the group who represents authority.

B. Fighting and controlling. Asserting personal dominance, attempting to get own way regardless of others.

C. Withdrawing. Psychologically leaving the group, being late or missing meetings.

D. Pairing up. Seeking out one or two supporters and forming a kind of emotional subgroup in which the members protect and support each other.

The Subject Problem

Choosing a subject for discussion should involve a real problem important to you. It might also be one that involves a policy, something that should or should not change, rather than one that deals with fact or value.

Clearly phrase the subject as a question. This helps the group focus on the issues which need solving and it encourages all possible solutions.

Six Steps Used in the Problem-Solving Process

1. Describe the problem.
2. Define the terms.
3. State the symptoms and the size.
4. Determine several possible solutions with the strengths and weaknesses that solutions must meet.
5. Suggest several possible solutions with the strengths and weaknesses of each one.
6. Select the best solution and ways to carry out this solution.

Here is a problem-solving practice sheet to help you.

Problem-Solving Practice Sheet

NAME ______________________________ DATE ______________

Subject question: ____

____

State the problem: ____

____

Define problem terms in the question: ___________________________

____

List symptoms of the problem: _________________________________

____

Describe the size of the problem: ______________________________

____

Analysis of the problem:
What are the causes of the problem? ____________________________

____

____

____

What criteria must the solutions meet? (What values, laws, or customs must not be harmed too much in solving the problem?)

____

____

Suggest several possible solutions:

A. Solution one ______________________________

____

B. Solution two ______________________________

____

C. Solution three ______________________________

____

D. Solution four ______________________________

____

Which solution seems the "best" and why? ______________________________

____

____

How can you put this "best" solution into operation? List specific things that can be done.

A. ______________________________

____

B. ______________________________

____

C. ______________________________

____

D. ______________________________

____

Formats of Delivery Used in Group Presentations

The Panel

The panel is a guided discussion held in the presence of an audience. Usually, the members are chosen because they are interested in, and well informed about, the chosen topic. Some professors offer lists of possible topics; others advise student committees preparing for a panel to select a topic of their own. The panel will consist of from four to six members sitting in a semi-circle with a discussion leader. The discussion proceeds among this group based upon an agenda previously planned, and is conducted with as much spontaneous presentation as possible. Obviously, all members should have adequate preparation following readings, research, and interviews.

The leader will introduce panelists to the audience, and offer a brief and clearly focused introduction concerning the choice of topic which is best presented in question form. This is called the "subject problem."

Arriving at the subject problem, or topic question, is an important step in the preparation process, for unless the question is well phrased and properly defined, a discussion cannot proceed with a clear view of the issues which that subject problem must raise.

The group might pursue discussion based upon:

- **a question of information** — What is the background of the struggle in Bosnia?
- **a question of solution** — What should the American position be in Bosnia?
- **a question of evaluation** — What would result from sending U.S. troops into Bosnia?

Therefore, unless the subject problem establishes the framework within which the panel discussion will take place, there is no orderly manner, or sense, to the entire role of mature and intelligent discussion. We cannot emphasize the importance of this step enough for here is where all troubles originate in the actual classroom performance. In a sense, it is the beginning of mature and intelligent discussion.

Discussion, furthermore, is a means of clarifying problems and seeking solutions, or possible solutions, wherein the members suggest or propose, but need not always advocate. This is not a debate, which is a way of advocacy based upon totally different rules and format. Discussion allows other voices to be heard, not merely one voice which issues orders. It is a democratic process.

Duties of Panel Members

Prior to the discussion, the members meet with the chairperson, moderator, or leader, for committee or pre-discussions and planning. It is in this period that the subject problem is shaped and the issues for the agenda selected. During the discussion, members give their opinions, use supportive materials, and are careful of their language, speech and voice. While discussing any individual point in a panel, members usually question and respond to one another without waiting for recognition from their chairperson. A new point from the agenda is always initiated by the leader; panel speakers do not interrupt each other.

After the panel discussion, in the forum or question period, the leader chairs the interaction of questions from the audience, and responses from the panelists to those questions. Both questions and answers should be brief and to the point. The objectives of the group are achieved when observation of the rules of good procedure are maintained.

The Chairman's Duties in a Panel Discussion

The chairman must help the discussion group achieve the most of which it is capable. This can be done by guiding, not dictating. Chairs assume all of the group responsibilities as well as carrying out the following duties as leader.

Study the problem thoroughly because without preparation you will be unable to guide and organize the group's thinking.

A Chair should prepare a series of leading questions for each step of the problem-solving process. Avoid all questions that can be answered by a simple "yes or no." Learn to use the five "W's" and one "H" for different types of answers. For example start with "what" for a reaction, or "why" to gather facts and reasons, or "who" to discover sources, or "how" to determine solutions.

The Symposium

The symposium differs in format and plan from the panel. Each participant makes a prepared speech on some aspect of the topic. At the end there are questions from the audience. It is more formalized than the panel because of the use of prepared speeches. No matter what type of discussion is used, it is always smart to do your research before you meet for performance in class.

The basic distinction to be made between the round table and the symposium is that the symposium replaces informal conversation among discussants with a series of short prepared speeches, presented in turn by members of the group. Usually the symposium topics represent a partitioning of a discussion problem into as many subtopics as there are to be speakers. Thus, a symposium might be set up as follows:

Problem: Can crime in schools be reduced?

I. Where do our delinquent children come from?
II. How extensive is our present problem?
III. Our courts and the handling of youthful offenders.
IV. The role of the church in combating crime in youth.
V. The role of the schools in combating crime in youth.
VI. The Police Department and the young criminal.

A symposium also can just present an informative issue. Sometimes the symposium divides into opposing views on a controversial issue. Under such circumstances, the symposium becomes a sort of informal debate, with the speakers taking specific positions and generally holding to those positions.

Symposium speakers presenting prepared speeches reduce the amount of interaction or interchange among the speakers. However, some interaction can be achieved through a brief period at the end of each symposium where questions or comments to the speakers may occur.

Speakers in a symposium make extended, prepared statements which enable each speaker to deal with the problem of projecting coherent, organized speeches to a sizable group. Symposia can be successfully planned without many meetings of the speakers. The symposium is a good form for bringing together the ideas of several persons, each of whom is prepared in some aspect of a broader topic. Symposia prepare the way to group discussion.

Here is an example of an informative symposium presentation given by an oral communication class at the Brooklyn Campus of Long Island University.

Celeste M. Banks — Chairperson/Moderator

A/G Witches, crystal balls, flying objects, black cats, and things that go bump in the night. These are all the things that people think of when they hear the word occult.

S/P To inform our audience about four popular aspects of the occult.

C/I Astrology, numerology, palmistry, and psychics are four popular aspects of the occult.

V/S By the conclusion of this discussion, the audience will have more knowledge about four aspects of the occult.

Celeste's Transition

Exactly what is meant when you hear the word occult?

Celeste's Body

I. What the occult is
   A. *Random House* dictionary definition: of magic and astrology
   B. Other alleged sciences claiming knowledge of supernatural agencies

Celeste's Transition

Today we are going to look at only four types of occult practices.

II. Astrology
   A. Introduce Rasheta
   B. Most popular — Horoscopes in media — everyone reads everyday

Rasheta

I. Introduction

A/G Vilified by science, ignored by modern learning, and scorned by the average man even as he looks for it in the newspaper everyday. You may ask, "What am I talking about?"

S/P I will discuss several aspects of astrology.

C/I I will discuss the history and sun signs of astrology.

V/S I want you to have an open mind and to make your own decision about astrology.

Transition

So, now I will begin...

II. History
  a. Definition of astrology
  b. Where it originated
  c. When it originated
  d How it was practiced

Transition

And now to modern astrology.

III. Aries
  a. Its astrological position
  b. Its ruling planet
  c. Its symbol
  d. Its characteristics

Transition

And now to the next sign.

IV. Taurus
  a. Its astrological position
  b. Its ruling planet
  c. Its symbol
  d. Its characteristics

Transition

And now to the sign, Gemini

V. Gemini
  a. Its astrological position
  b. Its ruling planet

c. Its symbol
d. Its characteristics

Transition

And now to the sign, Cancer.

VI. Cancer
  a. Its astrological position
  b. Its ruling planet
  c. Its symbol
  d. Its characteristics

Transition

And I'll discuss Leo.

VII. Leo
  a. Its astrological position
  b. Its ruling planet
  c. Its symbol
  d. Its characteristics

Transition

And now to Virgo.

VIII. Virgo
  a. Its astrological position
  b. Its ruling planet
  c. Its symbol
  d. Its characteristics

Transition

And now to Libra.

IX. Libra
  a. Its astrological position
  b. Its ruling planet
  c. Its symbol
  d. Its characteristics

Transition

And now to Scorpio.

X. Scorpio
  a. Its astrological position
  b. Its ruling planet

c. Its symbol
d. Its characteristics

Transition

And now to Sagittarius.

XI. Sagittarius
a. Its astrological position
b. Its ruling planet
c. Its symbol
d. Its characteristics

Transition

And now to Capricorn.

XII. Capricorn
a. Its astrological position
b. Its ruling planet
c. Its symbol
d. Its characteristics

Transition

And now to Aquarius.

XIII. Aquarius
a. Its astrological position
b. Its ruling planet
c. Its symbol
d. Its characteristics

Transition

And now to the last sign, Pisces.

XIV. Pisces
a. Its astrological position
b. Its ruling planet
c. Its symbol
d. Its characteristics

Transition

And so...

C a. Restate central idea and specific purpose
b. Closing

Celeste's Transition

Thank you Rasheta.

III. Psychics
   A. Introduce Tamir
   B. Gaining popularity — Dionne Warwick "Psychic Hotline"

Tamir

Introduction

A/G How many of you are familiar with psychic power?

S/P To inform my audience about psychic power.

C/I I am going to talk about the development of psychic powers, the use of psychic power, and the future use of psychic powers.

V/S I want you to recognize psychic powers.

Transition

I will now tell you about methods of developing powers.

Body

I. Methods of developing powers
   A. Concentration — think for a long period of time about subject
   B. Visualization — look at objects or persons, form mental pictures
   C. Handling metals and minerals, touch mental pictures
   D. Crystal Gazing — crystal ball that psychics use to tell us our future

II. The use of psychic powers
   A. Telepathy — use to read peoples minds
   B. Aura — all persons surrounded by emanations
   C. Crystal Gazing — easiest atomic molecular arrangements which promote the psychic powers

III. Looking into the future
   A. Dreams — during sleep they see events
   B. Awake — is able to impress this Astral Vision upon a wide physical brain

Conclusion

I hope that I have enlightened your psychic awareness, the development of psychic powers, the use of psychic powers and how psychics look into the future.

Celeste's Transition

Thank you Tamir.

IV. Palmistry
  A. Introduce Cynthia
  B. Neighborhood fortune tellers

Cynthia

A/G Do you believe that your hand can reveal your inner characteristics?

S/P To help my audience better understand the power of palmistry through natural procedures.

C/I To evaluate the hand using palmist method of lines, wrinkles, and the condition of hands and body.

V/S I feel it is important to acknowledge the existence of this psychic power and its wonders.

Transition

Now, let's look into the history of palmistry, and how and where it originated.

Body

I. History
  A. Began in ancient India
  B. Considered a natural phenomenon
  C. Witchcraft/condemned
  D. Inborn trait
  E. A science

Transition

Now, that we have insight on its history, let's move on to the hand, and its interpretation.

II. Hand
  A. Reveals fate/personality
  B. Describes job (hands rough, smooth)
  C. Predicts inner feelings
  D. Wrinkles on palms — lines
  E. Fleshy part — base to thumb
  F. Heartlines, lifelines, etc

Transition

Now, that we have a little more insight on hand interpretation, let's now look at the body.

III. Body
   a. Muscular contractions
   b. Nervousness
   c. Condition of clothes — style
   d. Condition of nails — hands
   e. Hairstyles/jewelry

Transition

Now, that we have an overall broad insight on palmistry let us recall some particular aspects.

Conclusion

Review central idea/specific purpose. Very interesting/very broad. Existed for years. Nature/science.

Celeste's Transition

Thank you Cynthia

IV. Numerology
   A. Introduce Fred
   B. Lucky numbers and days

Fred

A/G Imagine getting up in the morning and starting your day without numbers of any kind? For most people numbers are an intricate part of their lives.

S/P To inform my audience on the occult science of Numerology.

C/I To briefly introduce my audience to:

a. The history of numerology.

b. Expound on one particular method of numerology.

c. Mention briefly some of the different philosophies of numerology.

V/S Everything can some how or another be raised in mathematical terms and if that is so we can than relate everything through numerology.

Transition

Now let me begin with a brief history of numerology.

Body

I. A brief history
   A. Pythagoras "The Father of Numerology." Its hard to pinpoint exactly where, when, why, and how numbers and numerology truly began, and I quote, "In antiquity." Pythagoras was considered a master mathematician. Born in Greece in the 6th century B.C.
   B. Even though Pythagoras is called the "Father of Numerology" or rather the "Father of Modern Numerology," it has been recorded that he spent many years in Egypt learning the ancient science of numbers. If we study Egyptian philosophy we find that numerol ogy goes farther back than the 6th century and Pythagoras.

II. Fadic system—The most common method of addition in numerology is called the Fadic system, or natural addition. This simply means you keep adding two or more numbers together until you arrive at a single number or digit.

III. Pythagorean Approach
   A. Now I would like to give some insight on a method of numerology that uses the Fadic system of addition and it is called the Pythagorean approach.
   B. Pythagorean System—Pythagorean, or "modern numerology," as it's often called, is used in the majority of cases. This system is very popular because it's easier to learn how to translate letters into numbers, and to master their meanings. The name, when analyzed under this system, gives a psychological bent to what motivates you, what you best express naturally, as well as the impression you're likely to make on others. Thus, this method defines the natural talents, abilities, and tools that you were given at birth. This is why using the full name at birth is very important under this system.
   C. Pythagorean Number Values

1	2	3	4	5	6	7	8	9
A	B	C	D	E	F	G	H	I
J	K	L	M	N	O	P	Q	R
S	T	U	V	W	X	Y	Z	

D. Now I would like you to direct your attention to the handout sheet that shows the number equivalent for each letter using the Pythagorean number value system. Also on the same sheet is an example to follow on how to get the number equivalent for your own name. We are only going to deal with first names, so as to make things a little simpler to understand. After you have gotten a one digit number you can use this list of definitions for number values, which is also included in the handout.

1	2	3	4	5	6	7	8	9
A	B	C	D	E	F	G	H	I
J	K	L	M	N	O	P	Q	R
S	T	U	V	W	X	Y	Z	

V A N C E
4 + 1 + 5 + 3 + 5 = 18
1 + 8 = 9

L O U I S
3 + 6 + 33 + 9 + 1 = 22
2 + 2 = 4

W H E E L E R
5 + 8 + 5 + 5 + 3 + 4 + 9 = 40
4 + 0 = 4

First name clues

Number 1 Individualist, daring, straightforward, desire to be "first," a take-charge attitude.

Number 2 Peaceful, loving, friendly, considerate, desire for partnership, warm and gentle.

Number 3 Outgoing and expressive, cheerful attitude, desire to rise to the top, optimistic, youthful.

Number 4 Steadfast, dependable, unique way of doing things, deliberate, hard worker, serious minded.

Number 5 Changeable, carefree, strong desire for freedom and expression, quick thinking, ever alert.

Number 6 Sense of duty and responsibility, helpful, appreciative, affectionate, comforting.

Number 7 Need for privacy, analytical, unique way of thinking, intuitive, reflective, absorbing.

Number 8 Philosophical and mature, determined and intense with a desire to endure, religious, desire for the truth.

Number 9 Desire to inspire and lead, to control other's affairs, universal and giving, courageous and bold, action oriented, energetic, and strong willed.

Now you can determine the number and meaning to your first name.

IV. Different schools of philosophies of numerology
   A. Chaldean system, which takes both your name and birthdate into consideration. The analysis of your name under this system uses only the name you are most known by, instead of your original name given at birth (a requirement of the Pythagorean system). Also, the Chaldean system only uses the numbers 1-8, and not 1-9, thus making the number value for the alphabet very different.
   B. In ancient Japan there is a system known as Ki based upon certain numerical patterns found in the birth date (this system is coming back to popularity).

C. There is also the sacred system of Hebrew numerology, better known as the Kabalah which is based upon the meanings of letters and sounds.

Conclusion

I will conclude by stating that numerology is used in conjunction with other occult sciences such as astrology, which uses your birth date to determine your specific planets and signs, and palmistry, which uses certain numerical positions on the hand. Hopefully, you will be able to use the information I gave you today to further investigate the history, methods, and philosophies of numerology in more depth and reap the benefits of the wonderful and mysterious world of numerology.

Celeste's Transition

Thank you Fred.

Celeste's Conclusion

It is our hope that this symposium has increased your knowledge and understanding of astrology, psychics, palmistry, and numerology, the four most popular aspects of the occult. Here are visual aid handouts for your information. Do you have any questions?

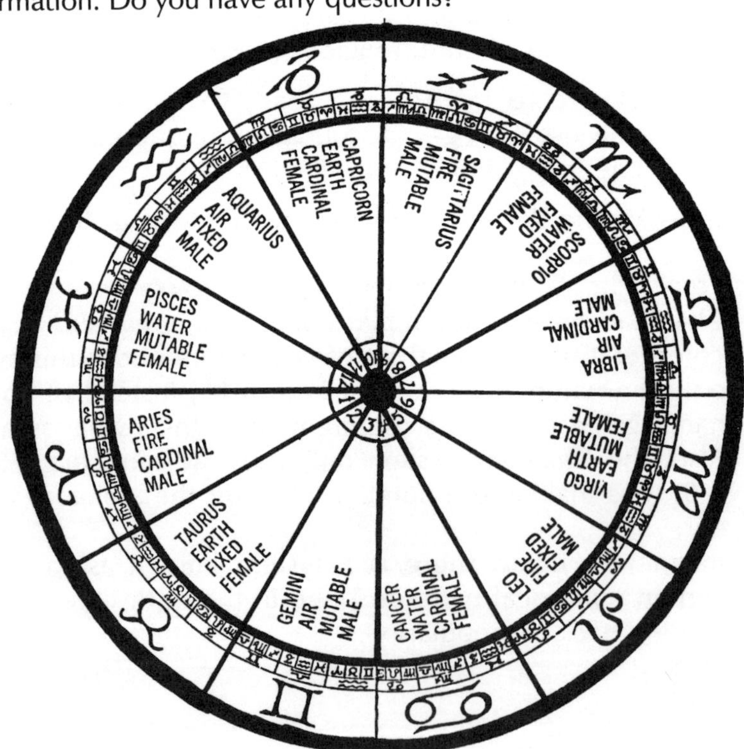

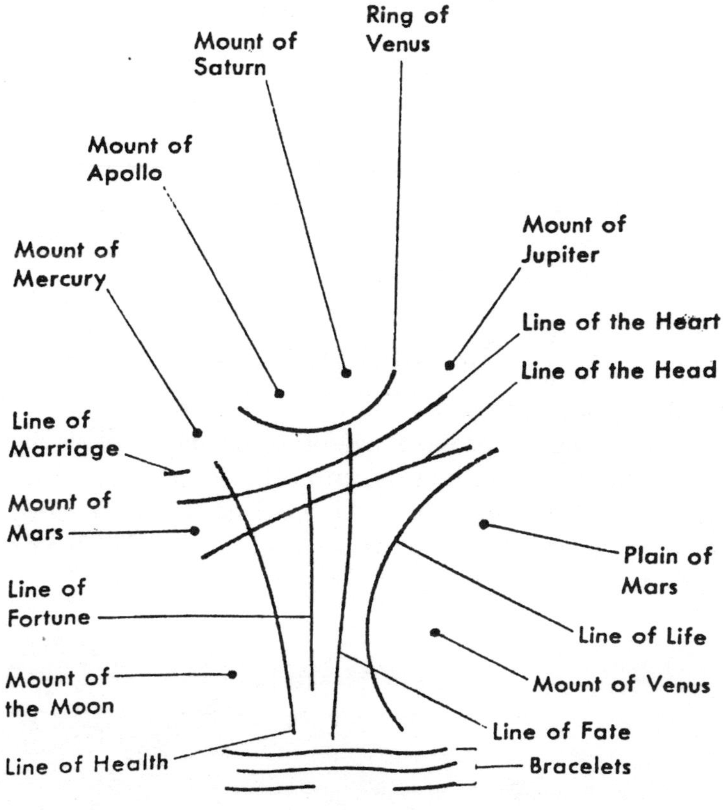

The Forum

The forum is an audience-questioning session that follows a panel or dialogue. To prepare the audience for the forum, at the beginning of the session the chairman should state that there will be a question period after the discussion. Once the discussion has concluded, the chairman should call for questions that pertain to the subject matter. He should indicate whether they are to be directed to individual members or to the members of the group as a whole.

When an audience is large, speakers should stand to be easily seen and when there is a small group they may remain seated. If the audience is slow to respond with questions the chairman should lead off with one or two.

When you respond to questions either as a discussion member or as a chairman, always be pleasant. If you do not understand the question, ask for it to be restated. If you can't answer it, admit it. Respond to hecklers politely but be firm. If the question is off the subject, point this out. A forum usually lasts about twenty to twenty-five minutes depending upon the length of the discussion.

The Colloquium

A colloquium is a public discussion in which a group of three to six persons discuss a problem among themselves and with the audience under the leadership of a chairperson or moderator. The colloquium is a hybrid in which the panel and forum are combined. The members of the group are experts on the problem or topic under discussion, and their views may be quite different. Representatives of the audience may sit with the experts in front of the audience to participate in the forum portion of the discussion.

The Round Table

The round table discussion is a small group that meets face to face around a table and there is no audience present. Members usually explore a subject or solve a problem. City councils, school boards, and other executive committees employ this type of small group. It is informal and consists of several people exchanging views. The entire discussion is spontaneous and can either be for sharing information or coming to a decision.

Class Discussion

A class discussion is an exchange of ideas. It explores the possible advantages or disadvantages, strengths and weaknesses, or pros and cons of a topic. There are differences between class discussions and small group discussions. Class discussions usually do not have to arrive at a decision and they attempt to develop a more complete understanding of discussion topics. They do not arrive at conclusions with which all discussion participants must agree. Small group discussions have the guidance of a leader or chairperson and the members discuss issues in order to find solutions to problems.

A class discussion is not an argument and students do not have to agree with one another. They should, however, make statements such as "I understand your point, but I don't fully agree because ..." when they don't agree. The only type of group discussion that uses argument is a debate.

There are many characteristics of class discussions. Students should talk as much or more than the teacher. Students who try to dominate may create problems for other students. The arrangement of chairs in the room should allow every person to see the faces of the other people. The topic for discussion is always clearly stated in the form of a question so that the goal of the discussion is clear.

For example:

- What is the background of the struggle in Haiti?
- What would result from sending U.S. troops into Haiti?

The statements and questions used are all directly related to the discussion topic and a summary may be used to explain relationships.

Students should make statements and ask questions. This discussion creates an understanding of the information that is needed to answer the question which was the topic of the discussion.

To prepare for a class discussion a student should read about the topic and make a list of the related important facts or opinions, as well as a list of questions.

Performance Tips for a Discussion

Most people are nervous when speaking within a group, because they worry about the impression they will make rather than concentrating on what they will say.

These are thoughts to keep in mind when speaking to a group:

- It is normal for you to be nervous when you speak in front of a group.
- As a participant, make sure you are fully prepared with notes and questions.
- Concentrate on what you want to say and not on your appearance.
- Active participation in discussions will help you gain experience for the future.

Strategies to Use While Contributing to a Discussion

A. If you do not fully understand, ask for a more detailed explanation. Additional information about the same topic is valuable to have and offer to fellow students. Ask and answer questions from the material you prepared while reading about the discussion topic.

B. Behavior that is inappropriate during a class discussion is not acceptable. For example, students who talk too much don't give others a chance to speak.

C. Students should read the required material about the discussion topic, instead of stating their own opinions and experiences.

D. Students should not interrupt others while they are speaking, or make distracting movements or questions.

E. Students shouldn't speak so softly that it is difficult to hear what they say, or engage in arguments with others, or make unkind statements .

F. It will rarely be possible to take detailed notes during a class discussion, but you should take some notes.

G. Group discussion leaders usually are confronted with situations or questions that need to be resolved.

For example:

1. When a point has not been considered he may ask "Has anyone thought about this phase of the problem?"
2. To question the strength of an argument he might ask "What reasons do we have to accepting this argument?"
3. To question the source of information he might ask "Who gathered those statistics?" or "Is that opinion quoted?" or "Is that as a fact, or is it your opinion?"
4. If the discussion is straying from the main idea he could ask "Can someone tell me what relevance this has to our problem?" or "Your point is a good one, but we need to get back to our subject."

5. If he wanted to call attention to the difficulty or complexity of a certain problem he could ask "Aren't we beginning to understand why a responsible party hasn't solved this problem?"
6. And if he wanted to suggest that no new information was being added he could ask "Can anyone add anything to the information that has already been given on this subject?"
7. To show agreement or possible disagreement he might ask, "Am I accurate in assuming that we all agree or disagree on this idea?"
8. And to suggest that a person may be prejudiced he might ask "Is our personal bias in this issue making us overlook something?"
9. If someone is talking too much he might say "Is there anyone who hasn't spoken who would like to contribute?"
10. If a compromise needs to be struck he might say "Do you suppose an answer lies between these two points of view?"
11. If someone speaks too long he might say "Let's hear from someone else, can you save your point until later?" To encourage further questions he might say "That's a good question and I'm really glad you raised it."
12. And to break up an argument he might say "I think we all know how so and so feels about this. Now would anyone like to comment on this?"

Helpful Tips for Group Members in Discussions

- You must listen critically to others and try to get the other person's point of view. Remember, don't accept unsupported theories.
- Be certain you understand the goal of the discussion from the beginning.
- Remember, say what you think since all discussion is based on the exchange of many ideas.
- Don't wait to be motivated to speak. Just go ahead and talk. But remember to let the other people speak as well. Try to make your point in as few words as possible.
- If you don't understand, ask questions and don't be afraid to disagree.
- Keep your comments relevant to the topic.
- Keep an objective, open mind.
- Be prepared to participate at any point.

- Avoid loud and unrelated side conversations with your fellow group members.
- Listen to what is being said and direct your remarks to the entire group.

Topic Selection

In choosing a topic remember that the problem should be important to society. For instance, problems of government, social institutions, family matters, interpersonal relations, or health and welfare are meaningful enough to talk about. The problem must be adapted to the group's reflective thinking. The problem must be limited to the group situation or it will take a long series of meetings to address it. A question like, "What changes could be made in our relations with Cuba?" is more suitable for a class group discussion. The task-oriented small group is usually composed of three to seven people working together to do a clearly specified job or to reach a common goal.

Suggested Topics for Public Group Discussion

1. Should mercy killing (euthanasia) be permitted? (What are the issues?)
2. How should juvenile offenders be treated? (What are the issues?)
3. What should be done to reduce child abuse? (What are the issues?)
4. Should capital punishment be mandated? (What are the issues?)
5. What should be done about pornography? (What are the issues?)
6. Should the Federal Government investigate cults? (What are the issues?)
7. Should abortion be outlawed in the U.S.? (What are the issues?)
8. Should a Federal gun control law be mandated? (What are the issues?)

Group Discussion Grading Sheet

Topic ______________________ Group Members ____________________

Moderator ____________________ ____________________

Chairperson __________________ ____________________

Leader ______________________ ____________________

Time taken __________________

Moderator

Introduces topic and panelists	1	2	3	4	5
Defines purpose of discussion	1	2	3	4	5
Stimulates discussion	1	2	3	4	5
Keeps discussion focused	1	2	3	4	5
Facilitates interaction between group members	1	2	3	4	5
Summarizes during and after discussion	1	2	3	4	5

Group Members

Listen actively (eye contact, facial expression, body language)	1	2	3	4	5
Interact with one another	1	2	3	4	5
Demonstrate knowledge of material	1	2	3	4	5
Speak clearly and include the audience	1	2	3	4	5

Evaluation of Group Discussion Leaders

Leader ______________________ Date __________

Evaluation ______________________ Grade __________

Subject ______________________

Leaders are rated 5 for excellent, 4 for Good, 3 for Adequate, 2 for Fair, and 1 for Poor.

I. Social Emotion Functions

A. Developing a Relaxed Atmosphere __________

B. Reinforcing Desired Behavior __________

II. Procedural Functions

A. Encouraging Participation __________

B. Getting Main Phases of Problem Considered __________

C. Clarifying and Summarizing __________

D. Seeking Information __________

E. Seeking Solutions and Evaluations of Solutions __________

F. Seeking to Resolve Differences __________

III. Problem-Solving Answers

A. Giving Information __________

B. Interpreting and Evaluating Information __________

C. Giving Solutions __________

D. Evaluating Solutions __________

E. Resolving Differences __________

Comments:

Evaluation of Group Discussion Members

Name of member ____________________

Evaluator ____________________ Date __________

Subject ____________________

Group members are rated in regard to the five general areas:
5 for excellent, 4 for Good, 3 for Adequate, 2 for Fair, and 1 for Poor.

I. Knowledge of Subject

A. Pertinent facts and authoritative opinions __________

B. Completeness and accuracy of information __________

C. Understanding of data __________

II. Analysis of Subject

A. Perceiving basic issues __________

B. Perceiving relationships among the parts or phases of the problem __________

III. Reasoning Ability

A. Reaching conclusions based upon evidence __________

B. Perceiving the probable consequences of solutions __________

C. Objectivity or absence of bias __________

IV. Discussion Sensitivity

A. Consideration shown toward the views of others and interest in a free exchange of ideas __________

B. Willingness to have one's ideas evaluated by others __________

C. Ability to perceive one's impact upon others __________

V. Communication Skills

A. Listening __________

B. Clarity of expression __________

C. Conversational quality __________

D. Interest — balance between abstract and concrete words __________

Remember!

From conversation to discussion, in a variety of forms, we are constantly involved with our whole social world in interpersonal communication. From the little private chat with your best friend, to that open rap session, to more formalized guided conversation, to group discussion in all its forms, we are always involved with the oral communication of our thoughts and feelings to the world around us. It is very useful as well as deeply important that you gain the techniques and power which classroom training in these areas can offer to you while you are in college.

Discussion does not just happen and much effort is required to solve the problem. Before you participate you must understand the procedure of group discussion and its responsibilities. If you follow these suggestions it will help you to become an effective participant. Participate with enthusiasm because your group needs your contribution. Don't dominate the discussion, but assume your share of the responsibility. Think before you speak! Listen carefully to what the others say so you can understand and evaluate. Be receptive to ideas by keeping your mind open. Always expect new ideas to evolve as group members contribute their knowledge. Stay objective and keep your emotions under control. Your purpose is not to win but to find the best solution to the problem. Remember differences of opinion will occur but you must handle them with respect.

Here are some student responses to working in a group.

- Maria Berthely

"My experience in the group was pretty positive. I had to control myself from being too domineering. I am aggressive by nature, so I had to learn to take a less dominant role in the group. This is one of the reasons why I chose to be an assistant leader. Each person knew their responsibilities within the group. LaTonya, the group leader, was very helpful. She didn't have to worry about reprimanding the others because everyone knew what was expected of them.

One good thing about our group is that we didn't have any personality conflicts. We all took part in choosing the group topic. I had suggested the topic—"hot" vacation spots—and everyone seemed contented with the idea. After we chose the topic, each person contributed by finding information for other members (including themselves) from various travel agencies.

By doing a group speech of "hot" vacation spots, I think each person enjoyed doing their specific place. They had identified themselves with the places that they talked about. Anthony is a native of Trinidad, so he was very enthusiastic about his topic. The other members picked places that they had been to or had visited. It was educational because they had now done some research on their own fantasy vacation.

I believe through this experience, it has taught us how to work well with others. We each learned how to take constructive criticism. No one felt threatened or insulted when another member had offered his/her suggestions. If we had to do another group topic, I believe each member would choose the same people because we worked so well together. As the professor said, this is a realistic scenario so we all have to learn to live with each other. In essence, we have learned a valuable lesson that will endure beyond this semester."

▶ Cynthia Audain

"Beginning from the first day the assignment was given, our group was ahead of the game.

The first day we discussed different topics and their subtopics. Then we voted on the most interesting topic possible, which was the occult, and broke it up into parts.

As a group, we helped each other gather resources and information. Then we began writing our central ideas and specific purposes and tried to connect all of them to see how well they flowed together.

We all agreed to meet several times in the library to put our outlines together, so the moderator would be able to proceed with her own outline. In the library, we made findings, talked, and finished our presentation. However, Fred missed one of our meetings. The next day, we gave Fred an alternative, we told him to 'shape up or ship out!' Guess what? He shaped up. No one was late to our meetings and everyone participated. We began to rehearse our speeches the last week of our meetings. Then we timed our speeches so we would not be under or over our time limit. At this time we found visual aids, which would enhance our speeches. Rasheda was a good leader. We told her to slow down when she spoke. Tamir had a low voice, so we encouraged him to speak louder. Celeste was very organized. She pushed those men to produce their share of the work. She emphasized that she will not get nor be satisfied with anything less than an "A." This threat seemed to work to our benefit.

Our last meeting was good. Fred could not make it because he had a class, but that did not bother us because his speech was complete. Tamir needed help with finding main topics, since his topic was very broad. After all the work, we finally rehearsed and rehearsed. Then we wished each other luck and went our own way.

I enjoyed myself because it pushed us to communicate and work together. It also placed responsibility on each of us which had a positive effect. The project created friends and developed teamwork. I found it fun and a challenge.

Why work in a group? The labor is divided, there is more comprehension of ideas, and a much greater commitment to a cause. Take a risk. Join a group."

▼▼▼ Chapter IX Key Terms

Empirical
Reflective thinking
Brainstorming
Maslow's Hierarchy of Needs
Authoritarian
Democratic
Laissez-faire
Task roles
Maintenance or support roles
Self-centered roles
Panel Symposium
Forum
Colloquium
Round table

▼▼▼ Endnotes

1. Ernest G. Bormann and Nancy C. Bormann. *Effective Small Group Communication.* Minneapolis: Burgess Publishing Company, 1972. p. 21-22.

Index

D

E

F

G

H

I

T

V

Y